THE SPORTS CAR

Sports car racing and design books available from Robert Bentley, Inc.

Design of Racing Sports Cars
Colin Campbell

The Design and Tuning of Competition Engines
Philip H. Smith and David N. Wenner

Porsche—The Man and His Cars
Richard von Frankenberg

Racing and Sports Car Chassis Design
Michael Costin and David Phipps

Racing Car Design and Development
Len Terry and Alan Baker

The Racing Driver: The Theory and Practice of Fast Driving
Denis Jenkinson

The Scientific Design of Exhaust and Intake Systems
Philip H. Smith

Seventeen Sports Cars 1919–1930: Landmarks in Automobile Design
Peter Hull and Nigel Arnold-Forster

Sports Car and Competition Driving
Paul Frere

The Sports Car: Its Design and Performance
Colin Campbell

The Technique of Motor Racing
Piero Taruffi

Tuning for Speed and Tuning for Economy
Philip H. Smith

THE
SPORTS
CAR
Its design and performance

COLIN CAMPBELL
M.Sc., C.Eng., M.I.Mech.E.

1978

ROBERT BENTLEY, INC.

872 Massachusetts Avenue

Cambridge, Massachusetts 02139

Library of Congress Catalog Card No. 77-94089
ISBN 0-8376-0158-4

First published 1954
Reprinted (three times) 1955, 1956
Second edition 1959
Reprinted 1960, 1961, 1962, 1965
Third edition (revised) 1969
Fourth edition 1978

Manufactured in the United States of America

To my wife

for her toleration of much fast motoring
and more slow writing

Preface to fourth edition

Preface to fourth edition

Some of the sports cars I wrote about a quarter of a century ago are still with us. I saw a few of them at the 1977 BARC Easter Monday meeting as they fought it out so valiantly over ten laps of the Thruxton circuit in the Classic Sports Car Race. It is a sobering thought that many of the readers of this new edition were not even born when I first attempted to analyse the technical make-up of such wonderful sports cars as the XK120, the Aston Martin DB2 and the Austin Healey 'Hundred'.

The greatest upheaval on the technical scene in recent years has been the challenge thrown out by government legislation around the world to increase safety and to reduce pollution. The former has virtually wiped out open-air motoring in several countries with warm climates, which is a pity. The latter has made it illegal in some countries for the enthusiast to tune his own car. This new edition therefore contains no advice on tuning, since this must now be considered as a professional prerogative demanding sophisticated and expensive instrumentation.

Apart from a general up-dating of all the subject matter we have added four design studies, partly historical, partly technical, on the *Jaguar*, the *Lotus*, the *Mercedes* and the *Porsche*. The author is particularly indebted to these four companies for their assistance in providing so much useful technical information on their products.

Grateful acknowledgement is also given to the many sports-car manufacturers who supplied technical data, drawings, photographs and handbooks, and to all the other component and specialist equipment manufacturers who gave such valuable assistance.

The question of units for this new edition is a difficult one. Great Britain, in theory at least, is now using metric (SI) units. Power should be expressed in kilowatts, torque in newton metres and speed in metres per second. Not only is the British motor industry reluctant to make the change, but the majority of our English speaking readers are in America, Canada and Australia where metric units are only used by scientists. In general in this edition we have given quantities in both SI units and in foot-pound-second units. There are exceptions. Motorists still prefer to think of speed in terms of miles per hour or kilometers per hour and engine speed will be quoted in terms of r.p.m. for many years to come. Eventually we shall become accustomed to saying that 'James Hunt wrecked his engine by using too many radians per second.' I do not think that 'Master James' will ever express it in such terms.

Suffolk   C.C.
July, 1977

Contents

1

The development of the sports car

'We are living in a time when
the plural is killing the singular;
nothing has real value
when everything comes in thousands.'
JEAN COCTEAU

Motor sport

Man is an adventurous and fun-loving creature. If we can bring ourselves to accept that we are descended from some branch of the monkey family, it is no longer difficult to understand that our boldness and our love of fun are instinctive. Our instincts are sometimes strong enough to break through that polished skin of sophisticated behaviour that we call civilized living, strong enough to make us do the most irrational things in the name of sport.

Nothing could be more serious than transport. Our modern suburban life would break down without it, yet we cannot resist any opportunity to create fun and sport out of this transport, whatever form it may take. Horse racing was inevitable, chariot racing irresistible and to those of us with muscles and wind enough the invention of the penny-farthing bicycle became just another thing to be raced. Who can tell what the next generation will do with space vehicles!

Motor sport is our immediate concern and with this particular form of transport we have given wide range to our faculty for invention. Not content with racing it round and about and up and down, we invent all manner of games of skill and chance, trials, rallies, gymkhanas, auto-cross, scavenge hunts and treasure hunts.

Sport and danger are often inseparable. Sometimes we seem to go out of our way to ensure this. The writer was a little horrified when he saw that the Kentucky Auto Speed Championship was to be fought out with old stock cars fitted with souped-up engines *around a figure-of-eight course.* The centre of the circuit was thus an uncontrolled crossroads to be negotiated at speeds approaching 60 m.p.h. with a field that soon became spread out, not only around the course, but on all sides of the cross-roads. If racing improves the breed, the future Kentuckians will be happy in the cut and thrust of modern traffic.

The sports car

Since motor sport embraces such a wide variety of games with the automobile, from the pure racing form of Formula I Grand Prix racing to the more bizarre antics of stock car Demolition Derbies, the reader might well ask, if this is motor sport what then is a sports car? And the answer is not going to be easy.

An examination of the writings of such renowned motoring journalists as Joseph Lowrey, Tom McCahill, Cyril Posthumus and Rodney Walkerley reveals only one thought in common. They all agree that a definition is difficult to find. As Cyril Posthumus dryly states: 'It is easier by far to decide what does *not* constitute a sports car — a hearse, a hotel brake, a limousine, a small economy car, for example; any vehicle, in fact, in which carrying capacity takes priority over performance.'

Significantly, if we reverse these priorities and add one word, we find that Posthumus has given us a very good definition. We can now say 'A sports car is any *road* vehicle in which performance takes priority over carrying capacity'. This simple definition brings us closest to what we call the Production Sports Car Class in modern racing. The prototype class of sports car was not seriously intended to be used regularly on the public roads. Such vehicles are designed to comply with the bare essential requirements of the class as defined by the current regulations of the FIA. They carry such lights as are demanded, a mirror and a barely audible horn. They measure up to the minimum windscreen height and door sizes, etc., but they never yield an extra inch to their competitors. Their suitability for normal road usage is always in grave doubt. Such vehicles usually arrive at the race meeting inside a van or on a trailer. It was inevitable that the relentless drive of all-out competition would lead to such a class of sports car. Many of us like to think that the real old-fashioned sportsman — my American friends call him 'the nice guy' — is so blessed by fortune that he can drive his honest roadworthy sports car to the races, put on his helmet and racing overalls and proceed to battle with the leaders. Was it not Leo Durocher of the Dodgers who first said 'Nice guys finish last'?

Despite these cynicisms the idea that a sports car is a dual purpose vehicle dies hard. Many still believe that the true sports car must be a road car and a racing car all in one package. Markham and Sherwin in *The Book of Sports Cars* suggested that 'pleasure' is the key word. 'A sports car,' they said, 'is an automobile designed for the enthusiast to whom pleasure is its paramount potential; pleasure in its performance and pleasure in its design. The sports car is a dual purpose car, it is equally at home in city traffic and in all-out competition and requires no essential modification to convert from one use to the other. It is, in short, a car that is meant to be driven to a race, in the race, and back home from the race.' This would have been a good definition thirty years ago. Today it is difficult to find any cars that are raced, even in the Production Sports Car Class, that could meet this specification to the full. When a production car has been prepared for racing it has usually become a noisy uncomfortable vehicle. The word 'pleasure' has been dimmed; only the sheer performance remains.

The history of the sports car

Nobody knows for sure who made the first petrol-driven automobile. The commercial success of Gottlieb Daimler and Carl Benz, separately and almost simultaneously in 1885 is undisputed, but there were earlier motor vehicles. Etienne Lenoir, for example, drove his horseless carriage for a distance of six miles in 1862. Unfortunately the records are not clear on one important point, the nature of the fuel used to propel this vehicle. There was also an Austrian called Siegfried Markus who drove his 'Strassenwagen' on the streets of Vienna in 1875, but again we know so little of its behaviour or reliability and nothing of its subsequent history.

The early history of the sports car is just as confusing. Probably the most confusing element is the lack of an agreed definition of the vehicle itself. For want of a sanctioned alternative, the writer proposes to use his own definition — any road vehicle in which performance takes priority over carrying capacity — as his specification by which to judge the validity of any early vehicle to the name 'sports car'.

At the turn of the century a man had to be a true sportsman to want to drive one of these self-propelled road vehicles that the general public still regarded as a great joke. For those with a belief in the future of the vehicle there was sufficient adventure, even danger, in a short cross-country journey to satisfy the requirements of a sport. There was no need to race, the competition lay in the journey itself. Despite all this, the continual breakdowns, the unreliable tyres, the dust and the panic-stricken horse-drawn traffic, it was inevitable that motorists would begin to race. The first race of any consequence was from Paris to Bordeaux and back again to Paris — in 1895. It was won by a 1¼-litre Panhard at an average speed of 15 m.p.h.

During the first ten years of motor racing great changes were made in the design of the cars that were raced. The flexible ash frames that had been satisfactory for the leisurely pottering around the town had to be replaced by steel frames that would stand up to the battering given by long distance racing on atrocious roads. Speeds rose higher and higher, far too high for the indifferent tyres of the period. By 1905 engines had grown to gigantic proportions. The racing Fiat of that year had a bore of 180 mm (7.08 inches) and a stroke of 150 mm (5.90 inches), giving a capacity of 16 litres (973 cu. in.) and a horsepower of 110.

A racing car was becoming a specialized and expensive vehicle, as different from the normal town carriage as Zsa Zsa Gabor is from the girl next door. Certain influential car manufacturers in Britain began to wonder if a racing formula could be devised that would give exciting and purposeful competition between ordinary touring cars. It could, of course, have been the poor showing of British cars in the fierce competition of the Gordon Bennett races for real racing cars that made them think along these new lines, but in all fairness there were good reasons for staging public demonstrations of the durability and road-worthiness of ordinary touring cars. Very few people believed that these noisy stinking oddities would really drive the horse-drawn carriages from the highways.

It was the Automobile Club of Great Britain and Ireland (later to become the Royal Automobile Club) that drew up the regulations for the first Tourist Trophy race which was held in the Isle of Man in September 1905. This was the first of a series of races that, in the opinion of several motoring historians, gave the impetus to European motor manufacturers to produce the sports car — a touring vehicle that could be raced. But if the T.T. saw the conception of sports car racing it was left to Le Mans to nurture it into blooming health with the assistance of that able French wet-nurse l'Automobile Club de l'Ouest, the club that organized the Le Mans race for sports cars, le Grand Prix d'Endurance des Quatres-Vingt Heures du Mans, run for the first time on May 26th and 27th in 1923. We owe a great debt to this enterprising French club for the work they have done in building up Le Mans into the greatest sports car race of them all. No club has fought so hard to prevent it from becoming a race for thinly disguised Grand Prix cars with one-and-a-half seats. That they have been forced to compromise at all in their concept of a true sports car has almost always been at the insistence of the entrants and usually with threats of withdrawal of popular contestants. The battle has been fought volubly for many years. The organizers on their side try in all good faith to define the cars to be raced and the essential equipment to be carried, to regulate minimum sizes for windscreens, seats, doors, ground clearance, luggage space, etc. etc. All this then only serves as a challenge to the cunning brains of a few of the competitors who search diligently for loopholes in the regulations to give them an advantage over all the others and then complain loudly the following year when the new regulations are several pages longer. Gamesmanship has been defined as 'winning without actually cheating'. I hope that Rodney Walkerley was going a little too far when he suggested it is 'cheating without being found out'.

The first sports car

It was Henry Ford who told us 'History is bunk.' A less destructive criticism might have been 'History is not yet an exact science and evidence is sometimes conflicting.' History was all so straightforward when we were at school. Our country was always in the right; Shakespeare was Shakespeare and Queen Elizabeth was a virgin Queen. Now we know our country was sometimes wrong, Shakespeare's plays could have been written by Sir Francis Bacon and the Earl of Leicester often stayed far too late after eating supper in the Queen's chambers. We once thought we knew the history of the sports car and its origins. Today we are not so sure.

There were sports cars around before anyone thought of the name. The name 'sports car' only appeared in catalogues after the First World War. The French had absorbed the English word 'sport' into their language and as early in 1921 Amilcar were advertising their tiny sporting vehicle under the model name of 'le Petit Sport'.

Sporting versions of the automobile appeared all over the civilized world in the first decade of the century. Since so many of these were made in twos and threes in back-street premises with no reliable documented evidence of their

Fig. 1.1 Aston Martin V8. Traditional front-engined luxury sports car.

Fig. 1.2 Ferrari Dino Type 308GTB. Typical modern mid-engined sports car.

dates of manufacture it is not likely that anyone will ever be able to name the first 'sports car' with any certainty.

William Boddy, the editor of *Motor Sport*, refers to the Mercedes 60 as the Daimler Company's first sports car. This car was first produced in 1903 and if we accept it as a sports car it must have been the first in the world. For the 1903 Gordon Bennet race in Ireland, the German Daimler Company, who made the Mercedes, had prepared three Mercedes 90 racing cars. These were destroyed in a fire at the Canstatt works a few days before the event and private owners handed over their 60's to be hastily prepared for the race. Jenatzy won this race with one of these fine cars and in the limited time available for preparation they must be regarded as production touring cars (or sports cars) with mudguards and lighting equipment removed. The Mercedes 60 had a 9.2-litre four-cylinder engine with push-rod-operated inlet valves. The chassis was of pressed steel with four semi-elliptic springs. Transmission was through a four-speed gearbox and final chain drive. This chain drive and the typical wooden wheels of the period were the only striking differences in the specification to divide it from the typical sports cars that followed twenty years later.

Cyril Posthumus traces the growth of the sports car in Europe to the impetus given by the early long-distance trials, the forerunners of the modern rally. The most famous of these were the Prince Henry Trials beginning in 1908 when Prince Henry of Prussia offered a prize for a long-distance rally round Germany in which bonus marks were awarded on the performance achieved over certain timed sections. The 104 horsepower Benz which won the first Prince Henry Trial had all the outward appearance of a sports car. It was reported to have good handling, would accelerate from 30 to 50 m.p.h. in 10 seconds and had a top speed of 90 m.p.h. The third and last of the Prince Henry Trials was won by an Austro Daimler, driven by 34 years old Ferdinand Porsche. This car, with a high-sided touring body and the performance of a sports car, had been designed by Ferdinand Porsche whose influence on sports car design was to grow and endure over half a century.

The 'Prince Henry' Vauxhall was one of the earliest British sports cars. Three of them competed in the 1910 Trial but were no match for the 5.5-litre overhead-valve-engined Austro Daimlers, having only 3-litre side-valve engines. Nevertheless the interest in sporting cars of this type had grown so much that both Austro Daimler and Vauxhall were offering for sale replicas of their Prince Henry models at the 1911 London Motor Show at Olympia.

It was in 1910 too that Ettore Bugatti introduced his 1.3-litre overhead camshaft Type 13, the forerunner of many much more elegant sports cars made by *le Patron* between the two World Wars. A modified 1.45-litre version of the Type 13 ran second in the 1911 Grand Prix de France at Le Mans. Its competitors were the 7- to 10-litre monsters of the period. Very few of the diminutive Type 13 were made and the first Bugatti sports cars to be made in what can be called production quantities were the 'Brescia' and 'Brescia modifié', types 22 and 23 made after the First World War.

A little study of the early American road racers shows that many of these roadsters, such as the Apperson, the Chadwick, the Colburn, the National, the Stutz and the Thomas measure up to our definition of a sports car. As the first American sports car the writer unhesitatingly awards the palm to the Apperson 'Jack Rabbit'. In the June 1964 issue of *Motor Trend* J.L. Beardsley is very persuasive in claiming the 'Jack Rabbit' as the world's first sports car, but the Mercedes 60 was one year, possibly two years, before the first Apperson sports roadster. This appeared in 1904, the name 'Jack Rabbit' being adopted a year later. A 1907 advertisement for the 'Jack Rabbit' gives us a very early definition of the sports car when the Apperson Brothers claim to 'cater to that limited class of owners who want a car that can be put to any service — racing or touring'. There is also a touch of modern snob appeal in their promise that 'only 15 cars of the type will be built for 1907'.

A close contender for the American title would be Stutz, since the 'American Underslung' was built in 1905. This was a low-built racy two-seater with a chassis that was underslung from the springs instead of being mounted high above them as in the prevailing fashion. It was not until 1914, that the famous Stutz Bearcat appeared, the most glamorous of all American roadsters — or should we say — sports cars?

Ken Purdy does not hesitate to use the name 'sports car' when writing of this great era in American automobile history. On the Mercer 'Raceabout' he says:

'There are American cars that rank higher in rarity than the Mercer Raceabout, but no car ever built in America is more sought after or more prized. There are two reasons: the sports cars of the years between 1900 and World War I were starkly functional, unburdened by frills and the weight of useless metal, a characteristic much to be desired; and of all the many contemporary two-seaters, the lean, high-striding Mercer is indisputedly the best looking. Second, most antique automobiles are not at all fast and this one is. A good Mercer Raceabout will cruise all day at 60, show 70 or more on demand, and it has the steering and road-holding to go with its speed.'

The fabulous years

No apology need be made for using such a threadbare adjective, since in its true sense we find that the passage of time is now weaving legends around the names Bugatti, Bentley, Mercedes-Benz, Alfa Romeo, Aston Martin; even the plebeian M.G. Fables are sometimes more popular than hard facts. Every year we see new books appearing to give us eye-witness, blower-by-blower accounts so to speak, of the mighty battles fought between Bentley and Mercedes-Benz, between Bugatti and Alfa Romeo; but we cannot let ourselves be tempted into such reminiscences, for our interest in this book is design and performance of sports cars and our interest in this chapter is the history of the forces and human foibles that have moulded the shape of the vehicle during the sixty years of its evolution.

The greatest influence of all has been Le Mans. A study of the rules for the first race for sports cars at Le Mans shows how the pattern was set for the design of a sports car that was to last for the first ten years. All cars were to conform

Fig. 1.3 Jaguar XJ-S. The latest Jaguar sports car has grown in size, has lost a little in sporting appeal and gained in effortless performance.

Fig. 1.4 MGB GT. Ageing in design, but still a popular formula. (Even the use of 'cheesecake' by Publicity Departments is becoming old-fashioned).

exactly to catalogue specification of the current year, with full touring coach-work including mudguards, running boards, headlights, side lights, tail light, a folding hood, a horn and a rear view mirror. All cars of greater capacity than 1100 c.c. had to carry a full four-seater body, those of lower capacity a two-seater body. Cars fitted with electric starters had to carry a starting handle in the tool-box. The only work done on the cars during the race had to be carried out at the pits and this only by the driver in charge of the car at the time. Only one of the two drivers travelled in the car at any one time, but ballast of lead or sand had to be carried in the car to represent the weight of one passenger. In later years limits were set on the internal dimensions of the body to ensure that the competing cars were sensibly-sized sports cars and not freaks. Mudguards had to be no less than a certain width and had to give a minimum angular wrap around the wheels. Even the type of headlamp bulb had to be the cadmium yellow specified for use on the public roads of France. To encourage reliability seals were placed on petrol and oil fillers, batteries and generators. The car that burned too much oil was disqualified for taking on oil too soon and the car that burned out its generator would have to retire during the night. Hard, you may say, but the organizers were not planning a Sunday School picnic, but a Grand Prix of Endurance. Their aim was to improve the new breed of sports cars, to force the automobile makers to develop engines and transmissions, lights and dynamos, wheels and tyres that would give trouble-free high-speed motoring to the new motor-minded generation that had grown up since the end of the war.

With no other thought in mind than the development of sturdy reliable weather protection, a new rule was introduced in 1924. All open cars had to come into the pits at the end of the fifth lap; there they had to erect the hood, then cover a further 20 laps of the old 10-mile circuit. At the end of this time they were allowed to come in again and stow away the hoods, but not until the scrutineers had examined the condition of the hood fabric and the state of the supporting frame. During the actual race several over-excited drivers, who no doubt had felt it beneath their dignity to practise anything so mundane as putting a hood up and down, made quite a comedy turn of the business. Others had difficulty in completing the requisite number of laps as they struggled to retain tattered fabric with one hand, while steering with the other.

Illogically the drivers were very angry with the organizers when they refused to drop this rule. The drivers and entrants agitated year after year until the rule was dropped. By this time, however, racing had improved the breed and by the end of the 'twenties the hoods on standard cars had become quite durable. Many years had to pass before really draught-proof weather protection was devised for the open sports car.

Over the years the organizers of the Le Mans race have been fighting a rearguard action, all the time resisting the changes that have gradually been made to the regulations, until today we see that the Le Mans sports car is a specialized sports/racing car designed to meet the Le Mans regulations, but no longer a car for use on the public roads. So, eventually they have failed, but they have left behind a long history of fine sensible sports cars that won races, yet were always sports cars. This in itself has been a fine achievement.

Le Mans has now lost its appeal. It is no coincidence that the 'sports cars' that race there now have lost all sense of identity with the sports cars we use on the public roads.

Historic sports cars

It is no mere cynicism that 'nobody remembers who came in second' and the cars we remember best are the ones that won races. Bentleys made a habit of winning races, even if they finally lost financially, and the writer would be no Englishman if he did not put the Bentley first. The Bentley is a cult in England as diehard and illogical as the Eton wall game or foxhunting. W.O. Bentley, who started it all, served his apprenticeship to locomotive engine design and there is little doubt that his cars bear the stamp of this well-engineered conservative branch of the mechanical arts. Here we find sound solid basic engineering with high factors of safety — no nonsense such as making one component serve two functions as we might see on a Lotus — every component designed specifically for its job, regardless of expense or weight, and presumably made to last for ever, or at least as long as the railway company stays in business.

The modern sports/racing car such as the Lotus is designed to be as light as possible, short of falling to pieces under more than average stresses, and to be as small as possible within the minimum dimensions of the current FIA regulations. In this way less power is needed to achieve a set rate of acceleration. With the minimum possible frontal area less power is required to reach the designed maximum speed. With less power, the engine is lighter, the transmission is lighter and the frame that has to support these components can be made lighter. Lightness can be said to breed lightness. As opposed to the usual vicious circle we could call this 'the benevolent circle' and no designer in modern times has used this technique with more success than Colin Chapman.

With Colin Chapman it was a matter of applying a very superior intelligence and a sound training in engineering to the problem of designing a car that would win races. With Ettore Bugatti it was more the artist's flair for doing the right thing and with Bugatti this intuition seldom led him to commit a gross error. Born in Milan, the son of an engraver and architect, he studied at first to be a sculptor. When his brother Rembrandt showed superior talent, Ettore's pride compelled him to abandon sculpture. He turned hopefully to the automobile and made his first car at the age of 18. At last he believed he had found an art form at which he could succeed. He left Milan for Alsace and in 1910 he rented a small property in Molsheim where he began to build what his advertisements called 'Le Pur Sang des Automobiles'. As a lover of horses he appreciated the full meaning of the words 'pur sang' or 'thoroughbred'. By the time he died at the age of 66 he had produced nearly 10,000 automobiles, less than one average day's output by General Motors Corporation. Names like Sheraton, Stradivari, Wedgwood and Bugatti will survive. The names of the members of Detroit design committees are as ephemeral as slogans chalked on wet pavements.

Fig. 1.5 Panther Lima. Sports car nostalgia is on the increase. When a Thirties replica is as beautifully finished as the Lima, a handbuilt copy of nothing in particular created by Panther Westwinds Ltd of Byfleet, Surrey, the appeal is instantaneous. The performance is electrifying.

Only once did Bugatti design big, when he made the Type 41 or Bugatti Royale. This car was so big and expensive that it excited the public imagination, but the car was so untypical that, for once, his intuition let him down. The brakes were woefully inadequate.

Many of Bugatti's sports cars started life as Grand Prix cars. These he would later detune and sell in modified form for use on the public roads. The Type 23, 'Full Brescia', as used so successfully by Ranmond Mays in his early days, was a racing car. The road version, sold in relatively large numbers for several years, was the 'Brescia Modifié'. The Type 23 was eventually replaced by the Type 37, a Bugatti that could be used by private entrants for road racing or could be fitted with road equipment and used as an everyday sports car. The beautiful chassis carried a simple slim body with a finely tapered bonnet behind a tiny horseshoe radiator. The 1½-litre engine had plain bearings (very unusual for Bugatti) and a relatively simple four-cylinder layout. Top speed was about 95 m.p.h. in road trim, with an acceleration time from zero to 60 m.p.h. of about 15 seconds.

No marque is more difficult to classify than the Bugatti, since so many of his pure racing cars were later converted to road use by their owners. A few of these might be regarded as sports cars, but in general they retained the harsh inflexible character of the Grand Prix car and were only regarded as sports cars by their loving owners. It could be a different story when the metamorphosis was carried out by Bugatti himself, or by his son Jean. The most desirable Type 55 is a case in point, being a Type 54 Grand Prix chassis fitted with a slightly de-tuned Type 51 Grand Prix engine — a double overhead camshaft, Roots supercharged engine, with ball- and roller-bearing crankshaft. With full road equipment top speed was about 110 m.p.h.

No matter what excuse we may give to our wives the sports car must always be classified as 'luxury consumer goods'. It was not surprising therefore that the economic blizzard that swept across the world after the Wall Street crash swept so many sports car manufacturers into oblivion. Oddly enough, Bugatti, whose cars were amongst the most expensive ever made, in terms of cost per pound, was not a casualty. Bentley, after the withdrawal of the financial backing of Woolf Barnato, the South African millionaire who had driven Bentleys to glorious victory at Le Mans, was forced into dismal bankruptcy.

Many manufacturers now completely abandoned active participation in motor racing — confining their activities to a little financial encouragement to the more promising private entrants. Such privately owned cars were usually tuned free of charge by the works before a race and, if necessary, straightened out before the next. No 'Clash of the Giants' now — with Blower Bentley battling 7-litre Mercedes-Benz. It was now the 'Battle of the Midgets' between such surprisingly fast small-engined cars as the J4 and R Type M.G. Midgets, the NA and K3 Magnettes, the Riley T.T. Sprite and the Singer 9 and 1½-litre. Handicap races were in vogue and to the imaginative spectator there was a Jack-the-giant-killer quality in the sight of a 2.3-litre Alfa Romeo, a magnificent car that could beat all-comers in such classic races as the Mille Miglia, the Targa

Florio and Le Mans, failing to catch a tiny M.G. before the checkered flag. Some day this spectator hoped to own an M.G.; they only cost about £200. The chassis alone of the Alfa Romeo cost £1,700 in Great Britain.

There was a growing demand for races for small sports cars and some of the international races were divided into classes. Others gave 'credit laps' to the smaller cars as a simple method of handicapping, while the organizers of Le Mans devised a complicated 'index of performance' to equalize, in theory at least, the chances of all sizes of car. This growing interest in small-car racing was a sign of the times. Millionaire sportsmen and wealthy noblemen had supported the game of motor racing from its earliest days, but there were not enough of these left to go around. It was a healthy sign for the future of the sport when the very cars that young men of modest income used for everyday transport could be modified at no great expense to be capable of winning races. Teams of such cars could be maintained at a cost of no more than £5,000 per annum, as against £50,000 per annum or more needed to maintain a team of Grand Prix cars.

After the reconstruction period following the Second World War we entered an era of economic prosperity in what was now known as the Western World. Never before had we had such a wide choice of exciting sports cars. Notable classics that appeared in this post-war period were the A.C. Ace, the Alfa Romeo Giulietta, in all its stages of tune, the Aston Martin 2/4 and DB3S, the Bristol 403 and 404 and Ferraris of so many types — we dare not suggest that any were not classics. We remember the 212 Inter that was invincible in its class, the 340 America, the 375 Mille Miglia, the 500 Mondial, the 500 Testa Rosa, the 750 Monza, all wonderful sports cars. Donald Healey made several models after the war, but the 'Silverstone' open two-seater, with its retractable windscreen and the spare wheel so neatly blended into the bodywork as to act as a rear bumper, is the most memorable. The Frazer-Nash 'Le Mans' was a superb achievement from such a small manufacturer and it is sad the marque has now passed into history.

The XK120 Jaguar was a post-war sensation and deservedly so. The successful C Type and D Type were developed from this basic design, but the emphasis had by this time shifted towards the sports/racing category. The XK120, however, was a very comfortable road car, luxurious in fact compared with the sports car we had known before. Despite this it could win races with little more than normal routine preparation. Contemporary styling connoisseurs judged it to have a beauty of line that has seldom been surpassed.

The Lancia Aurelia started life as an unpretentious Gran Turismo car, more remarkable for its advanced suspension system than for its performance. Eventually it grew into a sports/racing tiger that won the Mille Miglia and the Targa Florio and, in slightly tamer form, the Monte Carlo Rally.

The true genre of the Maserati Brothers was the Grand Prix car, but in the course of a long career they have made many fine sports cars. The Type A6GCS, with a 2-litre 6-cylinder engine designed by Colombo, was one of their more successful post-war designs.

The German contribution to the sports car revival was twofold: from

Porsche — as old as the sports car and from Mercedes-Benz, as old as the industry itself. With only Volkswagen parts available in a country smashed by war, Ferdinand Porsche and his son Ferry gave us a fine little sports car that was different, even though it was underpowered. The Porsche today is still different and the Porsche enthusiast would say 'Vive la difference', for the wide range of Porsche types today can offer everything from exhilarating sporty transport to the most formidable of turbocharged racing sports cars. Today they are all as far removed from the production VW as the Lincoln Continental is from the Model T Ford.

When Mercedes-Benz decided to make a new sports car after the war they waited until their manufacturing facilities were sufficiently re-established for them to design and manufacture as fine a vehicle as the pre-war SSK, of which they were justly proud. Nothing was spared in the choice of materials and in the manufacturing techniques used on this new 300SL. The engine was canted at 50 degrees to the vertical to achieve a low silhouette. Three Solex carburettors were used at first, later to be replaced by an expensive, but remarkably efficient direct fuel-injection system. Suspension was by double wish-bones at the front and swing-axle at the rear. It is doubtful if any model of sports car has ever had such an overwhelming history of victories. The 300SLR sports/racing car that followed the original design never lost a race.

For those of slender purse there has always been a wide selection of small sports cars, especially from Great Britain. There have been the TC, TD and TF Midgets, the MGA and MGB and, based on the Austin Healy Sprite, the new series of M.G. Midgets. The Triumph Company, who had made small sports cars before the war, entered the market again with the rugged conventional TR model which has been improved and developed up to the level of the current TR7. The latest Triumph is still reasonably priced for a 2-litre sports car and is still fun to drive.

The Lotus Company grew out of Colin Chapman's post-war 'specials' that were so successful that he had to make more to please the public. Tax could be saved in Great Britain by the use of 'build-it-yourself kits' and the early Lotuses were largely sold in this form. The modern Lotus is a luxurious creation, with electric windows, stereo radio and air conditioning; yet it remains a sports car. With an engine of only 2-litres it represents Chairman Chapman's thoughts on the car for the Eighties, when low fuel consumption and the long-life car will become an ecological necessity.

Detroit has been fascinated by the sports car for many years, but the market is relatively small by Detroit standards. The Corvette, for so long the only series-production sports car made in America, has had a strong following since it first appeared in 1953. In its latest Stingray form it is still a heavy car (over 3,000 lb) but the handling is now well above average for such a large car. The Ford Motor Company once made a sports car, the GT40, for the express purpose of winning at Le Mans. It was an expensive experiment and proved they had the expertise to win. The publicity was probably worth the effort. The Mustang is their most sporty product on sale today. It is popular and well suited to its environment. If only they would reduce the size and weight and improve the handling it could eventually make a very good sports car.

There have been a few good post-war American sports cars. Notable was Carroll Shelby's Cobra that was competitive enough to win the Manufacturers' Championship in 1965.

Pressures to meet future safety, emission and fuel economy regulations on their current models seem to be giving the Detroit top management all the signs of anxiety neurosis. In such a climate the word sports car or 'fun car' is never mentioned in the Board Room. Some of their younger executives still have the audacity to come to work in foreign sports cars. Perhaps there is some hope for the future, even in Automobile-City.

The future of the sports car

We face a future when 'conspicuous consumption', whether it be of expendable chrome-plated hardware or of irreplaceable fuel, will invoke public anger. There will be no need for laws to ban twenty-foot long gas-guzzlers. For those with no sense of public responsibility the very cost of burning vast quantities of fuel will make them 'think small.'

In such a climate thinking small could mean a 2-litre sports car, with good acceleration and sure-footed handling and a chassis and body so light and aerodynamically effective as to use no more fuel than the contemporary 500 cc motor-cycle.

The sports car of the future will be made to last twenty years or more, with all surfaces protected against corrosion and with mechanical components designed for easy maintenance.

We sometimes hear that this age of the throw-away component keeps us all in employment. We are forced to ask: for how long? Some day the materials to replace those throw-away components will no longer be found, even deep down in the ground.

Porsche are already at work on their Long-Life Car. Others will soon follow. If members of the Vintage Car Club can do it, many of them maintaining cars in excellent roadworthy condition that first left the factory fifty years ago, perhaps we could do the same.

2

The engine: combustion

'And now I see with eye serene
. The very pulse of the machine.'
WILLIAM WORDSWORTH

Cylinder head history

Where we burn the fuel and how we control its burning is so important, so crucial, to the whole science of the internal combustion engine that it is entirely fitting that we devote a whole chapter to the component where this burning occurs. Before the First World War the cylinder head was largely regarded as a convenient cover for the cylinder block and the actual shape of the combustion space was not considered to be of any importance. The superiority of the overhead valve cylinder head, especially the pent-roof twin overhead camshaft design, was appreciated by automobile designers, but only for its superior breathing and the low inertia of the valve gear. The excellent anti-knock characteristics were yet to be discovered. As early as 1908 Clement-Bayard won a Grand Prix using a 13.9-litre overhead camshaft engine fitted with inclined valves in a pent-roof head. For production touring cars, however, the T-head and L-head engines were almost universally used. Very low compression ratios were used, but despite this, detonation often occurred. Nobody knew what caused this knocking sound that came from the combustion chambers and in general it was ignored. Accessibility was everything to the early motorist and the T-head engine with its uncooled valve-caps placed over each valve head, seemed at the time the essence of good design.

After the war, a young experimental engineer, Harry Ricardo, was called upon to design an engine for the T.T. Vauxhall. This twin overhead camshaft 3-litre engine is still regarded as a classic example of the type. The superiority of this valve layout was now well established and several examples appeared during the 'twenties in Grand Prix cars. In 1926 the Riley Company introduced a cheaper form of valvegear, using twin camshafts, placed high on the sides of the cylinder block, and short push-rods to operate the inclined overhead valves. The classic hemispherical combustion chamber was used and the inertia of the valvegear was very little greater than with the Ricardo design. In the hands of enthusiasts such as the late Freddy Dixon, this design of engine was made to give remarkable power outputs all from an engine that in standard form was fitted to a car that sold for the modest price of £298.

Despite the work of such men as Ricardo and Whatmough and Janeway to refine the behaviour and efficiency of the side-valve combustion chamber, despite the attractions of its cheap and simple valve operation, the side-valve engine eventually disappeared from the scene.

The overhead valve engine

There are three major design decisions that confront the engine designer when he begins his preliminary layout of a new cylinder head:

(a) combustion chamber shape to promote efficient combustion,
(b) valve layout to give efficient induction and exhaust,
(c) valve operating mechanism to give reliable operation at the designed operating speed.

Experience has shown that aspects (a) and (b) call for great ingenuity if one is to achieve efficient combustion without making some sacrifice in breathing efficiency. Experience has also shown that the most effective method of valve operation, the provision of two overhead camshafts to each bank of cylinders, is also the most expensive.

In Chapter Three we discuss the all-important subjects of induction and exhaust. In Chapter Four valve operating mechanisms will be examined in detail.

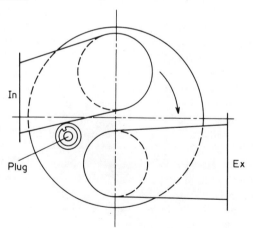

In

Plug

Ex

Fig. 2.1   Line drawing of induced swirl.

Combustion chamber research

In the combustion chamber of the modern sports-car engine one sees the embodiment of thousands of hours of research work, hundreds of patent specifications and countless academic theses and technical papers. The work on knock continues, but the excitement must surely be over. One could hardly hope for new discoveries in this field. If we hope to increase the output of the unsupercharged petrol engine we must strive for still higher volumetric efficiencies, leading in turn to higher engine speeds.

The work of Mercedes-Benz in Germany and the Texas Oil Company in America on the prevention of knock by means of directional turbulence and rotational swirl in engines using direct injection of petrol is not really a new discovery, since it is an extension of existing knowledge gained on compression ignition (Diesel) engines.

Volumetric efficiency

The volumetric efficiency of an engine is the ratio between the volume of air *at atmospheric pressure and temperature* drawn into the cylinder during the induction stroke to the volume swept by the piston, i.e. the piston area times the stroke. It is usually expressed as a percentage. The higher the actual pressure and the lower the temperature of the air at the point of inlet valve closing, the higher will be the volumetric efficiency. The power to be obtained from a given engine is largely a function of the *mass* of air it can breathe, since this within limits, controls the amount of fuel that can be burned.

Surprise is often expressed at the high compression ratios that were used in some side-valve engines. What is so often overlooked is that the compression ratio is not a ratio of pressures, but is a free volume ratio — a ratio between the cylinder volume at bottom dead centre to that at top dead centre. The side-valve engine usually gave a poor volumetric efficiency, seldom better than 70 per cent. A good overhead valve engine will give 85 to 90 per cent, with the hemispherical head engine approaching 95 per cent at maximum torque r.p.m. From this it is apparent that at the same compression ratio, the compression pressure will be much lower in the side-valve engine and, as a consequence, the brake mean effective pressure (b.m.e.p.) will also be lower.

The aim of the designer who wishes to achieve the highest possible volumetric efficiency in his engine is to get the air into the cylinder with as little drop in pressure as possible and in so doing to pick up as little heat as possible in the passage of the air from the atmosphere to the inside of the cylinder. The factors that influence the pressure drop and the charge temperature are discussed below.

(*a*) *Admixture of new charge with exhaust residuals.* At a compression ratio of 6 to 1, the admixture of the new charge of petrol/air mixture with the hot residual gases in the combustion chamber will raise the charge temperature by about 50°C. At 10 to 1 compression ratio the increase will only be about 25°C. In both cases the cooling effect of fuel vaporization is not taken into account, since this is treated separately under (*d*). Other things being equal, we can therefore expect about 7 per cent higher volumetric efficiency from a 10 to 1 compression ratio engine than a 6 to 1 engine.

(*b*) *Heat picked up from the induction manifold and hot-spot.* The hot-spot was invented by American automobile engineers to ensure a quick warm-up of the engine for the impatient American driver. It is a wasteful expedient and is to be avoided except on large engines of low specific power output. It was once thought that by collecting the fuel that could not be carried in suspension as fine droplets by the air stream, and by collecting these heavier drops in an exhaust gas-heated well in the floor of the induction manifold, the temperature of the main air stream would not be raised and the volumetric efficiency would not suffer in consequence. This is a fallacy. All the fuel in liquid form carried in the air stream must be regarded as a potential source of charge cooling, since the latent heat to vaporize these droplets comes largely from the air stream. To the designer of a high-output engine, any additional heat, whether applied at a hot-spot or in any other way, is anathema, since it represents a certain loss of power. In modern designs, where a heated induction tract is considered necessary to ensure a reasonably good distribution between cylinders before the engine has reached working temperature, there has been a return to the old water-heated manifold. Although not giving the rapid warm-up of the hot-spot it is effective in evaporating the larger drops that fall out of the air stream and those that fail to turn the bend where the carburettor branch enters the main tract On some modern engines a thermostatic control is used on the hot-spot. This arrangement, with careful design, is not as power-wasting as some of the older designs of simple hot-spot. In general we can state that the fewer cylinders sharing a carburettor the less will be the degree of induction heating required to give good distribution when warming up. With one choke per cylinder additional heat is not necessary.

(*c*) *Heat picked up from the cylinder head and walls, piston and exhaust valve head*. When the inlet valve opens directly into the cylinder, as in the overhead valve engine, this effect is reduced to a minimum. In some designs the inlet gases tend to impinge on the hot exhaust valve head more than in others. This is a mixed blessing, since the anti-knock properties of a cooler exhaust valve are obtained at the expense of a lower volumetric efficiency. In the average overhead valve engine heat picked up in this way will raise the charge temperature by about 30°C.

(*d*) *Latent heat of the fuel*. The temperature in the induction tract and in the cylinder is influenced to some extent by the latent heat of the fuel. With petrol and a maximum power mixture strength of about 12-13 to 1 a drop in charge temperature of about 25°C can be expected from this source. Methanol (methyl alcohol) has about four times the latent heat of vaporization of a normal petrol and, with a rich mixture strength of about 6 to 1, the *potential* lowering of the charge temperature is about 180°C. In this case only a fraction of the fuel droplets will be evaporated before the inlet valve closes and the actual drop in charge temperature resulting from this evaporative cooling will be about 50°C, giving an increase in volumetric efficiency of about 10 per cent when compared with a petrol/air mixture.

(*e*) *Port design*. One does not need a knowledge of fluid dynamics to see that a tortuous or restricted passage will reduce the mass of air drawn into the cylinder at high engine speeds. The series of right-angle bends we used to see on older designs of induction manifold were largely responsible for their poor volumetric efficiency.

Modern thoughts on port design, as exemplified by the work of Harry Weslake at Rye, suggests that efficient breathing comes from an experimental approach to the detail design of every obstacle that lies in the path of the gas, all the way from the inlet to the air cleaner to the cylinder itself. The use of a wooden model of the entire system makes it easy to modify the shape of any part in the search for the lowest pressure loss. This is a complete change from the old school of thought that insisted in abrupt changes of section in the main tract with buffer ends to promote turbulence. This certainly helped to break up fuel droplets and to equalise the distribution of mixture between cylinders, but the penalty was a greater pressure loss and a reduction in the maximum power output.

The inlet port is often given a tangential bias as shown in Figure 2.1. This creates a vortex flow which persists through the induction stroke and the compression stroke. The degree of spin influences the early stages of combustion. The importance of this induced swirl was realised many years ago by Harry Weslake and a swirl meter incorporating a tiny vaned spinner is inserted in the wooden cylinder head model used in the air-flow tests at the Weslake Laboratories.

(*f*) *Stroke/bore ratio.* Even without recourse to mathematics, one can see that a small stroke/bore ratio is likely to lead to a higher volumetric efficiency than a large one. For any basic head design, whether it be side-valve, in-line o.h.v. or hemispherical, the size of the inlet valve that can be accommodated is limited by the size of the cylinder bore. For the same bore dimensions, the volume of gas to be aspirated with a stroke/bore ratio of 2 will be twice that to be aspirated when the stroke/bore ratio is only unity. In the first case the mean gas velocity through the inlet valve would be twice that in the second case (if it could achieve the same volumetric efficiency). With twice the gas velocity, however, since the pressure drop across the valve orifice varies as the square of the velocity, the pressure drop will be four times as great. The volumetric efficiency of the long-stroke engine will always tend to be lower than that of the short-stroke engine. This factor, as much as the limitations imposed by the high stresses in the long connecting-rods, was responsible for the low practical engine speeds of the long-stroke vintage sports car.

Knock

To understand the phenomenon known as knock, or detonation, it is necessary to consider the manner in which the flame spreads from the plug points to the furthermost point of the combustion chamber. At first, after the ignition of the small amount of mixture close to the plug points, burning is relatively slow and depends in the main upon the speed at which the unburned charge is brought into contact with the expanding ball of flame. Without violent agitation, or turbulence, in the gas, combustion would be far too slow and if it were possible to make the gas perfectly quiescent only a small fraction of the total charge would be burned before the opening of the exhaust valve. Turbulence is present in varying degrees in all piston engines, being promoted in the first place by the passage of the charge through the relatively small restriction made by the inlet valve opening and in the second place by the 'squish' effect as the piston reaches top dead-centre and traps gas between the piston crown and portions of the cylinder head. In certain designs of side-valve and in-line overhead valve engines the clearance between the piston crown and a carefully chosen portion of the cylinder head is made small to increase the degree of 'squish' turbulence.

As the rapidly expanding ball of flame spreads outwards from the sparking plug, heat is radiated to the unburnt charge ahead of it. This accelerates the rate of burning since less time is wasted in raising the temperature of the unburnt charge to the temperature at which combustion takes place. Without this radiation, direct contact of the flame, i.e. mixing of the burning and the unburnt charge, would be the only way in which heat would be transferred. All the time that combustion is proceeding there is an exchange of heat energy throughout the whole combustion chamber. As fast as heat energy is liberated by the chemical reactions between the carbon and hydrogen of the fuel on the one hand and the oxygen of the air on the other — that complex reaction which we call burning — so this heat is spread to the unburnt charge and to the walls of the combustion chamber and the piston crown. This heat is transferred in two ways, by direct mixing of the flame front with the unburnt charge — this we called 'convection' in our physics class at school — and by radiation — the manner in which the earth picks up heat from the sun. All the time this extremely rapid interchange of heat is taking place the general rise in temperature of the gases while the piston is in the neighbourhood of t.d.c. causes a rapid rise in pressure. The pressure rise is greatest where the temperature is highest, i.e. immediately behind the flame front, where combustion is nearing completion. The temperature behind the flame front may be as high as 2000°C, while in the unburnt gas it will probably be about 500°C. Since, by Charles' law, a rise in temperature at a constant volume (all this happening within a few degrees of crank-angle movement) produces a rise in pressure, there travels outwards from the sparking plug, in company with the flame front, a wave of high pressure.

Towards the end of the combustion process, when nearly all the charge has been burnt, the pressure and temperature of the unburnt charge can sometimes reach critical values. This can occur despite the continuous loss of heat to the surrounding walls. If these critical values of temperature and pressure are reached, this 'end-gas', as it is called, explodes, or detonates, the whole volume of gas burning simultaneously. The pressure wave resulting from this detonation in striking the walls of the combustion chamber produces the characteristic metallic noise we call 'knocking' or 'pinking'. A third factor besides temperature and pressure decides whether or not the end-gas will detonate. This factor is *time*. Certain chemical changes are now known to take place in the end-gas before detonation takes place and time is required for these to occur. This is the reason why knocking occurs more readily at low engine speeds than at high.

At the General Motors Research Laboratory at Warren, Michigan, a special engine with a quartz window in the piston crown has been used to observe the

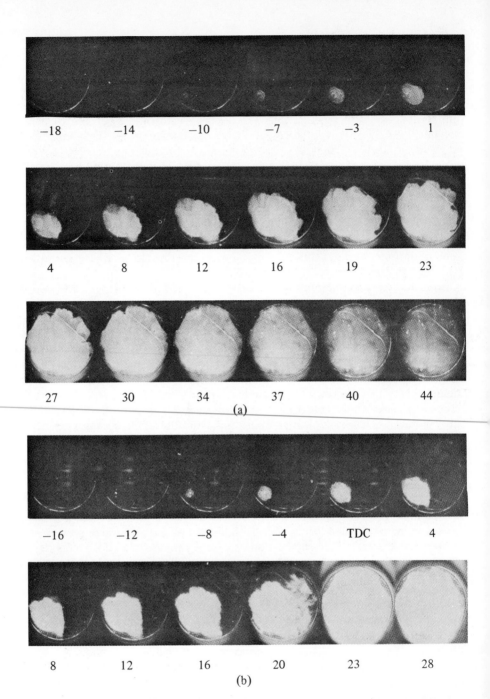

Fig. 2.2 (a) Non-knocking combustion (actual photographs). Note relatively slow controlled combustion of last 25 per cent of charge (from 19° to 34° after t.d.c.). (b) Knocking combustion. Note rapid combustion of last 25 per cent of charge (from 20° to 23° after t.d.c.). (c) Uncontrolled secondary ignition from hot spot.

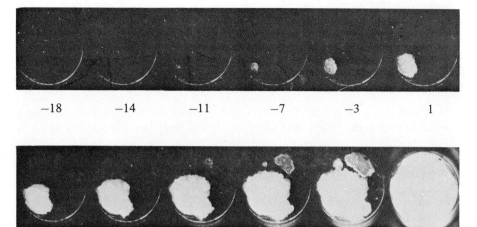

(c)

combustion behaviour in knocking and non-knocking engines. Figure 2.2(*a*) shows a sequence of high-speed photographs of the progress of combustion across a typical combustion chamber when combustion takes place in a normal non-knocking manner. The numbers are the crank-angle degrees relative to t.d.c., negative values being before t.d.c. Figure 2.2(*b*) shows what happens inside the same engine when the fuel is changed to one of lower octane value, so low that knock occurs. From the point where the flame front has travelled about half-way across the chamber (16 degrees after t.d.c. in both cases) the non-knocking engine takes about 18 more degrees to pass right across the chamber. The knocking engine completes this distance in about 7 degrees.

The burning of a liquid fuel is a very complex multi-stage process. Preparatory oxidation reactions must occur before what is called the 'cool flame' stage is reached. The third stage, 'blue-flame formation' is the first visible stage and is followed by 'auto ignition', the final phase. While all these complex, but extremely rapid, reactions are taking place organic peroxides are forming and are decomposing into formaldehydes. Knock is now believed to occur only when the concentrations of these compounds reach certain critical values in the end-gas. These undesirable reactions occur more readily with a detonation-conscious 'straight-chain' paraffin than with a high octane 'branch-chain' paraffin. Tetra-ethyl lead considerably reduces these undesirable reactions in the cool flame period, the peroxides particularly appearing to be de-activated by minute quantities of tetra-ethyl lead.

Iso-octane is a well-known example of the 'branched-chain' paraffins that are used in fuels with high anti-knock rating. One particular isomer of octane, known to the chemist as 2,2,4-trimethyl pentane, has been standardized throughout the world as the 100-octane reference fuel. Thus a fuel which gives the same degree of knock in the C.F.R. (Co-ordinating Fuel Research) engine as an 80/20 mixture of the good-reference fuel, iso-octane, and the poor-reference fuel, normal heptane is called an 80-octane fuel. The octane rating scale is no longer adequate, since many branched-chain hydrocarbons have been developed with far higher anti-knock properties than iso-octane. New test methods have been developed for rating these fuels, which explains the appearance since the end of the Second World War of '110 Octane' and even '125 Octane' fuels. Benzene and toluene, and the commercial mixture of benzene and toluene known as Benzol, are ring compounds and show much of the stability and resistance to knocking of the branched-chain paraffins. Methyl and ethyl alcohol are almost knock-free, but in certain engines at compression ratios of about 15 to 1 they produce a type of 'rough-running' that sounds a little like the knock associated with Diesel engines. This is called pre-ignition and, as the name implies, it is ignition of the mixture occurring ahead of the spark. This phenomenon can also occur with petrol, but in this case the pre-ignition is usually produced by a glowing piece of loose carbon, an overheated sparking plug, or the glowing edge of a badly-seated exhaust valve.

Limiting compression ratio

In the majority of engines the practical limit to the torque, which is proportional to the b.m.e.p., is set by the highest compression ratio that the engine can use without knock occurring on the particular fuel used.

Violent knock will quickly wreck an engine. When knock occurs a large part of the energy normally released by the burning of the end-gas is wasted and does no useful work. This is revealed by the drop in b.m.e.p. indicated on the dynamometer when serious knock occurs. The wasted energy results in a rise in cylinder head temperatures, piston crown temperatures and exhaust valve temperatures and in bad cases engine failure can occur by piston seizure or exhaust valve burning. In some cases the rising temperatures lead to pre-ignition and the resulting uncontrolled rise in pressure before t.d.c. may overstress a component such as a connecting-rod or the already overheated and weakened piston. Knock is a serious matter and should be avoided at all costs.

Let us not, however, develop a neurosis about every little ping or tinkle we hear from our engine. There is a world of difference between the barely audible knock we hear when an engine is a little over-advanced and the kind of knock that punches holes in the crowns of pistons. This latter type of knock can be heard quite clearly about a hundred yards away.

The following are the major factors that have been shown to have an influence on the knock resistance of any design of combustion chamber:

(*a*) *The maximum distance to be travelled by the flame front.* The shorter the distance between the sparking plug and the end-gas, the less will be the tendency to knock. This means that engines with small bores can use higher compression ratios than those with large bores, all other things being equal.

(*b*) *The relative positions of the plug(s) and exhaust valve(s).* The plug (or plugs) should be placed in the cylinder head with a decided bias towards the hot exhaust valve. This is an obvious requirement, since temperature is one of the factors influencing knock. It is obviously desirable for the end-gas to be situated near the inlet valve rather than the exhaust valve.

(*c*) *The end-gas should be situated in the coolest part of the combustion chamber.* This would appear at first sight to be another way of stating (*b*), but in some designs an attempt is made to cool the end-gas by trapping it between the relatively cool large areas of the piston crown and the part of the cylinder head immediately above it. In this position the end-gas is not only provided with large cool surfaces for the extraction of heat from the small mass of the trapped gas, but the position also tends to shield it from direct radiation from the flame front.

(*d*) *A certain amount of induced turbulence is required.* The importance of turbulence and its influence on the combustion process was first stressed by Ricardo. Turbulence in a gas may be regarded as the extent to which individual eddies are rotating and intermingling. The more violent the turbulence, the more rapidly will the eddies rotate, intermingle, break up and reform. Turbulence is used to mix the sugar which is at the bottom of our teacup. Left to itself in perfectly still tea, the sugar would slowly diffuse through the tea by simple 'molecular diffusion', i.e. the molecules of sugar would slowly diffuse away from the strong concentration near the bottom towards the weak concentration at the top. When we stir the tea we produce turbulence and the sugar is mixed by 'eddy diffusion'. In the Ricardo turbulent head designed for the side-valve engine and on almost all side-valve heads made since the early 'thirties a portion of the cylinder head is brought low enough to the piston at t.d.c. to form an area of 'squish'. Since the piston approaches this portion of the head at a very high speed the effect is that of an air ejector squirting this small volume of trapped gas into the man body of gas in the combustion chamber. This squish effect results in a great increase in the turbulence in the combustion chamber, this occurring when it is most required, speeding up the rate of burning in the middle phase. The cooling effect of the adjacent surfaces on the gas remaining in the squish gap, after this ejection has occurred, has been mentioned under (*c*) above, but the effect of the ejected gas on the turbulence of the main gas was the subject of Ricardo's original patents.

The final phase of burning, the critical phase when detonation can occur, is slowed down by the lower temperature of the end-gas left in the squish gap. Ricardo also showed in his experiments that a practical limit existed to the amount of turbulence that should be induced. With excessive turbulence, the rate of pressure rise could be so high that rough running was given. Another disadvantage of excessive turbulence has since been shown to be an increase in the heat losses to the cooling water. The need for induced turbulence becomes less at high compression ratios, since the high pressures and temperatures at these higher ratios increase the speed of propagation of the flame front.

Types of combustion chamber

In general, combustion chamber designs can be classified in terms of the valve layout. For simplification and low cost, all valves in the same bank can be placed with the valve stems in a straight line. Valve operation can be by a single overhead camshaft or by pushrods that transmit the motion from a single camshaft near the base of the cylinder block.

The Wedge head

A wedge-shaped chamber as shown in Figure 2.3 has been popular for many years. It fulfills the four requirements for good combustion:
  (a) short flame travel to farthest point,
  (b) short distance from plug to exhaust valve,
  (c) well cooled end-gas and
  (d) a degree of squish turbulence.

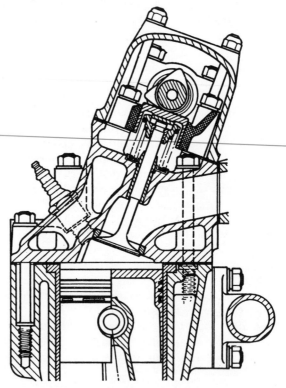

Fig. 2.3   A good example of a wedge head: the FWA
Coventry Climax.

The squish area can be chosen to give the required pressure rise during combustion. For a high compression engine this area is usually smaller than one with low compression. In this excellent Coventry-Climax engine, once used in several racing sports cars, the valve ports are given a downward inclination of 10 degrees. Since the valves are inclined at 20 degrees in the same direction the gas flow path into the cylinder (or exit the cylinder in the case of the exhaust valve) is only diverted 60 degrees, against the 90 degrees change of direction with vertical valves and horizontal ports.

The Heron head

The 'bowl-in-piston' or Heron head has achieved a reputation for efficient combustion. When Jaguar Cars Ltd. decided to develop a V-12 engine for their cars they made two prototypes, a double overhead camshaft engine (with two camshafts per bank) and a single cam design with a shallow bowl-in-piston combustion chamber. This design is very attractive to the production engineer. By transferring the combustion chamber to the piston crown the cylinder head face becomes a flat machined surface. The problems of matching combustion chamber volumes are considerably eased when the volume is transferred to the piston crown.

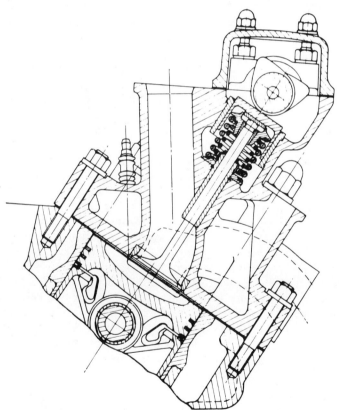

Fig. 2.4 The Heron (bowl-in-piston) Head; a cross-section of the Jaguar V-12 single cam engine.

A cross-section of the single cam V-12 Jaguar cylinder head is shown in Figure 2.4. The prototype had a squish clearance of 1.25 mm (0.050 in). Cutouts were required in the outer rim of the piston crown to clear the valve heads. Improved combustion was given with reduced squish and the final design had a squish clearance of 3.8 mm (0.150 in) and no valve cutouts. Harry Mundy, the Chief Engineer in charge of Power Units at Jaguar Cars was much impressed by the potential of the Heron head, in particular when used on an over-square engine. The single cam engine has a cylinder bore of 90 mm and a stroke of 70 mm.

The Hemispherical head

Perhaps the most successful engine in all sports car racing has been the 4.5 and 5-litre flat 12 engine in the Porsche 917 (see Figure 2.5a). In its final stage of development as an unsupercharged engine it was producing 125 bhp per litre and seemed to prove conclusively that the hemispherical head was indeed the ultimate power producer. The two valves per head in this Porsche 917 were indeed enormous. The inlet valve was 47.5 mm (1.87 in) in diameter and the exhaust 40.5 mm (1.6 in). Their combined diameters exceeded the bore size of 86.8 mm (3.42 in). For an unsupercharged engine it does not, however, now appear to be the ultimate since the 4-valve-per-head design has now become the norm in racing engines.

A good example of the modern hemispherical head is that used in the Lancia Beta 2000, shown in cross-section in Figure 2.5b.

Much ingenuity is often shown when designing down to a price. Paradoxically the Chrysler Hemi-head V-8, introduced as a moderately-priced production engine as long ago as 1951 (see Figure 2.6) was so successful in American stock car racing that the finally developed competition engine was very expensive.

The hemispherical head and its close approximation, the pent-roof head, when used with very high compression ratios does not give a compact combustion chamber and at ratios of 11.5 and 12 to 1 as used in Formula 1 engines it begins to look in cross-section like a piece of orange-peel. In this respect only can the Heron head be said to be superior. If one discounts the large concentric ring of squish area, the cylindrical combustion chamber in the centre of the piston can be made quite compact.

The ability to produce power depends upon the ability to breathe in a high mass flow of fresh charge and to discharge the exhaust gases freely. A high mass throughput of mixture largely depends upon the provision of large valves. This then is where the hemispherical head scores. The valve area, depending upon the included angle between the valves, can be anything from 25 to 35 per cent greater than that of a typical flat-head engine. The specific power (the power per litre) is correspondingly greater.

Fig. 2.5   (a) The Hemispherical Head: two-part cross-section of the Porsche 917 5-litre engine. (b) The Hemispherical Head in production: cross-sections of the Lancia. Beta 2000.

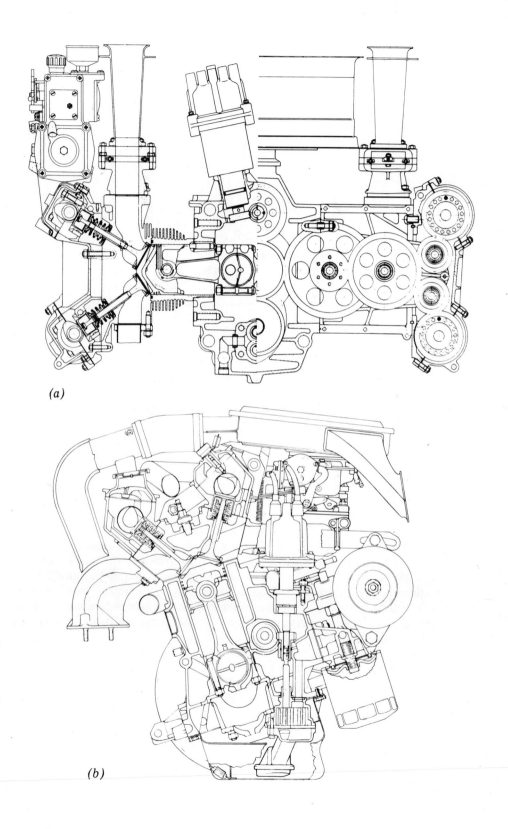

(a)

(b)

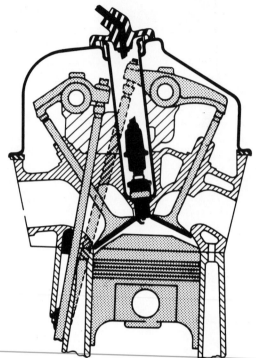

Fig. 2.6   The Chrysler Hemi-Head V-8, in which
a single camshaft in the valley between
the banks operates inlet and exhaust
valves on both banks through push-rods.

The Pent-roof head

The alternative shape to the hemispherical head resembles a typical roof of a
house with the inlet valve (or valves) on one side and the exhaust on the other. It
is the logical shape to choose for the power-producing 4-valve head, although a
four valve head has been made by BMW that approximates to a hemispherical
design by arranging the valve stems to radiate outwards from some central point
in a three-dimensional plan. This creates something of a headache for the valve
gear designer. The pent-roof, with inlet valves on one side and exhaust on the
other, is well-known in racing circles and is usually associated with the name
Keith Duckworth of Cosworth fame.

    After blowing the dust off the 1925 catalogue for W.O. Bentley's new 3-litre
sports car we see that particular attention is drawn to the provision of 'four
valves in each cylinder'. One reason given for using four instead of two valves is
given as 'efficiency — namely, to get the gas in and out of the cylinders as
quickly as possible.' Another reason, so the catalogue states, is 'reliability' and
this reason applies as much to a lorry engine as to a private car. By using two
valves instead of one the seating area is increased by 50 per cent, and in

consequence the cooling surface is greater, and a greater volume of water can be circulated through the space surrounding the seatings. Further the hammering effect on the seating of a single large valve with a strong spring is greatly diminished by using light valves with light springs.'

Who could have put the case for the 4-valve head better, even after more than sixty years of automotive progress, than the great 'W.O.' himself? In 1925 W.O. Bentley was not only the engine and chassis designer, the chief salesman and financial director. He was also the copywriter for the catalogues.

The 4-valve head became associated for many years with that other famous long-stroke engine, the 4-cylinder Offenhauser, so successful for so long at Indianapolis. As stroke/bore ratios gradually decreased and engine speeds went up from 4,000 rpm to 8,000 rpm and higher there became established a general belief that the 4-valve head was an unnecessary complication. The Ford Motor Company of America changed our thinking with a sharp jolt when they designed an engine for Indianapolis competition with a 4-valve head. The logical successor to this was the Ford-Cosworth Type DFV V-8 Formula 1 engine which completely overwhelmed the opposition for a decade and is still used in the majority of Grand Prix cars.

The Type DFV has a shallow pent-roof head with an included angle between valve stems of only 32 degrees. The traditional pent-roof head, as used by Ferrari and Maserati in the past had an included angle of 65 to 80 degrees. The provision of two separate rocker boxes to each bank of cylinders gave these engines a distinctly top-heavy appearance. The Cosworth design with its smaller valve angle gave the designer the chance to enclose the two camshafts in a single neat cambox and cover, giving a substantial saving in weight and bulk.

A larger included angle would, of course, have permitted the use of even larger valves and this alternative is always a future possibility. The Cosworth DFV engine was given two inlet valves of 33.5 mm (1.32 in) and two exhaust valves of 29.0 mm (1.14 in) for a bore of 85.7 mm (3.38 in). In its first year of competition the engine gave its peak power at 9,000 rpm. This has now been increased to 11,000 rpm with the provision of larger valves.

As a typical sports car alternative to this very expensive machinery we should examine the latest 2-litre Triumph engine. Taking the advice of such old hands as Walter Hassan and Harry Munday, who had already opted for a 2-valve Heron head on the V-12 Jaguar, Spencer King decided that a 4-valve head would be commercially viable on an engine with only 4 cylinders. A cross-section of the Triumph Sprint engine is shown in Figure 2.7. As shown here the head joint face is horizontal. When fitted to the canted engine block however it is inclined 45 degrees to the right, i.e. with the inlet port almost vertical. Only one camshaft is used with 8 cams. Each cam serves to open an inlet valve and the transversely located exhaust valve. The inlet valve is opened directly via a bucket tappet, the exhaust valve via a rocker.

As in the Cosworth engine the included angle between the valves is low, only 35 degrees and the camshaft and rockers can be enclosed under one cover. The sparking plus is at the centre of the four valves, the obvious location but one

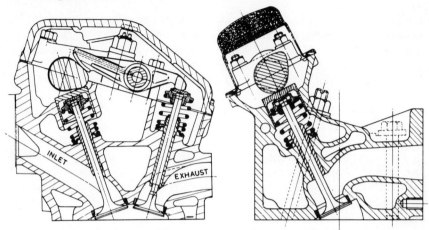

Fig. 2.7 The 4-valve Pent-roof Head of the Triumph Dolomite Sprint. (a) Because steel — instead of cast iron — rocker is used, end wiped by cam has to be lubricated. Seal over exhaust valve is to prevent oil dropping down into it under idling conditions. (b) Comparison of four valve head with earlier two valve design shows both to be identical height.

difficult to achieve. 10 mm sparking plugs have been used in such tight locations in the past, but they are known to be troublesome, with a very narrow heat range. The Triumph solution is novel. A special 14 mm plug is used but slimmed down to take a 16 mm A/F spanner. This plug is screwed into a boss at the bottom of a tubular housing.

3

The engine: induction and exhaust

'There the thundering strokes begin,
There the press, and there the din.'
THOMAS GRAY

The induction system

The basic principle of induction in the four-stroke engine is simplicity itself. Efficient induction, however is not as easy, especially at high engine speeds. On a two-stroke engine, where we lack the positive displacement of the descending piston to induce the charge, a clear understanding of gas dynamics with a little dash of witchcraft is needed to induce even half the charge captured by the four-stroke.

Fortunately, in the modern sports car engine, we are only concerned with the four-stroke cycle. We are, however, concerned with a mixture of air and fuel, much of this fuel being in the form of finely divided liquid droplets that are carried by the air stream into the cylinders. At light loads and at idle about 25 to 30 per cent of the fuel is in liquid form as it enters the manifold. At full power, even though engine temperatures are higher, the flash-boiling effect of a liquid entering a region of low pressure (the induction manifold) is lost, since the throttle plate is wide open, and the amount of liquid fuel is much higher, as much as 60 per cent in some cases.

The more bends there are in the induction system the more danger there is of the mixture segregating into richer and weaker streams, some cylinders receiving the former and the others the latter. In a competition engine the problem of segregation is solved by the provision of individual induction pipes and individual fuel metering jets. The Porsche 917 induction pipe shown in Figure 2.5a is a good example. Production engines do not usually have one carburettor (or one induction pipe) to each cylinder and the behaviour of an induction system can make or mar an engine.

A designer must strike a satisfactory balance between the conflicting requirements of providing easy passage for the air flow to achieve a high volumetric

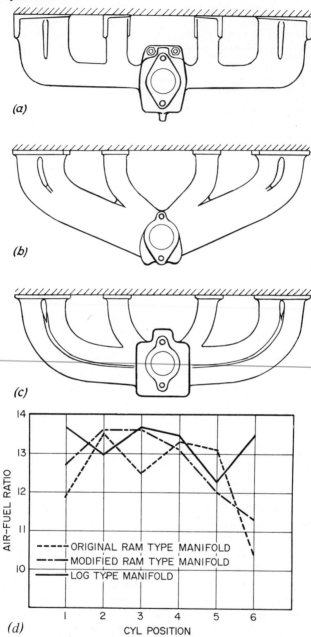

Fig 3.1 (a) Production 'log-type' intake manifold for American Motors Rambler
6-cylinder engine. (b) Full ram manifold for Rambler. (c) Modified ram
manifold for Rambler. (d) Air-fuel ratio comparison of experimental
and production manifolds. Tests conducted at 1,000 r.p.m.

efficiency and providing passages that impart sufficient turbulence to keep the liquid droplets in suspension. Good distribution means supplying equal quantities at the same mixture strength to all cylinders. It was not uncommon in the past to find induction systems that collected pools of liquid fuel on the floor of the manifold at low engine speeds. Figure 3.1 shows the poor distribution given on several experimental manifolds used on an American Motors Rambler 6-cylinder engine fitted with a single carburettor. A log-type manifold, i.e. straight pipe with right-angle bends, gave the best distribution but the lowest volumetric efficiency. The more streamlined 'ram' manifolds gave good volumetric efficiency, but unacceptable distribution.

Good distribution would present no problem if we were to heat the manifold, especially where the carburettor branch enters the main gallery. Enough heat applied here would vaporize all the fuel and the distribution of a gas mixture presents few problems. Unfortunately we cannot do this, particularly on a sports car engine, where performance is so important. The maximum power developed by an engine depends upon the mass of air it can breathe in a given time. By heating the air density is reduced and the mass air flow is reduced in direct proportion. For power considerations, then, we have no escape from the problems of handling wet mixtures, unless we inject the fuel directly into the ports.

The 4-cylinder in-line engine

Turning now to a typical system as used on a 4-cylinder sports car engine, the twin-carburettor manifold, we find that our efforts to distribute the mixture evenly between cylinders are hindered by the firing order, i.e. the order in which the induction pulsations occur. Taking the usual firing order of 1-3-4-2 we see that the negative pressure pulse caused by No. 2 cylinder's induction is immediately followed — and indeed slightly overlapped — by that from No. 1 cylinder (see Figure 3.2). On the other hand, No. 1 pulse is followed by a period of about 360° before the next No. 2 pulse occurs. From this we see that the beginning of induction on No. 1 cylinder will tend to rob No. 2 cylinder of charge at the critical stage when No. 2 inlet valve is on the point of closure. This effect will be greatest with siamesed ports; the shorter the distance between adjacent valve seats the greater the chance of mutual interference during this

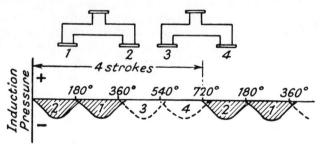

Fig. 3.2

period of overlap. The system is asymmetrical and it is not to be expected that equal charges will be drawn into Nos. 1 and 2 cylinders over a reasonably speed range. The same state of affairs will of course exist in Nos. 3 and 4 tract. A good solution to this distribution problem was found many years ago in a simple bleed or balance pipe between the two parts of the induction system. In this way when No. 2 cylinder is being robbed of charge as its inlet valve is closing, there is a flow of gas along the balance pipe or duct from the inner end of the opposite tract. Since the induction in No. 3 cylinder does not occur immediately after No. 2, this does not rob No. 3 cylinder of charge. The diameter and length of the balance pipe is usually determined on the test-bed by trial and error. This system gives satisfactory distribution, but by no means perfect distribution. An excellent 4-cylinder manifold giving good power at high speed and acceptable low speed distribution is shown in Figure 3.4 (modified).

We must state, at this stage, that our analysis contains a simplifying assumption in that the more complex effects of pressure waves or pulses in the inlet and exhaust systems are neglected. The special cases of 'tuned' or ramming induction pipes and exhaust pipes will be treated fully later in the chapter.

The 6-cylinder in-line engine

When we turn to the 6-cylinder engine, in its more popular in-line arrangement, there are three cases to be considered, the twin carburettor, the triple carburettor and the six-carburettor. At first sight it would appear that the triple carburettor system is a better one than the twin. In Figure 3.3 (a), however, it is seen that while no actual overlap occurs between the opening periods of paired cylinders, the induction pulses for Nos. 1 and 2 pair and Nos. 5 and 6 pair do not occur at regular intervals. The pulses for the centre pair, Nos. 3 and 4, do occur at regular time intervals. The irregular pulses of the two outer pairs would be of no great importance if it were not for the complex wave system that persists in the induction tract and which influences the pressures in the cylinders, in particular at the crucial moment when the inlet valve is nearly closed. With an irregular pairing of cylinders it is not difficult to see that the charging of one cylinder might, at one particular engine speed, be helped by the residual pressure waves in the induction pipe, while the paired cylinder might have its charging impaired.

In some 6-cylinder engines using three carburettors slightly smaller main jets are used in the outer carburettors to compensate for the irregular pulses. At first sight this appears odd, but tests have shown that *for a given mean air rate* a steady air flow through a choke induces a lower mean fuel flow from a given jet than an irregular flow; the more irregular the air flow, the greater the mean fuel flow from the jet. Thus to obtain the same mean mixture strengths throughout, smaller main fuel jets are required on the outer carburettors where the air flow is more irregular.

Figure 3.3(b) shows diagrammatically the twin carburettor system. With the usual engine timing of 1-5-3-6-2-4 the induction pulses are symmetrically at intervals of 240°. The induction tract itself, however, cannot be made

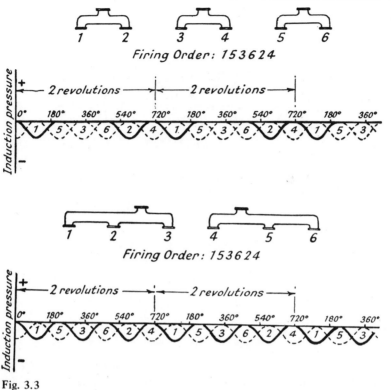

Fig. 3.3

symmetrical. If the carburettors were placed directly opposite Nos. 2 and 5 inlet ports the volumetric efficiencies would be slightly higher on these two cylinders than on the other four. This in itself would not be a serious fault, but the more direct flow in to these two cylinders would cause them to receive a disproportionate amount of fuel in the form of droplets, especially when the engine was cold. A good compromise is shown in Figure 3.3 where the carburettor branch enters between Nos. 2 and 3 cylinder ports on the front manifold and between Nos. 4 and 5 on the rear manifold. With this layout, Nos. 1 and 6 cylinders are the only ones in which the induction process is not preceded by a reversal of flow in the manifold. The flow of gas into No. 2 cylinder helps the beginning of induction on No. 1 cylinder. Similarly the flow of gas into No. 5 cylinder assists the start of the induction process in No. 6 cylinder. It is reasonable therefore to compensate for this advantage by making the overall path to Nos. 1 and 6 cylinders greater than the paths to the other four cylinders.

From the above it would appear that neither twin carburettors nor triple carburettors can guarantee perfect distribution to a 6-cylinder engine. The triple system gives the shortest and most direct path from carburettor to valve and is usually the best power producer. The twin carburettor system is usually the most economical. While the earlier Jaguar engines had twin carburettors the search

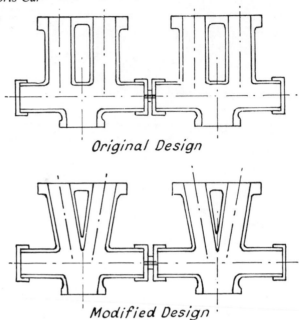

Original Design

Modified Design

Fig. 3.4   Changes to 4 cyl. Coventry Climax F.W.A.
engine to increase power.

for greater specific power outputs in the later versions such as the 3.8 and the
4.2-litre E-Type engine led to the fitting of three H8 S.U. carburettors. Curved
Y-pipes were used between each carburettor and the ports in the head, the curves
being asymmetrical and of differing lengths for the outer pairs.

To extract the maximum power from a given size of engine a separate fuel
metering system must be provided for each cylinder. The fuel metering system
may take the form of three twin-choke carburettors, six single carburettors, or a
system of individual fuel injection in which a high-pressure pump meters fuel to
nozzles fitted in the valve port or into the cylinder head itself. Using multiple
carburettors is a clumsy and heavy solution now that several makes of fuel
injection are available and have proved to be reliable. The beauty of the
individually metered system lies in the smooth unbroken passage from intake to
valve head. There are no branches, no subdivisions of the gas flow to upset
distribution of the fuel, no possibility of one cylinder interfering with the
breathing of the next. A good distribution is assured with a much lower heat
input to the charge than is possible with any other system.

The V-8 engine

The V-8 engine is the popular choice in America today, despite the rising cost of
gasoline. Three types of carburettor and manifold system are in common use on
American V-8's. The oldest system, as one might expect, is the single carburettor with one choke tube or venturi. Later came the two-barrel, then the

four-barrel carburettor. For competition use, as in stock car racing or drag racing, it is common to see three two-barrel carburettors feeding the eight cylinders through a plenum chamber. A more logical scheme is seen on a recent Ford competition engine in which two four-barrel carburettors are used.

For a sports car engine we need not consider the single- or the two-barrel carburettor. Four-barrel types usually have two float chambers, each with its own float and needle valve, an idle circuit with two branches (feeding only the primary venturis) a main discharge circuit (feeding all venturis) four throttle-plates (one to each venturi) and one accelerator pump. The manifold is arranged with galleries at two levels as shown schematically in Figure 3.5, each level

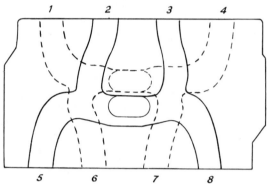

Fig. 3.5 Layout of manifold used with single 4-choke (four-barrel) carburettors on Ford V-8.

feeding two cylinders on one side and two on the opposite side. The two venturis provided with both idle and main metering circuits are called 'primaries'. The other two are called the 'secondaries'. Each primary and secondary pair feeds the outer cylinders of one bank and the inner cylinders of the other. The throttle-plates on the secondaries remain closed at low air velocities. In this way a high gas velocity is maintained through the primary venturis even at low engine speeds, thus helping to break up the fuel spray effectively and to maintain good distribution. The opening of the secondary throttle-plates can be controlled by a mechanical delay mechanism or, as is becoming more common, can be triggered by a second pair of weighted auxiliary throttle-plates that only open when a critical differential pressure exists between the atmosphere and the manifolds. In this way the four-barrel carburettor is a fine, though complicated, instrument, designed to give good torque at low speeds and low pressure drop at high speeds.

The dual four-barrel manifold, as used on the Ford 427 cu. in. (7 litres) single overhead cam engine, is shown schematically in Figure 3.6. Each four-barrel carburettor was designed so that the primary and secondary venturis diagonally opposite each other feed two cylinders, one in each bank. The firing order of this engine (using the Ford System of cylinder numbering) is 1-5-4-2-6-3-7-8. By

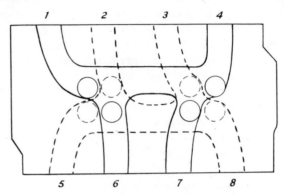

Fig. 3.6   Layout of manifold used with dual 4-choke
(four barrel) carburettors on Ford V-8.

feeding cylinders in the chosen pairs, successively firing cylinders are fed
alternately from upper and lower galleries. The improvements in torque and
power given by this system over the single four-barrel manifold is shown in
Figure 3.7. To European ears the sound of a V-8 engine giving an output of
616 b.h.p. at 7,000 r.p.m. (albeit S.A.E. horse-power) is an awesome thing. It is
also impressive that the power does not appear to be limited by breathing, since
the power curve is still climbing at the Ford-imposed limit of 7,000 r.p.m.

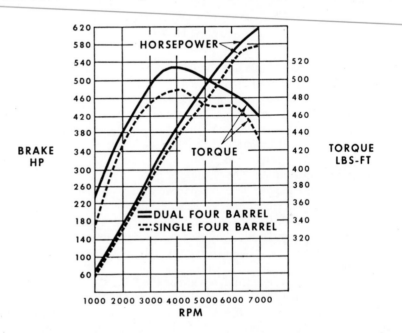

Fig. 3.7   Full throttle performance of 427 cu. in. single o.h.c. Ford V-8

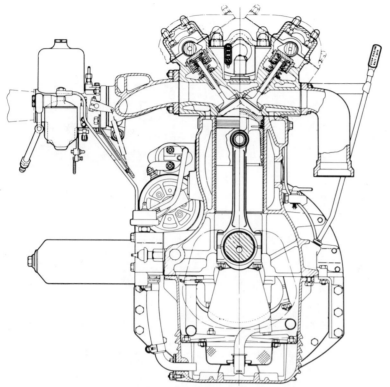

Fig. 3.8   Cross-section of Jaguar twin o.h.c. engine.

One choke per cylinder on the V-8

One cannot attempt to predict what the ultimate development might be in the breathing of the overhead valve engine when fitted with one choke per cylinder. Many believed that the hemispherical and pent-roof head design was reaching its limit of development and that the classical twin o.h.c. two-valve head as seen in the Jaguar, the Aston Martin and the Ferrari could only enjoy marginal improvements in the future. It was known that the Offenhauser engine which has powered so many successful Indianapolis cars for so long was limited more by the high inertia loadings of its big-bore long-stroke design than by the breathing potential of its 4-valve cylinder head. The Ford Motor Company were well aware of this when they decided to make a V-8 engine to challenge the Offenhauser. They made an engine with two overhead camshafts to each bank of cylinders and two inlet and two exhaust valves to each cylinder, thirty-two valves in all. Careful calculations had shown that a higher output would be given by such a head than could ever be achieved by a 2-valve head.

Two port layouts were tried, as shown at the left of Figure 3.10. In both systems the exhaust ports turned outwards and can be referred to as 'horizontal ports' if we regard the cylinder axis as vertical (actually 45° to the vertical on a

Fig. 3.9   Cross-section of Mercedes 350SL V-8 engine. Note the downstream fuel injection directed into the inlet port.

90° V-8). In the upper case shown in Figure 3.10 the inlet port is also 'horizontal'; in the lower case it is 'vertical'. The tests on the air-flow rig showed superior breathing with 'vertical' inlet port.

Ramming induction pipes

The use of ramming induction pipes, 'tuned' lengths of inlet pipe, to enhance the output of an engine over a limited speed range is no new discovery. It was used on stationary constant-speed Diesel engines before the war, a well-known case being the two-stroke Diesel engines designed by Kadenacy for Messrs Armstrong Whitworth. By 'tuning for ram' one means that the lengths of both inlet and exhaust pipes have been varied experimentally until the optimum lengths have been found which give maximum power. The engine has, of course, been fitted to a dynamometer while these experiments were carried out. In this

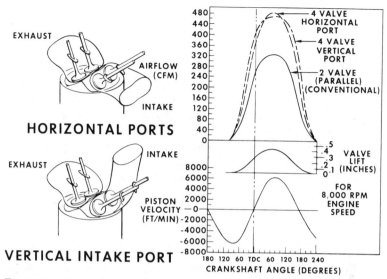

Fig. 3.10   Air flow comparisons on Ford d.o.h.c. engine.

way the peak power can sometimes be increased by as much as 15 per cent over that given by an engine with two or three carburettors and the usual standard exhaust manifold and silencer. About 10 per cent of this gain can come from the adoption of a separate carburettor per cylinder, with a tuned inlet pipe either beyond the carburettor or between the carburettor and the engine.

The late Freddy Dixon always fitted a separate carburettor to each cylinder on his racing Rileys and, despite the great air of mystery surrounding all his work and the padlocks always fitted to the bonnets, there is good evidence that he used tuned lengths of inlet pipe to give him that little extra power to beat the works team. The designer of the modern unblown Grand Prix engine makes full use of induction ram, and exhaust ram too, to fatten the torque curve exactly where the extra torque is most needed. Sometimes the lengths of the intake trumpets on the carburettors are changed between races. For a fast circuit with long straights, short intake horns will be fitted to give maximum ram at peak r.p.m.; for a twisty circuit, where acceleration is more important than top speed, longer intake horns will be fitted to improve the torque curve in the middle of the operative speed range. The use of ramming induction pipes has now spread to sports cars and is seen on all serious competition machinery.

Let us now consider what is happening to the pressure waves in the induction system to make them have such a profound influence on performance. We could, of course, blindly install our engine on a test-bed and lengthen and shorten the pipes until the brake readings tell us we have got the right answer. Indeed when a dynamometer is available there is no doubt that the correct induction length can be found in this way, but the man who is not so blessed must depend upon theory alone, hoping that the theory is not too far from the truth.

Ramming pipe theory

Induction and exhaust ramming have been the subjects of much research spread over almost a third of a century. As yet we cannot say we have the complete answer to all its problems; its full possibilities are not yet exhausted. Many years ago the author worked under Dr G.F. Mucklow, a British authority on the subject. Later, during the last war, the author was able to apply the knowledge thus gained to the analysis of several experiments carried out on ramming induction pipes fitted to two sizes of single-cylinder engine. From these experiments the author evolved a simple general formula for the design of ramming induction pipes. The formula is fairly accurate and in the majority of cases has been found to give quite close agreement with test-bed measurements. When abnormal valve timings are used the formula is less accurate.

It is the inertia of the atmosphere that usually prevents us from achieving a volumetric efficiency of 100 per cent. There are ways, however, in which we can make this inertia work for us. Inertia may be defined as *an inherent property of all matter by which it tends to remain for ever at rest, unless acted upon by an external force. When in motion, its inertia tends to maintain it at the same velocity, unless acted upon by an external agency.* This universal objection to being pushed around is shared by solids, liquids and gases (and quite a large part of mankind too!).

The external force to persuade the air to enter the cylinder comes from the downward motion of the piston. This creates a depression in the cylinder and this depression is, in effect, the driving force to move the air, since the pressure in the induction pipe is now higher than that inside the cylinder. The higher the speed of the engine, the greater must be the depression in the cylinder before the volume of air in the induction pipe can be accelerated. As the piston passes midstroke and begins to decelerate the inertia of the air column makes the air tend to 'pile into the cylinder' at a greater rate than the displacement rate of the descending piston. At b.d.c. the depression is much reduced, but air still continues to flow into the cylinder as the piston is rising again on the compression stroke. This is when the inertia of the air is 'working for us'.

In a typical modern engine the inlet valve will start to open about 20° before t.d.c. and close about 50° after b.d.c. This valve timing is a compromise since the inertia lag between the acceleration of the piston and that of the air column increases with speed. If we choose an inlet valve closing time to give maximum volumetric efficiency at 3,000 r.p.m., at lower speeds there will be a back flow of mixture from the cylinder into the induction pipe just before the inlet valve closes. At higher engine speeds than 3,000 r.p.m. mixture will still be flowing into the cylinder at the point of closure. Thus we find an early 'inlet valve closing' in an engine designed to have a good torque at low speeds. Where torque at low speeds is sacrificed in order to boost the power curve at high speeds the i.v.c. is late.

In ramming-pipe theory we are interested in the effects of inertia in the induction pipe itself. When the inlet valve opens just before t.d.c. and the piston begins to descend on the induction stroke a negative pressure pulse is created at the valve port which begins to travel outwards towards the open end of the induction system at the velocity of sound (about 335 metres per sec or 1100 ft per sec). For simplicity we are considering the induction system to consist of a single straight pipe of unvarying cross-section. This negative pressure pulse is similar in character, though not in magnitude or sign, to the positive pulse that would travel down the pipe if a small explosive charge were detonated behind the valve head. If we were to fit a pressure/time recorder at the valve, it would trace a curve roughly of the form shown in Figure 3.11 as 'actual pressure diagram'. To the non-scientific man, whose mind usually becomes a little

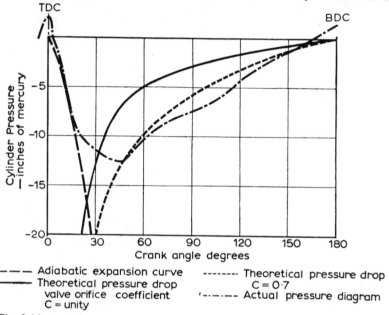

— — — Adiabatic expansion curve

——— Theoretical pressure drop valve orifice coefficient C = unity

······· Theoretical pressure drop C = 0·7

·—·—·— Actual pressure diagram

Fig. 3.11

stubborn when the scientist or engineer begins to talk about waves or pulses, it is sometimes helpful to imagine the column of air in the pipe as a long line of railway trucks standing behind the shunting engine (the piston). The downward movement of the piston may be compared in this simile to the sudden pull of the shunting engine on the first truck. The initial 'plug' of air rushing through the inlet valve to try to fill the depression left by the descending piston may be likened to the leap forward made by the first truck. This stretches the spring coupling between the first and second truck and after about half a second the second truck leaps forward to follow the first. In a similar manner a second 'plug' of air may be considered as leaping forward to fill the depression left by the first. The impulse travels down the whole line of trucks in just the same manner as the negative pulse travels down the induction pipe, only much more slowly. In both cases it should be noted that it is the movement of matter in one direction (the movement of air towards the piston and the movement of trucks towards the locomotive) that causes the disturbance or pulse to travel in the opposite direction.

When the negative pulse reaches the open end of the pipe it will produce a rarefaction in the atmosphere near the end of the pipe. The surrounding air will rish in to fill this depression and by virtue of its inertia will produce a *positive* pulse which will travel back up the pipe with the speed of sound in air. This, in the language of physics is called a 'reflected' pulse, the first reflection. This reflected pulse, when it reaches the cylinder again, is reflected back towards the open end. The summation of these and subsequent pulses, recorded by suitable instrumentation, is seen as a complex wave form. Since the wave length is proportional to engine speed and the length of the induction system, it is possible to change the frequency and magnitude of the wave system by altering the length of the induction pipe. The science of ram tuning is to choose the pipe length so that these pressure waves assist the charging process. In simple terms a

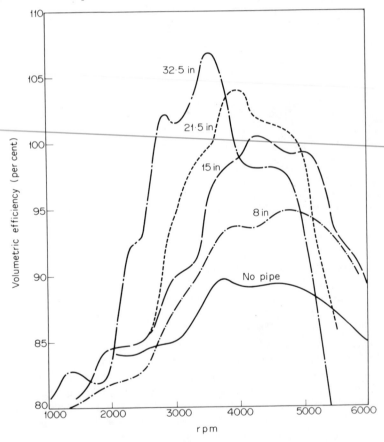

Fig. 3.12   Effect of intake pipe length on volumetric efficiency (D Type Jaguar engine).

positive pressure behind the inlet valve towards the end of the induction stroke assists charging by 'ramming' additional charge into the cylinder before the valve closes; a negative pressure lowers volumetric efficiency by extracting mixture during this critical period.

Ram charging is most effective on engines with a separate induction pipe to each cylinder, although experiments carried out at Southampton University on a Ford Cortina with a single carburettor gave a power increase of about ten per cent by the provision of separate long branches to each cylinder.

The effect of induction pipe length on an engine with individual pipes and a separate metering system to each pipe is well illustrated by Figure 3.12. Short pipes sacrifice power at all speeds, but the choice of a very long pipe such as 810 mm (32.5 in) would cause a serious loss of power at 5,500 rpm. A length of about 430 mm (17 in) appears to be a good compromise for the D Type Jaguar and this was the length usually used when racing.

Figure 3.13 is the author's guide to the best ram length for a particular engine speed. It is only a rough guide since the length of the exhaust pipe and the pressure waves existing there also influence the shape of the volumetric efficiency curve. This is the cause of the modulating wave-form clearly seen on the curves in Figure 3.12.

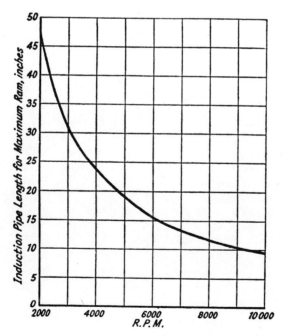

Fig. 3.13

Forward-ram intakes

The forward-ram intake is an expedient sometimes used to utilize the forward motion of the car to ram air at a higher pressure than atmospheric into the carburettor intake. The device has appeared on a few sports cars, but in the majority of cases the external scoop seen on the bonnet top is simply a 'cold-air intake', since the air duct between the scoop and the carburettors is freely vented to the engine compartment. With a true forward-ram intake the duct is sealed against leakage into the engine compartment. To prevent a serious disturbance of the carburettor metering the carburettor float chamber must also be sealed and the cover balanced to the pressure in the duct. On rear-engined cars the forward ram intake is usually placed just ahead of the rear wheel arch.

Theoretically one can recover all the velocity head of the airstream, but in practice, since the duct must turn through 90° to enter the carburettors, the most we can hope to recover is about 90 per cent of the total velocity head.

This velocity head is

$$p = \frac{\rho v^2}{288g}$$

where p = the velocity head, lb per sq in., ρ = the air density, lb per cu. ft, v = the car velocity, ft per sec, and g = the acceleration due to gravity, ft per sec.^{2}.

If the car is travelling at 150 m.p.h. (229 ft per sec)

$$p = \frac{0.076 \times 220^2}{228 \times 32.2} = 0.4 \text{ lb per sq in.}$$

This represents a gain in power of about 3 per cent. Several years ago the Car Division of the Bristol Aeroplane Company carried out special tests on a forward-ram intake and confirmed that a forward-ram intake would give an improvement of 4 b.h.p. at an air speed of 150 m.p.h., or an improvement of 2.7 per cent on the normal test-bed 145 b.h.p. Only high-speed sports cars can gain much from such an intake. At 75 m.p.h. the ram would be reduced to a quarter of the above value and the gain in power would be less than one per cent.

Cold-air intakes

At the beginning of the chapter we mentioned the loss of power that a heated induction system would entail. The same objection applies to heated air entering the carburettor intake. Under-bonnet temperatures as high as 70°C have been measured on older designs of sports car. Apart from serious power loss, temperatures as high as that would probably cause vapour-lock in the fuel system. It is now generally appreciated that the carburettors can benefit from a separate cool air supply and with the provision of large low pressure-drop air cleaners there is no need to fear any increase in bore wear from the intake of fine

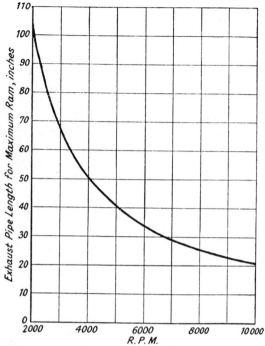

Fig. 3.14

road grit. In many cases the placing of the air scoop on the top of the bonnet has resulted in an improvement in the cleanliness of the air fed to the carburettors. The cold-air intake can be used alone, or combined with the forward-ram intake. If required to function without ram effect a free flow of air is permitted out of the air box which feeds the air filters.

The gain in power from fitting a cold-air intake must obviously differ from car to car, since under-bonnet temperatures differ widely. If we take an average under-bonnet temperature of 40°C, with an atmospheric temperature of 15°C, the gain can be calculated from Charles' law:

$$\frac{\rho_c}{\rho_h} = \frac{273+t_h}{273+t_c}$$

where ρ_c = the density of air with a cold-air intake, ρ_h = the density of air with a hot-air intake, t_c = atmospheric temperature, °C, t_h = under-bonnet temperature, °C.

$$\rho_c = \frac{273+40}{273+15} \times \rho_h = 1.09\rho_h$$

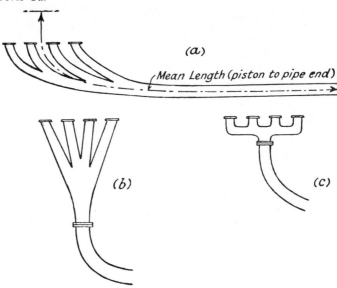

Fig. 3.15   Good and bad exhaust manifolds

This represents a gain of 9 per cent in air density, or 1 per cent for every three degrees drop in aspirated temperature. The gain in power will be the same, provided the mixture strength is adjusted to allow for the change in density and also provided there is no detonation limit or other limit preventing achievement of this power. In some countries a cold-air intake is not advisable owing to the danger of carburettor icing.

The exhaust system

In 1911 the late L.H. Pomeroy, designer of the Prince Henry Vauxhall said: 'Getting the gas out of the cylinder is a simple pumping action, but it is getting it in that makes the engine either a pig or a horse.' Today with our knowledge of the interaction between intake and exhaust we would go further. It is a poor exhaust system that only gets the gas out of the cylinder; a good exhaust system should help the fresh charge into the cylinder.

It is not possible to design an exhaust system on steady fluid flow theory. If the gas were flowing at a steady rate the branches and the main pipe could easily be sized so that a chosen total pressure drop was not exceeded. The flow is not steady and in the branches it is not even continuous. In the individual branches it is flowing for about 35 per cent of the time. Peak velocities in the branches therefore tend to be higher than in the main pipe unless their cross-sectional area is made at least 75 per cent of the main pipe area.

The silencer

For maximum power we require a straight-through system. The use of an absorption type silencer (glass-pack of Hollywood) provides the system with the lowest pressure drop, but the effectiveness as a silencer is often in doubt, especially in the low-frequency end of the audible note range. Glass fibre is almost invariably used as the absorbent material in the annular chamber around the perforated centre-tube. This has inadequate strength at the operating temperatures of most sports car exhaust systems and the weakened glass fibres soon disintegrate and disappear out of the tail-pipe.

In figure 3.15 we show three types of exhaust system. Either type (*a*) or type (*b*) are good smooth flowing designs that lend themselves to pulse tuning. Type (*c*) is shown more as a warning. Cast manifolds of this type used to be popular on mass-produced cars and only helped to cut down the power output of the engine.

Ramming exhaust pipes

The same principles of ramming pipe design as were discussed earlier in the same section on ramming induction pipes can also be applied to the exhaust pipe. With a straight-through silencer only a small fraction of the amplitude of the original pulse is damped by the absorption material of the silencer, although the amplitude of the pulse does become of negligible size after three or four reflections. To obtain ram from an exhaust system our aim is to make the exhaust system extract residual gas from the cylinder head during the period of overlap between the opening of the inlet valve and the closing of the exhaust valve. Overlap may be a modest 30 to 40 degrees on a touring engine. On a competition engine it can be as much as 120 degrees. A depression in the exhaust port at this time helps to extract the hot residual gases from the combustion chamber thus helping to lower the charge temperature. By creating a depression in the cylinder it also helps to start the movement of the new charge into the cylinder through the already open inlet valve. With normal overlaps an increase in volumetric efficiency of from 5 to 7 per cent can be obtained in this way. If we are willing to sacrifice fuel economy and a smooth idling speed, greater gains are possible by using overlaps of 50, 60 and even 80 degrees. In this way the last traces of the residual gases can be sweapt out of the combustion chamber at the expense of a certain amount of the new charge going to waste down the exhaust pipe. Unfortunately when very large overlaps are used the smooth running of the engine is adversely affected at engine speeds where a positive pressure is produced in the exhaust port during overlap. Extreme overlaps are therefore not conducive to good idling.

Figure 3.14 is the author's attempt to provide a rough guide to the ramming-pipe length for an exhaust system using separate pipes to each cylinder. This would make a very bulky exhaust system on a sports car where every pipe would require a separate silencer.

Branched exhaust pipes

A tuned length of pipe is still possible with a multi-branch exhaust system. The modern rear-engined GP car is now a familiar sight with its 'bunch of snakes' system. Care is taken to tune the lengths of the branches as well as the two main exhaust pipes. Branches are grouped in fours on the V-8 engine, the two inner pipes from one bank of cylinders being carried across to join up with the two outer pipes from the opposite bank. In this way even pulsations occur at the point where the four branches join their main pipe. The dynamometer is the best instrument we can use for this determination of optimum lengths, but Figure 3.14 will be of value to the tuner of modest means.

4

The engine: valve gear

Perhaps it is nothing more than a piece of English folklore, but it is told of the early days of Steam that the first valve gear was invented by a lazy boy whose job in life was to pull the right rope at the right time to admit steam to the valve chest and to pull the other rope to cut it off again when he saw the cross-head begin to reverse its direction. He must have been a very thoughtless child. Automation has put many of us in later generations among the ranks of the unemployed — but this is material for a different sort of book.

Push-rod valve operation

Push-rod valve operation is a little more sophisticated than using ropes. The cams operate tappets (cam-followers) and these transmit motion to tubular rods which in turn transmit the motion via rockers to the valve stem ends. To replace the rope to close the valve a coil spring or springs perform the closing operation. The system appeals to the cost-conscious production engineer since the camshaft can be placed low down on the engine to be operated from the end of the crankshaft by a relatively short chain drive. The disadvantage lies in the long distance between the camshaft and the valves it has to operate. This increases the inertia of the valve mechanism on high-speed engines. There is also a certain springiness in the whole system that leads to a distortion of the valve opening period and rates of opening and closing as defined by the shape of the cam.

On a V-8 engine a single camshaft can be placed in the valley between the banks of cylinders and used to operate valves on both banks. This, naturally, brings a glow of happiness to the heart of the production engine. Even so the ingenuity of master tuners like Harry Weslake has demonstrated what can be done with this simple basic layout if you only have a 'quick inventive brain.'

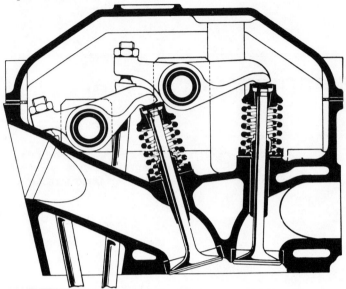

Fig. 4.1   Four-valve Chevrolet head designed by Harry Weslake using
a single camshaft to operate 32 valves through push-rods.

Figure 4.1 is a cross-section of the prototype 4-valve head designed at the
Weslake establishment at Rye in Sussex for the 5-litre Chevrolet engine. In the
standard engine the sequence of valve operation along the length of the
camshaft for the 16 valves (4 inlet and 4 exhaust per bank) is *exhaust, inlet,
inlet, exhaust*, etc. To operate 32 valves from a single camshaft, a new camshaft
carrier casting was made to accommodate forked rockers in two rows. The cam
sequence was also changed to *exhaust, inlet, exhaust, inlet*, etc. The porting and
valves were developed by the well-known Weslake gas-flowing technique
described in Chapter Two. In 1974 when this work was undertaken the current
racing 5-litre Chevrolet with 2-valve head developed 490 bhp. The Weslake
4-valve head turned out 600 bhp at 7500 rpm. This is an interesting case-history
to illustrate that push-rod valve operation is not to be dismissed too lightly, even
though no one in his right mind would attempt to design a competitive Grand
Prix engine using push-rods. The Weslake engine delivered 120 bhp per litre,
while the current GP engine has a specific output of 179 bhp per litre and
operates at speeds up to 12,000 rpm.

The double overhead camshaft valve operation

The double overhead camshaft (DOHC) cylinder head has a long racing
tradition. Figure 4.2 shows how the two camshafts were often driven by a very
complex gear train in the traditional DOHC racing engine of the Fifties. The
method was noisy but very reliable. In the cross-section of the Jaguar engine
shown in Figure 3.8 in the previous Chapter the typical valve operation through

Fig. 4.2   Twin overhead camshaft Aston Martin engine used in DBR1 racing
sports car. Note complexity of gear train to take drive from
crankshaft to the two camshafts.

bucket tappets is shown. Not all designers have adopted the bucket tappet.
Daimler-Benz (*see* Figure 3.9) prefer to use a rocker between the cam and the
valve stem. Adjustment of valve clearances on the bucket tappet system is very
time-consuming. Circular shims of different thicknesses are placed inside each
tappet until the correct clearances are obtained throughout. The rocker on the
Mercedes engine pivots at one end on a spherically-ended stud. Adjustment of
valve clearance is a simple matter of screwing the stud in or out and re-locking in
position with the lock-nut.

The single overhead camshaft head

When Jaguar introduced the 3.4 litre XK120 sports car in 1949 with a DOHC engine, many automotive production engineers asked the question, 'How on earth do they do it at the price?' Even so when those two experienced engine designers Harry Munday and Walter Hassan began to work on a new V-12 Jaguar engine about twenty years later they found the prospect of providing four overhead camshafts and all the attendant drive gear a little daunting. They knew how to do it of course but there were still two problems to be solved; the obvious question of cost and the sheer size of the DOHC layout which had to be accommodated between the front wheel arches.

As a design exercise they started by making two engines, one with DOHC and the other with SOHC. The first engine was such a power-producer that the Company was tempted to develop the engine as a dual-purpose power-unit, an engine good enough to return to the field of sports car racing again, yet satisfactory in a de-tuned form, as a very attractive production sports car engine. The provision of camboxes, tappet carriers and cylinder heads for a DOHC was no problem and followed established practice. The drive train to operate four camshafts at the top of the engine from a crankshaft at the bottom was no mean problem. For a pure competition engine they used a combination of two chain drives, followed by two separate gear trains as shown in Figure 4.3. This gave reliable service during the development period and a specific power of

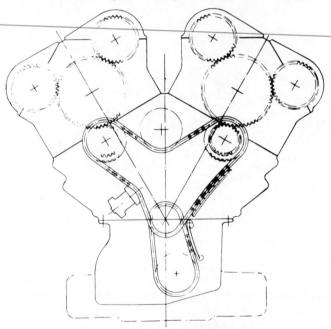

Fig. 4.3   Camshaft drive on Jaguar DOHC competition engine
using two chain drives and two gear trains.

100 bhp per litre was soon attained. A boardroom decision however prevented further work on this racing engine and an attempt to reduce cost for a production version by the provision of multiple chain drives resulted in the layout shown on the right in Figure 4.5. This was not a reliable drive system and gave a noise level that was considered unacceptable for a luxury car.

The SOHC engine was given a larger bore, 90 mm against 87 mm for the DOHC, but the valves were still smaller in the SOHC design and the air flow at maximum lift was reduced by about 30 per cent. The highest power output reached on the testbed with fuel injection to individual intakes and with open

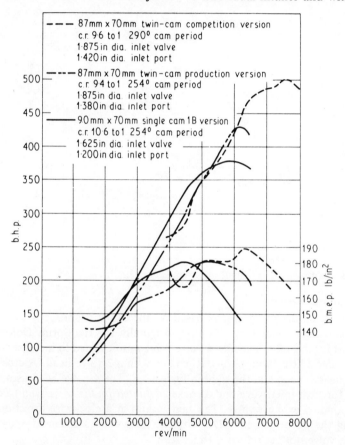

Fig. 4.4   Power curves of single and twin-cam Jaguar engines.

exhaust was still only 75 per cent of that reached by the DOHC engine (*see* Figure 4.4). The advantages of the SOHC design are summarised by Harry Munday as:

(a) cheapness and lightness,

(b) reduced engine bulk, in particular of the critical width across the exhaust manifolds, since this limits wheel-lock angles with the wide tyres fitted to the modern Jaguar,

(d) more space between the cylinder heads to accommodate a 12-cylinder ignition distributor and an air-conditioning compressor.

In its final production form the SOHC engine with a compression ratio of 9.0 to 1 gives 272 bhp (DIN) at 5850 rpm, a modest output of 51 bhp per litre, but a silky smooth torque flow reminiscent of a steam engine.

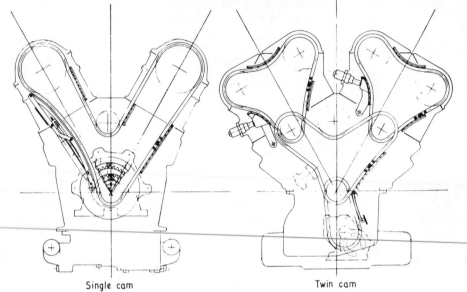

Single cam   Twin cam

Fig. 4.5   Comparison of single and twin-cam chain drives.

The four-valve head

An interesting design of engine based on the SOHC concept is the 16-valve, 4-cylinder engine made by Triumph, originally for the Sprint Dolomite and intended for the TR7. The new 4-valve head was designed to increase the power of the older 2-litre Triumph SOHC engine with a 2-valve head. A cross-section of this head is shown at the right in Figure 2.7. The 4-valve head uses a bucket tappet for each inlet valve and a rocker *actuated by the same cam* to open the corresponding exhaust valve. The cam rotates in a clockwise direction. In the drawing the piston is near TDC with the inlet valve starting to open and the exhaust valve not yet returned to its seat.

The ideal place for the sparking plug on a 4-valve head in the centre. To reach this difficult spot special plugs are used having 14 mm diameter screw threads where they enter the head, but with a hexagon size reduced to that of a 10 mm plug. This reduces the maximum plug diameter and of the tubular housing in which it fits. The plus is of the conical seating type to obviate the need for a gasket. The problems associated with retrieving a gasket from the bottom of this long narrow tube are obvious. (*See* Figure 4.6.)

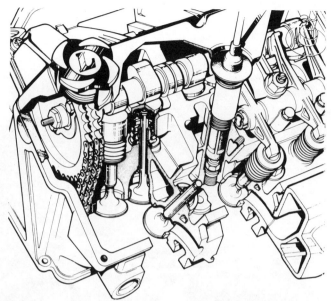

Fig. 4.6   Triumph 4-valve head. 10 mm hexagon on 14 mm
sparking plug makes a very compact design.

Another successful 4-valve head is that used in the 2-litre Lotus Elite, Eclat
Esprit sports cars. It was built originally for the Team Lotus racing cars. The
engine is a slant-four canted at 45 degrees and using two overhead camshafts to
operate the 16 valves. The manner in which the two camshafts are driven by a
single timing belt (toothed belt) from a pulley on the end of the crankshaft is
shown in Figure 4.7. The small pulley on the crankshaft nose is barely visible in
the illustration, being shielded by the outer pulley that drives the alternator and
water pump by means of a V-belt. The toothed pulley vertically above the end of
the crankshaft drives a jackshaft to drive the oil pump and a horizontal
distributor. The timing-belt is tensioned by an external jockey-pulley situated
between the driving pulley and the jackshaft pulley.

The downdraft carburettors shown here are not those used in the production
engines, where horizontal twin-choke Dellorto carburettors are used to fit below
the low bonnet-line. For safety reasons a sheet metal guard is fitted over the top
of the belt drive on production engines.

The timing belt gives a very neat inexpensive drive for the camshaft or
camshafts and with the now proven reliability of the latest belts we can
anticipate more designers turning to this system in the future. Modern timing
belts use helically-wound polyester as tension members and polychloroprene as
the basic compound. External abrasion is resisted by a two-ply nylon facing. As
an example of what can be done if one is not afraid to festoon the front of the
engine with whirling belts and pulleys we have given a front view in Figure 4.8 of
'the poor man's instant Grand Prix engine' as designed by Keith Duckworth.

Fig. 4.7   Lotus LV/240 engine. Use of timing belts (internally toothed) to give inexpensive and reliable drive to DOHC engine.

This Cosworth engine uses the 3-litre V-6 British Ford 'stock-block' as a basis for a 3,412 cc engine that develops 'more than 400 bhp' at 8,500 rpm.

The combustion chamber shape, valve and port configuration is based on the victorious Cosworth 3-litre Grand Prix engine and all is achieved using the bottom end of a perfectly ordinary mass produced push-rod engine. It is interesting to note that Mike Hall who was in charge of the development of this particular engine has found that timing belt drives are not only cheap and reliable, but they help to isolate camshaft and crankshaft vibrations. Many an expensive gear-train drive has foundered on that very problem. Gears provide great strength and reduce timing variations to a minimum, but there have been

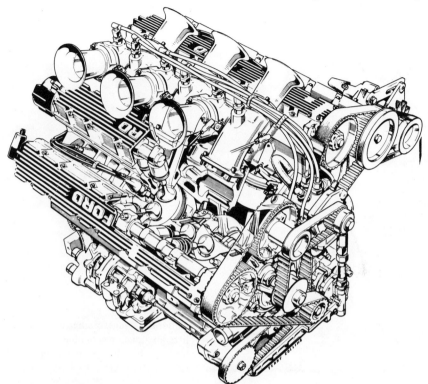

Fig. 4.8   Cosworth-Ford V-6 with 4-valve DOHC arrangement using a multiplicity of timing belt drives.

occasions when destructive interaction of torsional vibrations has been transmitted through the gears between the two vibrating systems, the crankshaft and the camshaft. In theory, a designer should be able to use the computer to eliminate this possibility. In practice, being only human, he is happy to use a drive that automatically absorbs these torsional vibrations.

Desmodromic operation

Older readers, and perhaps more youthful followers of the sport of motorcycle racing, might well ask: what happened to desmodromic valve operation? On a conventional engine the cam only opens the valve, closure being brought about by the action of the spring or springs. As engine speeds rise so do the inertia forces and the only way to prevent the valve from bouncing off the end of the rocker or the top of the cam is to increase the strength of the springs. This increases the loads on the valve seats at lower engine speeds and is a source of valve-seat sinkage that calls for special valve-seat insert materials to resist this continual hammering action. Figure 4.9 is a plot of actual valve lifts as measured on a push-rod ohv installation. The upper plot shows that the cam profile is faithfully followed at an engine speed of 2,000 rpm. At 4,800 rpm (camshaft speed of 2,400 rpm); however, the valve bounces away from the

(a)

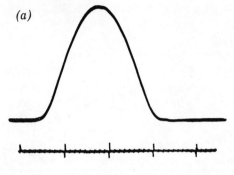

a

(b)

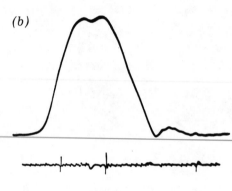

Fig. 4.9
Laboratory measurements of valve
lifts on a push-rod engine with
inadequate valve spring strength:
(a) at 2000 r.p.m.; (b) at 4000 r.p.m.

b

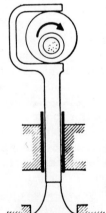

Fig. 4.10
The desmodromic valve operation used by
Delage in 1914 on their GP racing car.

rocker before reaching full opening, then falls back momentarily only to ricochet again off the nose of the cam. Contact is made again with the rocker end just before the point of closure. After a momentary closure the valve bounces again for a few degrees of crank rotation, making the actual point of closure an uncontrolled variable. Desmodromic valve operation is the logical solution, a solution that has been a long-standing challenge to our engineering ability. *Desmodromic* is a word created from two Greek roots: *desmos* meaning a band and *dromas* meaning running. It is therefore a valve gear confined to run in a band. When it first appeared on the 1914 Delage GP car the band was provided by a rectangular stirrup on the valve stem that embraced an eccentric cam (see Figure 4.10). A small 'tolerance spring' was used to pull the valve finally on to its seat, since the desmodromic cam mechanism only brought the valve within a few thousandths of an inch of the closed position. This problem of tolerance has been the downfall of so many attempts to provide a practical system. If, for example one were to provide a total clearance between the cam and the stirrup of, say, 0.10 mm (0.004 in) and this value was exceeded due to the sinkage and erosion on the valve and its seat, plus the differential expansion due to temperature changes between a cold engine and a hot engine, the valve could fail to reach its seat. This would naturally result in a burned-out valve in a very short time.

Delage soon abandoned their 'push-pull' system, but there were many other attempts during the next forty years with no design reaching the level of reliability to warrant its adoption for a production engine. In 1954, however,

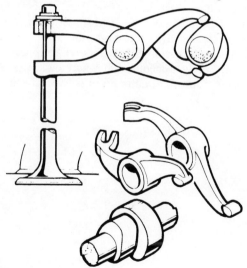

Fig. 4.11   Desmodromic valve operation used by
Mercedes-Benz on their 1954/55
GP cars.

Daimler Benz entered the Grand Prix arena with their world-beating Formula 1 car fitted with a 2.5 litre straight-eight engine with a reliable desmodromic valve gear. Even so they never attempted to introduce desmodromic operation in a production engine and the suspicion remains that the excellent reliability was dependent upon meticulous attention to valve clearances by their team of dedicated racing mechanics. We need hardly mention that some production engines receive no attention until they fail to start. The prototype Daimler-Benz design used light springs for the final closure of the valves, but experience during development allowed them to dispense with these. With a fairly generous, *but carefully maintained*, clearance, the pressure inside the cylinder closed the valve on its seat. From a study of Figure 4.11 it will be seen that two cams per valve were used, one to close the valve, the other to open it. Each cam had its own rocker, positioned side by side on the same rocker shaft and with the forked ends turned inwards to bring them axially together. Extreme accuracy in cam machining is essential with such a system to maintain a close tolerance on clearances at all times if the valve is to follow the cam profile accurately.

This was the last desmodromic system to be seen in motor racing to our knowledge, but the application to motor-cycle engines has proceeded apace. Modern racing motor-cycle engines reached *permitted* speeds of 20,000 rpm and will sometimes overspeed by as much as 3,000 rpm when going down through the gears when slowing down for a corner. In 1958, Norton modified their 'Manx' racing engine to a very promising system but the necessary money to develop this desmodromic Norton was not available. In more recent times the Italian Ducati Company have spent many years developing a successful system. Unlike Daimler-Benz they were not able to dispense with 'tolerance springs' since, without these the engine gave no compression when cranked over slowly.

The desmodromic system has so much to offer and we appear to be so close to a satisfactory solution. Surely someone somewhere can release a little brain-power from the pressing problems of anti-anti-missiles to give us a reliable valve gear?

5

The engine: fuel metering

'So once it would have been - 'tis so no more:
I have submitted to a new control.'
WILLIAM WORDSWORTH

THE CARBURETTOR

The carburettor, like King Charles the Second, is 'an unconscionable time a-dying.' It has been developed over the years into an accurate and relatively inexpensive fuel metering device. In recent years the carburettor manufacturers have striven very hard to meet the increasingly stringent American emission-control regulations and their success has been not without some compensation, since they have not yet been put out of business.

The simple carburettor uses a venturi to meter the fuel supply to match the mass air-flow and by a complicated system of compensating jets, emulsion tubes, accelerator pumps, idling circuits and other gadgetry it has for many years been able to match the air/fuel ratio requirements demanded by the project engineer over the whole operating range of the engine to an accuracy of plus or minus 5 per cent. Unfortunately, the project engineer who is responsible for getting his baby through the emission control tests now knows the acceptable limits on metering accuracy must be reduced to no more than plus or minus 2½ per cent, day in and day out, over wide ranges of ambient temperature and barometric pressure. This is the challenge that has faced the carburettor experts in recent years.

The S.U. carburetter*

The S.U. Carburetter Company have worked diligently for many years to eliminate or reduce many sources of mixture variation that are intrinsic in the basic method of metering by venturi. Since the S.U. instrument has been so popular in the past with sports car manufacturers it will serve to illustrate some

*There are two English and one American way to spell this word. The S.U. Carburetter Company have always used this one.

of the problems encountered when the metering band has been tightened to plus or minus 2½ per cent.

For those not familiar with the working principle of the S.U. carburetter here is a brief resume:-

The modern S.U. carburetter comes in several different designs but the basic metering system is similar to that illustrated in Figure 5.1. At idling engine speed

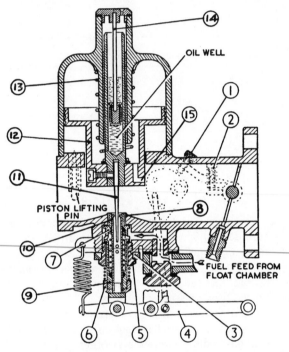

Fig. 5.1   Cross-section of basic S.U. carburettor.

the base of the piston (12) rests on the bridge (8), a small opening for the idling air supply being created by the provision of two small projections on the base of the piston. The depression downstream of the piston is in constant communication with the upper part of the piston, the suction disc, through the passage (15). As the throttle is opened, the air flow through the gap between the piston and the bridge increases. This causes the depression downstream of the piston to increase. This increased depression causes the piston to rise, since the higher depression is transmitted to the top of the suction disc through passage (15). With an increased area at the choke (the choke being the space between the bottom of the piston and the bridge) the depression tends to fall again and the final new position of the piston is an equilibrium position where the depression above the suction disc exactly balances the weight of the piston, plus the additional load of the light spring (13). Without the damping action of the oil damper unit (14) any sudden change in throttle position would be followed by the oscillation of the piston as it overshot the equilibrium position at least once. As the throttle is opened and closed under the varying load demands dictated the the driver, the piston rises and falls to new equilibrium positions, the depression between the choke and the throttle always remaining constant close to the usual design value of eight inches of water head. As the piston rises and falls in this way under the influence of the changing air consumption of the engine, the position of the tapered needle (11) also changes, the annular space between the needle and the jet (10) being smaller for low air rates than for high. By choosing the profile of the needle to suit the mixture requirements of the engine at the various air rates almost any desired mixture can be metered over the whole range from idle up to full-throttle at the highest operating engine speed.

The damper in the S.U. carburetter, besides its obvious action in preventing undue oscillations of the piston, has a secondary function in that it enriches the mixture during acceleration. Without an acceleration enrichment device a flat-spot would occur in carburation every time the throttle was suddenly opened. The effect of the damper on the S.U. carburetter is to delay the rise of the piston slightly when the throttle is snapped open. This causes the depression to rise above the normal steady value, and this enhanced depression acting on the fuel in the jet induces a greater flow of fuel. It will be seen that the delay in the rising of the piston will also keep the needle at a lower position in the jet, which in itself should tend to reduce the flow of fuel. The effect of the enhanced depression, however, is much greater and the combination of the two effects is still an increase in the strength of the mixture.

In general, with a perfectly standard engine, only the maker's recommended needle need be considered. If however the engine is modified in such a way as to increase the power output it becomes necessary to make dynamometer tests to choose a more suitable needle. It must be stated though that any form of modification to the fuel metering system, even a change in jet size or in needle profile, has become illegal in some countries where strict emission control regulations are enforced.

We have described the simple S.U. carburetter as we have known it for half a century. We can now consider the modifications that were found necessary to give the more precise metering demanded by the current US Federal exhaust emission laws. Cars exported to North America are fitted with the HIF (Horizontal Integral Float Chamber) model.

The HIF model incorporates the following eight new features:

Spring-loaded jet needle. Readers familiar with the older S.U. carburetter will know how important it was to centralise the needle in the jet, or should we say *try* to centralise the needle. S.U. engineers working on the new problems set by the emission control requirements discovered that a needle set to be clear of the jet wall, but slightly off-centre (case *a* in Figure 5.2) would pass slightly more fuel under a given head than a perfectly concentric needle (case *b*). To remove this tuning anomaly they decided to spring-load the needle so that it always touched the side of the jet. The pressure is very light but contact with the jet wall is maintained over the entire range of needle movement. No jet centring

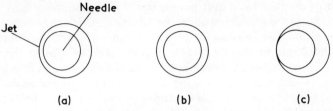

Fig. 5.2 Influence of needle centring on fuel flow. An off-centre needs (a) gives a higher flow than one perfectly centred (b). For consistent performance the latest carburettor has the needle spring-loaded to touch the jet wall (c).

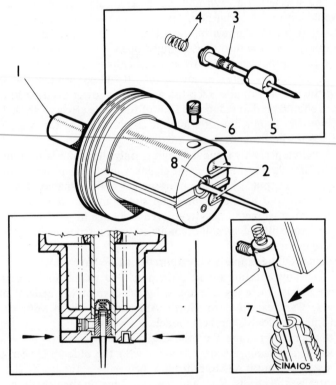

1. Piston rod
2. Transfer holes
3. Jet needle
4. Needle spring

5. Needle guide
6. Needle locking screw
7. Needle biased in jet
8. Etch mark

Fig. 5.3 The spring-loaded jet needle.

is required with this HIF model and one source of variation from specification is removed.

Concentric float chamber. With the float chamber placed in front of the main jet assembly (or the venturi in a fixed venturi carburettor) there is a tendency to enrich the mixture when accelerating and to give a leaner mixture when braking. Before emission control this was acceptable. In fact, in earlier days before we had acceleration pumps or other acceleration devices we considered it to be a very elegant solution to the problem of mixture enrichment during acceleration!

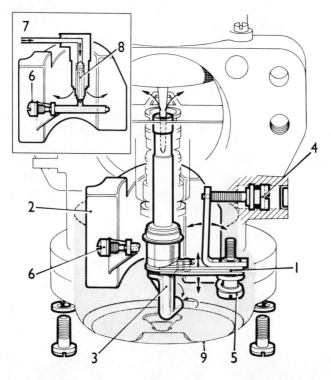

1.	Bi-metal assembly	4.	Jet adjusting screw	7.	Fuel inlet
2.	Concentric float	5.	Bi-metal pivot screw	8.	Needle valve
3.	Jet head	6.	Float fulcrum screw	9.	Bottom cover-plate

Fig. 5.4   An enlargement of the float-chamber in the S.U. Type HIF carburettor.

The HIF float chamber, shown in Figure 5.4, is designed to prevent such variations from forward, backwards or sideways accelerations of the car. The bowl is concentric with the jet assembly and the semi-circular float is shaped to surround the jet tube. The float pivot is parallel to the inlet flange.

The concentric float is not a new idea and will surely become the normal pattern on all future designs.

Fuel viscosity compensator. Even changes in fuel viscosity have created problems. As the temperature of the fuel rises, the viscosity is reduced and more fuel is metered through the jet at the same effective jet area. This means that the mixture tends to be weaker in winter than in summer. In the HIF carburettor the jet head is attached to a bi-metal strip (Part 1 in Figure 5.4). This strip is immersed in the fuel and lifts the jet to a slightly higher position as the fuel temperature rises. Temperature compensation makes it possible to pre-set the mixture setting (or during the official agent's pre-delivery checks) and to seal this setting against illegal mixture adjustments.

Part-throttle by-pass emulsion. The makers of fixed choke (venturi) carburettors, such as Solex, Zenith and Weber have made great improvements in the degree of atomisation achieved during idle and part-throttle running. In the older S.U. carburetter the fuel is atomised fairly effectively at the jet. Unfortunately the throttle-plate is some distance downstream and tends to collect the spray of fine droplets on its front face and cause them to agglomerate into larger droplets as they are re-entrained in the airstream at the throttle-edge. In the new carburettor a small-bore passageway carries the mixture created at the top of the jet to a discharge point at the throttle-edge. A slot is provided in the base of the piston (*see* Figure 5.5) to direct the mixture into the small-bore passageway. During idle and slow-speed running the air velocity through

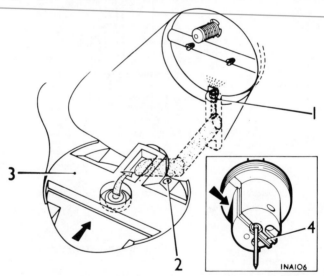

1. By-pass emulsion outlet
2. Cold start enrichment outlet
3. Carburetter bridge
4. Slot in piston

Fig. 5.5   Part-throttle by-pass emulsion system in the S.U. Type HIF Carburettor.

the passageway is much higher than the velocities achieved on the older carburettor design. Higher air velocities give more effective atomisation and this in turn leads to improved distribution between cylinders.

Cold start enrichment. The traditional method of providing a rich mixture on the S.U. carburetter was to provide a lever to pull down the jet-head, thus increasing the area between the needle and the jet. The latest device is a rotary valve which admits augmented fuel supply to a drilled passage that emerges behind the jet bridge (2 in Figure 5.5). The action of the rotary valve is progressive and controlled manually.

Overrun valve. During overrun, i.e. deceleration with a closed throttle, manifold depression can rise to as much as 25 inches Hg. The level depends upon the size of the engine, the weight of the car and the design of carburettor. Good combustion is difficult to maintain with such a high manifold vacuum. Under such conditions the hydrocarbon and carbon monoxide levels rise to unacceptable levels. The simple solution is to bleed mixture into the manifold through a spring-loaded valve located in the throttle-plate to limit the manifold vacuum to the chosen value. This value will be slightly higher than the normal idle vacuum.

Sealed mixture adjustment. Mixture adjustment in the HIF model is achieved by moving the jet tube up or down relative to the needle as in all previous models. A screwdriver adjustment is provided on the new carburetter (4 in Figure 5.4). This acts on a right-angled adjusting lever, attached to the body-casting by a spring-loaded screw (5 in Figure 5.4). The bi-metal strip responsible for temperature compensation (1 in Figure 5.4) is riveted to the horizontal arm of this lever. It is therefore capable of moving the jet head up or down independently. When screw 4 is turned inwards the jet tube is lowered and the mixture is enriched. To prevent unauthorised changes in the pre-set mixture strength in countries where the emission laws make it illegal to do so the mixture adjusting screw is in a recessed boss which can be sealed with a metal plug.

Crankcase emission control. One of the early requirements for cars supplied to the smog-bedevilled State of California was a system to prevent the escape of blow-by gases from the crankcase. Since the gases that escape past the piston rings are very rich in unburned hydrocarbons they contribute considerably to the sum of all other hydrocarbon pollutants in the urban atmosphere. In the S.U. installation these fumes are drawn from the crankcase into the constant depression zone between the throttle-plate and the carburetter piston. An oil separator is provided to prevent oil droplets from entering the induction system. Small variations in the amount of blow-by gas passing the piston rings does not have an appreciable influence on the strength of the mixture fed to the engine since these gases are largely unburned mixture. Since the whole system is sealed, the mixture that leaks past the rings was metered by the carburetter in the first place. The only contaminant is the small percentage of partially burned mixture present in these gases.

The work carried out by S.U. to produce the HIF design is typical of the ingenuity demonstrated by other carburettor designers throughout the industry. Unfortunately the emission levels demanded in the future will be even lower than those of today. I say, unfortunately, simply because I hate to see so much effort unrewarded. If the final result is a cleaner environment, the result will obviously be fortunate.

Several sports car manufacturers have abandoned the use of carburettors and, despite the increased expense, they now look to fuel injection to give them the ultimate answer.

FUEL INJECTION

As every motor racing enthusiast knows the battle between the carburettor and fuel injection was decidedly won by the latter about ten years ago. Even with a separate carburettor (or individual venturi) to each cylinder there is always a small drop in volumetric efficiency when a venturi is placed between the cylinder and the air intake. Moreover the carburettor has only a small pressure available (a fraction of one atmosphere) to break up the fuel into a finely divided mist. With fuel injection the pressure can be several atmospheres depending upon the design of the pump.

For a sports car, especially a moderately priced production sports car, the need to extract the ultimate power from a given size of engine is less vital. There is really no need to provide a separate choke (venturi) to every cylinder. It is much less expensive to give the customer a 4-cylinder 3-litre engine with two twin-choke carburettors than a 2.2 litre engine with 8 cylinders and four twin-choke carburettors. The road performance of the two cars would hardly differ, even though the aficionado will always prefer the latter.

Why then need we bother with the complexity and high cost of fuel injection? To find the answer we must travel, in mind at least, to that sprawling urban community called Los Angeles, the super city that gave us Sam Goldwin and Shirley Temple, stole the Brooklyn Dodgers for a handful of silver and finally paid the price of sin under the affliction of photo-chemical smog. They were indeed the first to experience this phenomenon since their peculiar geographical location and climate prevented the dispersal of exhaust fumes and encouraged the photo-chemical reactions. In the last twenty years we have seen the gradual spread of smog to other American cities, to Tokio and to other warm countries where the automobile density is high.

The automobile industry began to work, half-heartedly at first, and more in earnest when prodded by the California State Legislature, on the problems associated with the reduction of hydrocarbon and carbon monoxide levels in the exhaust gases. Later, it was realised that certain nitrogen oxides, that are produced when nitrogen and oxygen are subjected to the high temperatures existing during combustion, actually encourage the smog reactions. Nitrogen oxides were then added to the list of undesirables.

To improve combustion they experimented with many types of combustion chamber, notably the stratified charge-engine, but as work continued through the sixties there grew an increasing awareness that a reliable system of fuel injection was a necessary corollary to successful emission control.

In 1957 the Bendix Corporation of America published an SAE paper on their Electrojector fuel injection system and this was the basis of the electronic metering system developed by Robert Bosch of Germany under the trade name 'Jetronic' and first used on a production car, the VW 1600, in 1967 to meet the 1968 U.S. Federal Law for emission control. Variations on the Bendix/Bosch system have since been produced under licence by AE-Brico and the Lucas Electrical Company in Great Britain. Figure 5.6 shows the basic metering system applied to a 4-cylinder engine.

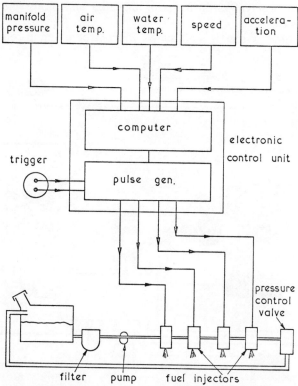

Fig. 5.6   Application of electronics to control fuel injection.

Port injection is used since the injectors are not then subjected to the high temperatures and carbonising problems associated with direct injection into the combustion chamber. Metering of the fuel quantity is controlled on a pulse-time basis. When more fuel is demanded the pulse is of longer duration. To give the reader an idea of the maximum time available for this pulse we can state that the time taken for all four strokes of one cylinder at 6,000 r.p.m. is only 20 milliseconds. Experience has shown that the pulse need not be timed relative to any point in the induction stroke. In fact for convenience it is normal to operate injectors in two groups. In the case of a 6-cylinder engine all 3 injectors in the same group will operate simultaneously. In a V-12, all cylinders on one bank of six will receive a pulse into the valve port at the same time. Some inlet valves will be open at the time, others closed. In the latter case the fuel will pass into the cylinder several milliseconds later when the valve opens. No detectable differences in mixture strength or combustion behaviour have been observed between cylinders with inlet valves open during injection and those with the valves closed.

The pulse-time system is well suited to control by mini-computer. The

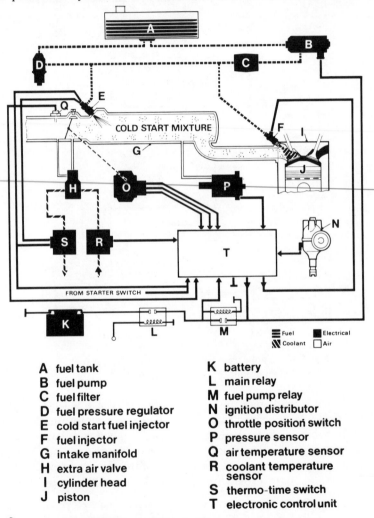

A	fuel tank	K	battery
B	fuel pump	L	main relay
C	fuel filter	M	fuel pump relay
D	fuel pressure regulator	N	ignition distributor
E	cold start fuel injector	O	throttle position switch
F	fuel injector	P	pressure sensor
G	intake manifold	Q	air temperature sensor
H	extra air valve	R	coolant temperature sensor
I	cylinder head	S	thermo-time switch
J	piston	T	electronic control unit

Fig. 5.7   Lucas Electronic fuel injection

important parameters of engine speed, manifold vacuum, induction air temperature and engine water temperature can be measured. This information can then be fed into the computer designed specifically for this purpose. After processing all the information this mini-computer then transmits the correct pulse-times to the solenoids that operate the injectors. Other data processed by the computer are signals for mixture enrichment when starting from cold and during warm-up, for full-throttle operation, for acceleration and to cut off fuel during overrun.

Lucas electronic fuel injection

The Lucas system now fitted to the Jaguar XJS is shown diagrammatically in Figure 5.7. Metering accuracy depends primarily on two elements, *time* and *pressure*, this being the pressure maintained in the supply lines to the injectors. The fine control of the pressure from the fuel pump (B in Figure 5.7) by means of the regulator D to the correct pressure of 28 lb.f./in² (2 kg.f./cm²) is as vital as the correct functioning of the computer circuits. Excess fuel from the regulator is returned to the fuel tank. The fuel line is manifolded to each injector with an additional line feeding the cold-start injector on the inlet manifold.

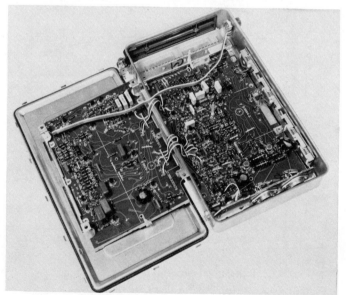

Fig. 5.8   Inside the Lucas fuel injection control unit.

The heart of the control system is the computer. Figure 5.8 shows the computer opened up for inspection. The two major control parameters are the pressure in the induction manifold and the engine speed. For every new model of engine the mixture requirements must be determined by dynamometer tests and these result in a family of curves of the type shown in Figure 5.9. From this set of curves the analysing circuits of the control unit are tailored to trigger the output circuits to generate the pulse-times requested by the combined signals of manifold pressure (plotted here in mm Hg) and engine r.p.m. An inductive transducer operated by evacuated aneroids is used to produce the pressure signal and reed switches in the ignition distributor indicate engine speed and camshaft timing. The current pulses sent out from the control unit energise the solenoids in the appropriate group of injectors. When a solenoid is energised the magnetic field attracts the plunger and lifts the needle valve from its seat. For the duration of the pulse the pressurised fuel is injected into the inlet port as a finely atomised spray.

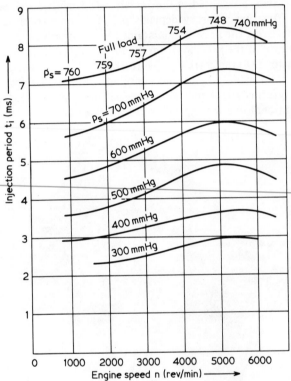

Fig. 5.9   Engine fuel demands are established by dynamometer tests to produce a family of curves relating the precise injection period for every engine speed and manifold pressure.

The basic family of curves in Figure 5.9 only apply to a specific operating temperature. Corrective signals are given to the computer circuits for variations in air intake temperature (Q in Figure 5.7) and for variations in coolant temperature (R in Figure 5.7). Mixture enrichment for cold starting is given by energising the cold-start injector, E. The thermo-time switch, S, cuts off this

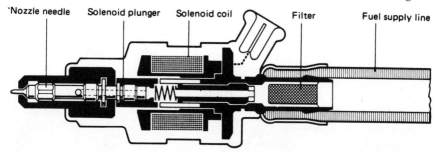

Nozzle needle   Solenoid plunger   Solenoid coil   Filter   Fuel supply line

Fig. 5.10   Schematic diagram of the solenoid-operated injection valve.

injector when the engine coolant temperature reaches a certain value. The correct mixture for smooth idling is obtained by the provision of an extra air valve, H, which permits a controlled amount of air to by-pass the throttle. Cylinder head coolant temperature controls the exact quantity of extra air. The addition of extra air with a cold engine raises the manifold pressure. This in turn acts on the induction pressure sensor, P, which automatically increases the duration of the injection pulse and enriches the mixture. Warm up of the engine reduces the quantity of extra air, reduces the degree of enrichment and thus maintains the correct mixture for good combustion.

During overrun the fuel supply is cut off, re-commencing when the accelerator is depressed or when the engine speed has fallen to a certain value.

A throttle-position switch is required to indicate to the control unit that the throttle is almost closed (idle or overrun). This switch is designed to transmit three distinctive signals. Besides the closed position contacts there are other contacts to indicate the final stages of throttle opening. At a chosen point near full-throttle contacts are closed that signal a demand for mixture enrichment, a necessary precaution to prevent damage to exhaust valves and pistons by burning a lean mixture at full-throttle. At all other throttle openings between the idle position and this point the mixture is lean, economical and controlled to give low emissions of hydrocarbons, carbon monoxide and nitrogen oxides. The third signal given by the throttle switch device indicates acceleration by a wiping action over a set of comb-like strip contacts. These contacts generate additional injection pulses to provide acceleration enrichment.

This then is the highly sophisticated Bosch-Lucas fuel injection system. Even this description is not complete since the needs of other devices to improve combustion may be controlled from the fuel injection computer. When exhaust gas recirculation is used to reduce nitrogen oxides signals from appropriate contacts are needed to cut off the exhaust gas recirculation system when it is not required.

The Bosch K-Jetronic mechanical system

The Robert Bosch Company have been making fuel injection equipment longer than we care to remember. The jerk type pump used to operate the fuel injection

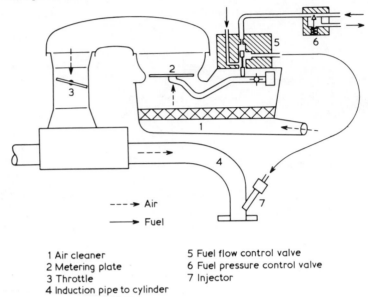

1 Air cleaner   5 Fuel flow control valve
2 Metering plate   6 Fuel pressure control valve
3 Throttle   7 Injector
4 Induction pipe to cylinder

Fig. 5.11   Diagram of Bosch 'K-Jetronic' fuel injection with mechanical control, as used by Porsche.

on the famous Porsche 917 racing engine was a development of the Bosch Diesel injection system. The latest K-Jetronic system however bears little resemblance to the traditional mechanical system where individual reciprocating plunger pumps supply fuel at a timed injection point to separate injectors. In this new system the injectors supply a continuous spray of fuel into the inlet ports, the injection rate being based on a measured mass air-flow. This is the system that Porsche adopted in 1974 when they needed a new metering system to meet the American exhaust emission laws. Porsche are unsurpassed as mechanical engineers and the author sympathises with their apparent distrust of the 250 to 300 components in the electronic control unit. Mechanical engineers have a natural predilection for mechanical gadgets, since they can understand how they work! Even so the K-Jetronic system is not exactly simple, but the Porsche organisation have a very well equipped research and development centre at Weissach near Stuttgart-Zuffenhausen and the development of a reliable application to all the new production Porsches, even to the Turbo model, will have been no great challenge to such dedicated professionals.

Figure 5.11 is a simplified line diagram of the system. Air enters a plenum chamber (1) after filtration. The pressure of the air as it passes over and round the metering plate (2) is used to measure the mass air-flow into the engine. The metering plate is attached to a counterbalanced lever which moves the control valve (5) to regulate the fuel flow to the injectors (7). This is the basic system. As in the electronic system it requires auxiliary devices to cope with cold starting, warm-up, idle and overrun.

All future sports cars will carry suitable fuel metering equipment and improved combustion techniques. It will be fascinating to see what will eventually emerge as the most acceptable solution from the plethora of ideas under investigation. Perhaps it will be an improved Stirling engine, or a more effective stratified charge-engine. Perhaps it will be an electric car and this chapter will then become redundant in our next edition!

The engine: miscellaneous components

'Every instrument, tool, vessel, if it does
that for which it is made, is well.'
MARCUS AURELIUS

THE CRANKCASE

In the beginning the crankcase was simply a convenient enclosure to prevent the splash fed oil from escaping from the confines of the engine. Cylinder pressures were low and any crankcase with thick enough walls to produce a good casting was stiff enough for the purpose. Today with the increased stresses and higher rotational speeds it is rigidity we require before all else in a crankcase. A crankcase is never stressed near the limit in normal operation, since the deflections produced by such stresses would seriously overload the main bearings by the malalignment that would be produced in the crankshaft journals.

The crankcase in this respect is analogous to the chassis frame, for in both Rigidity is next to Godliness. Weaving and lozenging of a chassis frame can upset the most carefully planned suspension layouts and, with even more devastating results, can a well-conceived set of main bearings be reduced to molten metal by a crankcase lacking in stiffness. The crankcase in the modern engine is almost invariably combined with the cylinder block and the whole casting is a carrier for both reciprocating and rotating components. It is designed to withstand the explosive loads from the combustion processes, these acting not only outwards, but upwards on the cylinder head holding-studs and downwards on the main bearings, tending to pull apart the top and bottom parts of the crankcase. Other loads are imposed by the centrifugal forces acting on the main bearings and, of a lesser magnitude, the torque reaction which the crankcase transmits through the mountings to the frame. Very few of the early designs of petrol engine had crankcases that were rigid enough and the life of the main bearings occasionally suffered as a consequence. A common fault in 4-cylinder engines with three main bearings was a movement of the centre main bearing under load. Eventually, wear in this centre bearing caused loss of oil pressure, followed by failure. The cause in part was a lack of stiffness in the crankshaft, but an equal contribution to the failure came from crankcase flexibility. Without rigidity between the front and rear main bearing housings the benefits of the centre main bearings are lost. The principle remains when more cylinders and more bearings are involved. The crankshaft is designed to resist both bending and twisting. With an absolutely rigid crankcase, bending of the crankshaft would only occur between adjacent bearings. Absolute rigidity is impossible, but the greater the deflection the greater is the span over which bending of the crankshaft takes place.

In some modern engines the necessary rigidity is obtained by making each section of the crankcase between main bearings, in effect, a separate compartment with dividing walls between the bearing housings. The loads imposed on the main bearings are often transferred to the heavier portions of the crankcase through suitably placed webs.

Engine designers have not always thought it necessary to place a main bearing between each cylinder. Torsional vibration can be reduced by the use of the

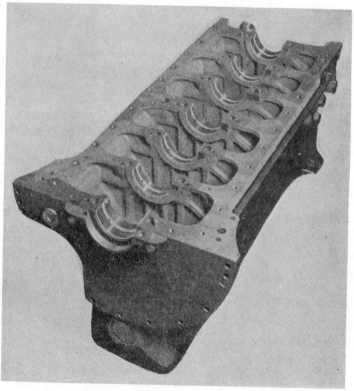

Fig. 6.1   The 6-cylinder Jaguar crankcase.

shorter crankshaft of the four-bearing 6-cylinder engine. The makers of the pre-war Riley 9 claimed that its two-bearing 4-cylinder engine had a much stronger crankshaft with this arrangement since the crankshaft was so much shorter and stiffer than with the three-bearing arrangement. With 100 horse-power per litre produced today from 4-cylinder sports car engines it would be difficult to design a two-bearing crankshaft of robust enough proportions to withstand the bending moments over such a wide span.

A typical modern crankcase for a 6-cylinder engine is shown in Figure 6.1. With the provision of transverse walls at each main bearing housing, four sides of a box are established between bearings to create a very rigid structure.

A system known as 'cross-bolting' is used on some American competition V-8 engines. As engine speeds increased above 6,000 r.p.m. it was found that the horizontal vectors of the inertia loads could no longer be adequately contained by the bearing caps. A cross-bolted system is shown in Figure 6.2 this being a

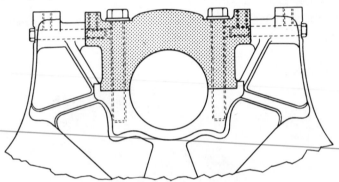

Fig. 6.2   Cross-bolting of main bearing caps to increase rigidity of crankcase on Hemi-Head Chrysler V-8.

scrap section of the Chrysler Hemi-Head crankcase. Two horizontal bolts are fitted into tapped holes in the sides of each bearing cap and are tightened to a pre-determined torque. Horizontal inertia loads are thus distributed between the bearing cap and the crankcase walls. Cross-bolting is usually confined to the more highly loaded intermediate bearings.

THE CRANKSHAFT

The design of the crankshaft for a modern high performance petrol engine is a challenge to the designer, especially if the number of cylinders is six or more. The success or failure of the whole engine may rest on the ability of the designer to achieve a satisfactory compromise between the conflicting requirements placed on this component. To illustrate this point let us consider the problem of the number of main bearings to be used. At first sight one is tempted to reject out of hand the four-bearing design for a 6-cylinder engine. The seven-bearing design will re ult in a longer engine, but this we might accept if satisfied that seven bearings give the better design. A longer crankshaft unfortunately has a lower natural frequency of torsional vibration and, if the crankshaft is too long, this natural frequency can become low enough to enter the range of frequencies of the explosive and inertia force cyclical variations. If resonance occurs between this natural frequency and the applied frequency of the combustion and inertia loads the torsional stresses in the crankshaft can build up beyond the safe limit. A good vibration damper would mitigate this, but the possibility of fatigue failure would remain. If we reduce the projected area of the main bearings in order to shorten the crankshaft, the bearing load factor (pressure times surface velocity) can become too high. We are therefore forced to use a much larger journal diameter on a seven-bearing crankshaft than on a four. This increases the general stiffness and raises the natural frequency of torsional vibration to a safe level.

The short-stroke crankshaft is inherently stiffer than the long-stroke design. Figure 6.3 serves to illustrate why this is so. With a long-stroke design there is

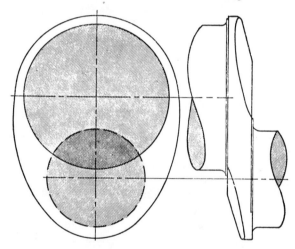

Fig. 6.3   Overlap of crankpin and main bearing journals on a short-stroke engine increases stiffness of crankshaft.

very little overlap of crankpin and main bearing journal, when viewed from the end. The amount of overlap is dependent upon journal diameters as well as stroke dimensions. In older designs with small diameter journals there was usually no overlap at all. Flexing of the web under bending moments is obviously much greater when the overlap is small. The V-12 Jaguar engine has a relatively short stroke (70 mm against 106 mm in the 6-cylinder engine). This gives the new crankshaft even greater stiffness than that in the older engine.

CRANKSHAFT BEARINGS

Bearing pressures

When speaking of the pressures in a set of bearings with a forced lubrication system we must distinguish between the pressure supplied by the oil pump to force oil through the bearings and the self-generated pressures created by the rotation of the journals in their bearings. The pump pressure controls the flow through the bearings, a higher pressure giving a greater flow in gallons per hour. Bearing temperatures can be controlled in this way. The hydrodynamic pressure created by crankshaft rotation is the pressure that keeps the metal surfaces apart, even under the high peak loads imposed by the combined combustion and inertia forces.

Two Englishmen gave us our first insight into the phenomenon of hydro-dynamic bearing pressure. Beachamp Tower in 1883 discovered the existence of

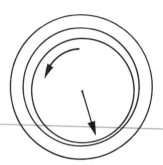

Fig. 6.4
Rotation of crankshaft journal inside its bearing creates a wedge action in the oil film to build up a hydrodynamic pressure. The peak value of this pressure is far greater than that created by the oil pump. The clearance is, of course, exaggerated in this drawing.

a fluid film pressure in a bearing and three years later Osborne Reynolds made a brilliant mathematical analysis of the forces that produce it. In simple terms we can say that the rotating action of the journal makes it climb slightly (within the confines of the existing bearing clearance) up the side of the bearing (see Figure 6.4). The oil film is pulled round in the direction of rotation by the viscous drag at the surface of the journal and a pressure build-up occurs in the wedge-like part of the oil film where the minimum clearance exists. The pressure gradient created in this way depends upon the speed of rotation and the viscosity of the oil. It is at its highest value just before the point of minimum clearance and drops away rapidly after this, even becoming slightly negative at one point. A typical pressure profile is shown in Figure 6.5. The negative pressure area is an obvious point on the bearing for the introduction of the pressure oil feed. Since maximum pressures can be as high as 5,000 lb per sq in. and pump delivery pressures are in the range 80-120 lb per sq in. we could hardly hope to maintain an oil flow through the bearing with an oil feed at the bottom.

The simple case of Figure 6.5 assumes a steady vertical load. In practice the load is fluctuating and changing in direction with the angular changes of the connecting-rod. As the load direction changes, so does the maximum pressure point move and with an adequate bearing area, correct clearances and the right

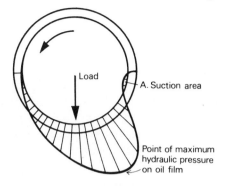

Load

A. Suction area

Point of maximum
hydraulic pressure
on oil film

Fig. 6.5
Typical pressure profile near
loaded area produced by
wedging action. Note slight
negative region.

lubricant, the wedge action of the rotating film prevents metal-to-metal contact at all times, with the single exception of the initial slow-speed rotation when the engine first turns under the action of the starter. At this time we depend upon 'boundary lubrication' to save the bearing from damage. This type of lubrication will be discussed later.

Bearing failure will occur when:

(a) bearing clearance becomes so great that too much pressure is lost by leakage at the sides of the bearing.

(b) the oil viscosity becomes so low, from overheating, contamination or other means, that the bearing pressure falls below the critical value required to offset the load

(c) the oil flow through the bearing becomes so much reduced by blocked oil feed lines, or similar obstruction, that the surface temperature becomes too high for the particular bearing alloy. In such cases failure is by melting of the bearing metal, which in turn increases the clearance and leads to case (*a*).

It is well known that the load that can safely be carried by a bearing becomes less as the speed increases. The heat generated by a bearing is a function of both pressure and speed. The running temperature is controlled by a balance between the rate at which heat is generated and the rate at which it is removed by a combination of air cooling and oil cooling. The more heat we can remove by the flow of lubricant, the higher will be the load the bearing can stand without failure. This is the reason for the use of oil-coolers on competition engines, since a cool oil will remove more heat than a hot oil. Moreover a cool oil will have a higher viscosity, leading to higher hydrodynamic pressures.

The expression one sometimes finds in engineering textbooks:

$$\text{pressure} \times \text{rubbing velocity} = \text{a constant}$$

cannot be of universal application, since the degree of oil cooling influences the value of the constant. An important implication of this relationship is that an increase in bearing diameter will not increase the load-carrying capacity of a bearing. The pressure is reduced, since the projected area of the bearing is increased, but the rubbing velocity is increased in the same ratio and the load factor remains unchanged. We therefore see that the critical dimension is the width of the bearing. Since the available space between cylinders is limited, there is a limit on all engines to the width of the main bearings. Any increase in main bearing width entails a decrease either in big-end bearing width or in crank web thickness. Thus, unless we are prepared to increase the spacing of the cylinders and to increase the overall length of the engine, there is a fairly close limit set to the width of the bearings that can be used in an in-line engine. On a V-6, V-8 or V-12 the available space is much less, but the main bearing loads are substantially reduced since the thrusts imparted by paired cylinders partly cancel one another out.

When we speak of the hydrodynamic pressure exerted by the oil film of a bearing we must remember that this pressure is not constant across the width of the bearing. It is at its highest at the centre and falls to a negligible pressure at the outside edge. This is illustrated in Figure 6.6 for the case of a typical bearing

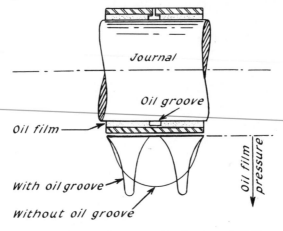

Fig. 6.6   Improved pressure distribution of oil film
when oil groove is eliminated.

with an oil groove around the centre and a plain bearing with no oil groove. The traditional oil groove, originally intended to distribute oil around the bearing, is now condemned by most authorities since it breaks the pressure profile into two peaks as shown in the diagram. When the Chevrolet Company were developing their 265 cu in engine they also had doubts about the efficacy of the oil groove, so they took the trouble to measure oil film pressures in all five main bearings at different loads and speeds.

The reduction in mean pressures in the grooveless bearing was approximately equal to the increase in bearing area that this modification provided. Endurance testing showed that the grooveless bearings were superior in service and, at the same operating clearances, would carry almost twice the load without failure. As a result of these experiments Chevrolet adopted a design in which the oil groove was omitted from the lower half. It was retained in the more lightly loaded upper half.

Bearing metals

The properties we value in a bearing metal are as follows:-

(a) High mechanical strength to resist the maximum loads imposed in service.

(b) High melting point to resist damage by high temperature lubricants and to resist bearing failure.

(c) High resistance to corrosion from degraded acidic lubricants.

(d) Good 'embeddability' to absorb particles of dirt smaller than the bearing clearance (larger particles should have been trapped by the oil filter).

(e) Good comformability to yield slightly when the mating shaft is misaligned.

(f) Sufficient hardness to resist abrasive wear and erosion.

(g) Good compatibility with the shaft material to prevent seizure when oil has drained away after prolonged standing and before rotational speeds are high enough to provide hydrodynamic pressure.

This is a formidable list and it is difficult to find a bearing material that scores highly on all of them. The type of bearing alloy that has been demonstrated over the years to possess the apparently conflicting requirements of 'conformability' and 'hardness' consists of a relatively soft matrix in which are embedded crystals of a harder metal. During the running-in period the soft matrix of a good bearing alloy flows slightly under pressure leaving the harder crystals to act as load bearing members. The depression left in the matrix acts as an oil reservoir to help establish an oil film over the whole surface during the critical period when starting the engine.

White metal bearings

The original white metal, introduced about 1860 by Isaac Babbitt, is thought to have contained about 85 per cent tin, 10 per cent antimony and 5 per cent copper. How right he was in choosing this alloy has been proved over and over again and the composition of the white metals used for the first fifty years of this century differed only slightly from his original specification.

The older brasses of the vintage era have given place to the modern steel-backed bearing in which a high degree of strength and stiffness is obtained from a thin steel shell covered with a film of bearing metal. The shell is usually about 0.9 mm (0.036 in) thick with a bearing metal lining of about 0.4 mm (0.015 in) thick. The bearings are stamped from large bi-metal strips, pressed to shape and indented at one corner to provide a location against rotation. They are cheap and reliable. Quality control was never very high with the old vintage hand-poured, cast, white-metal bearings.

Metallurgists have developed several improved bearing alloys to withstand the increased bearings loads that have resulted from the higher compression ratios and higher operating speeds used on modern engines.

Copper-lead and lead-bronze bearings

The introduction of the high-speed Diesel engine for heavy transport in the early thirties, where compression ratios as high as 18 to 1 were used, brought in its wake a crop of bearing troubles, for the load carrying capacity of the white-metal bearings was sometimes exceeded. The answer was found in mixtures of approximately two-thirds copper and one-third lead and similar mixtures of lead copper and tin, usually called 'lead-bronzes.' These copper-lead and lead-bronze bearing metals are not alloys but mechanical mixtures of the powdered metals and great care is required in the casting operation to prevent segregation of the components.

The one advantage over white metal is the higher limiting load factor. Two disadvantages are that they tend to wear the crankshaft more readily and they require higher running clearances. The former can be countered successfully by the provision of hardened journals and crankpins; the latter calls for a higher oil pressure and a larger capacity oil pump to compensate for the increased oil flow from the sides of the bearings. A minor disadvantage of these bearings are their poor resistance to corrosion by the acidic oxidation products in the lubricating oil. Frequent oil changes are beneficial in reducing this corrosion, but an answer was found in a protective layer of tin of indium. This coating is only about 0.025 mm (0.001 in) thick and without regular attention to the air filter and regular changes of the oil filter the accumulation of road dust and combustion contaminants in the oil will gradually wear away this protective skin.

Aluminium-tin alloy bearings

Aluminium alloy crankshaft bearings are not new. High Duty Alloys of Slough developed good bearings of this type to carry higher loads than white metal about forty years ago. The new aluminium-tin alloys are far superior in load-carrying capacity than these earlier alloys, this being almost as great as the lead-bronzes. The tin content can be as little as 6 per cent or as high as 20 per cent. The attraction of these new alloys lies in their superior resistance to corrosion.

Aluminium-silicon alloy bearings

A new bearing alloy has been developed to cope with the very high loads imposed on connecting rod bearings in turbocharged Diesel engines. This new aluminium alloy contains 11 per cent silicon and 1 per cent copper. The alloy has excellent strength and its chances of survival under severe conditions are exceptionally high. It requires no protective overlay against corrosion and has been shown to have a high resistance to seizure when hydrodynamic lubrication is almost non-existant. For all very high performance engines, in particular for turbocharged competition engines, this new bearing alloy holds great promise.

GENERAL LUBRICATION

The majority of motorists have at least been educated to change oil filter elements at the recommended mileages. It is not always realized that contamination of the lubricating oil can come as much from the air entering the cylinders as from the burning of oil and fuel in the combustion chambers. Neglect of air filtration admits abrasive dust particles which are deposited by the highly turbulent conditions in the cylinders on to the cylinder walls. The oil film on the walls is being continually renewed from below and being scraped off again into the sump by the action of the rings. We must therefore regard the air filter as our primary oil filter — the first line of defence against contamination.

The importance of adequate *flow* as well as adequate pressure is now appreciated by engine designers. The oil pumped through the bearings serves to cool them, the higher the flow rate the lower the operating temperature. With true film lubrication, as distinct from boundary lubrication, the surfaces of the bearing and journal are held apart by a film of oil. Since the two metal surfaces have a high relative speed it is obvious that adjacent layers of this oil film are suffering a continuous shearing action. This shearing action, usually called viscous drag, is manifested in the form of heat. *Given good filtration*, there is nothing to be lost and everything to be gained if the output of the pump is made as large as possible.

The lubrication circuit for the V-12 Jaguar engine is shown diagrammatically in Figure 6.7. The oil pump is exceptionally large, but at low speeds the entire

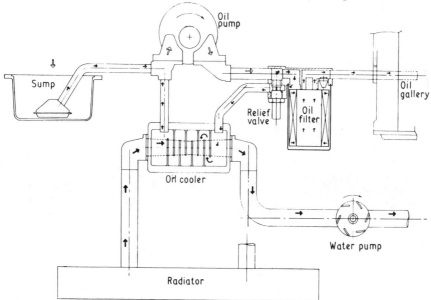

Fig. 6.7   Layout of Jaguar V-12 oil cooler circuit.

output passes through the filter to the main oil gallery. As the speed increases the relief valve opens to by-pass surplus oil through the cooler. This cooled oil is returned to the pump inlet. At about 2500 r.p.m., as much oil is by-passed through the cooler as the amount delivered to the main gallery and at higher engine speeds the flow through the cooler is appreciably greater. The oil cooler is an aluminium oil-to-water heat exchanger bolted to the front underside of the sump (oilpan). From the base of the radiator cooled water passes through the water passages in the cooler before entering the water pump. At speeds of 130 m.p.h. a temperature reduction of 23°C (41°F) has been recorded with the engine fitted to the XJ-S sports car. Without the oil cooler the temperature of the oil delivered to the bearings would be about 140°C (284°F) which is a little higher than that recommended as an upper limit by the bearing manufacturers. Bearing failure can in general be anticipated when the temperature of the oil film at the bearing surface reaches about 170°C (338°F) and the temperature measured at the bearing is usually about 30°C (86°F) higher than that measured in the main gallery.

The complexity of the lubrication system in a modern engine is shown in Figure 6.8. From the main gallery oil is fed at full pressure via the six

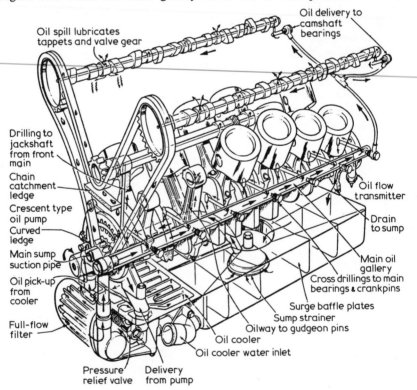

Fig. 6.8   Diagram of oil system in Jaguar V-12 engine.

cross-drillings to the main bearings. From the main bearings the oil enters the drillings in the crankshaft to provide a copious flow to each connecting rod bearing. The connecting rods are drilled to convey oil to each gudgeon pin (wrist pin) and a metered supply of oil is piped to the camshaft bearings. In general, it can be said that all rotating, sliding or rubbing parts in an engine must be lubricated if they are to survive. Small lightly loaded components are occasionally made from graphite-impregnated porous metals or from low-friction plastics, such as PTFE, but a continuous supply of lubricant is required when loads are high. Pistons have always been lubricated by splash from the oil that squirts from the sides of the connecting rod bearings and the sides of the main bearings. This does appear to be a hit-and-miss method since an increase in bearing side clearances can overtax the ability of the oil control rings on the pistons to prevent excessive oil consumption. Despite this lack of engineering finesse the designers of pistons and rings have achieved miracles of oil control in modern engines.

Engine oils

It is self-evident that a relatively high viscosity is one of the essential properties of an automobile lubricating oil. Not all viscous liquids are lubricants, however, since they do not all possess the property of 'oiliness'. The peculiar property of oiliness is associated with the way the molecules of a lubricant in contact with a metal surface form an intimate bond with the metal molecules. This 'boundary layer' is believed to be no more than one molecule thick. It is this surface effect that is so vital when an engine is being started, since the hydrodynamic pressure to hold the surfaces apart is only produced when the journals are rotating at a fair speed. Boundary lubrication can also postpone bearing failure for a short time after the flow of lubricant has been cut off. It can only be a postponement at best, since the heat cannot be easily dissipated when the flow of lubricant has stopped. This property of boundary lubrication is exhibited by all oils, but is much stronger in some than in others. Castor oil and rape oil are two outstanding examples. The strength of the molecular bond established by these two oils is so great that it resists repeated washings in petrol and other solvents and can only be completely removed by scraping or grinding the metal surfaces. It is this property that makes rape oil such a valuable constituent of certain proprietory upper-cylinder lubricants. In certain circumstances, notably when starting from cold, the piston rings are starved of oil and only boundary lubrication prevents partial seizure of the rings and the cylinder walls. A lubricant such as rape oil or colloidal graphite serves to strengthen the boundary lubrication. Special lubricants containing molybdenum disulphide are now on the market. Rather extravagant claims are made in some of the advertisements, but tests have shown that this substance does in fact help to reduce scuffing of tappets and cams and such components as may be imperfectly lubricated. Some proprietary engine oils contain very small amounts of metallic compounds that are claimed to reduce wear by improving boundary lubrication. Castrol, for example, add an oil-soluble long-chain compound with the popularised name of 'liquid tungsten'. Such additives do not work miracles but there is good evidence that they do reduce cylinder wear during the crucial period after a cold-weather start when oil is washed from the cylinder walls by liquid petrol.

Another property demanded from an engine lubricant is a high 'viscosity index'. The older types of lubricating oil can be blended to have a high viscosity at low temperatures, but as the oil temperature rises to its working temperature, the viscosity usually falls to a very low value. This was obviously a bad feature and the oil technicians have now developed oils with much higher viscosity indices. This simply means that the viscosity does not fall so rapidly with rise of temperature. The scale of viscosity index is purely arbitrary; asphaltic Gulf oil being taken as zero and the excellent Pennsylvanian oil as 100. The so-called multi-grade oils are simply oils with a high v.i. The S.A.E. specifications for automobile engine oils only call for an oil of medium v.i. and by blending special oils or by using special additives called v.i. improvers a normal oil can be improved in v.i. until it has the viscosity of an S.A.E. 10W Grade oil at 0°F, that of a 20W Grade oil at 100°F, that of a 30 Grade oil at 210°F and that of a 40 Grade oil at 300°F. Such an oil possesses the low oil drag of a winter grade oil to assist winter starting, at the same time it maintains a high enough viscosity to prevent loss of oil pressure under arduous hard-driven conditions.

Resistance to contamination

In general two kinds of contamination can occur in an engine oil that arise from chemical breakdown of the oil itself. Slow oxidation of the oil and the emulsification of atmospheric condensate can form thick acid sludges. The older motorist will remember how the walls of the crankcase, even the insides of the pistons, became plastered with the stuff. The second kind of contaminant comes from the burning of oil in the combustion zone, on the piston rings, lands, etc., to form carbon. There is also a third contaminant which is formed by chemical breakdown, but is different in composition and appearance. This is the brown lacquer which is formed on the skirt of the piston. Sludge formation is now combated and almost completely prevented by the addition of certain chemicals which have been proved by full-scale engine tests to discourage oxidation of oil. Improved ventilation of the crankcase has also reduced the tendency for water vapour to condense on the crankcase walls. The chief danger of sludge formation, apart from the gradual reduction of the general oiliness of the lubricant, is the possibility of oilways becoming blocked or seriously restricted. The sludge is also difficult to disperse and in sufficient quantities can choke the surface of an oil filter.

The carbon deposits in the combustion chamber and on the piston crown are partly formed from lubricant which splashes past the top ring of the piston or is drawn past the inlet valve guide during the induction process. A small amount of this carbon comes from the incomplete combustion of petrol. The deposits also contain small amounts of other elements, such as silica and calcium coming from road dust which has passed through the air filter. The more oil passing the top ring, the softer will the deposit be and, what is more important, the faster will the deposit grow. Carbon deposit is known to encourage knock. Calculations show that the effect cannot be fully explained in terms of the increase in combustion temperatures caused by the heat insulating properties of the layer. There is strong evidence that the carbon layer takes part in the combustion processes in a catalytic manner. One theory, advanced by a Canadian research worker, is that the carbon particles picked up by the turbulent flaming gases act as nuclei for the detonation of the end-gas. One of the petroleum companies has followed up this work by developing an additive which it is claimed 'fire-proofs' the carbon. Another harmful effect of carbon is the manner in which it can accumulate on the compression rings, in the grooves and on the lands, especially at the top ring, until at least one of the rings becomes stuck in its groove and inoperative. The majority of the oils now sold are strongly detergent, i.e. they wash the carbon from the pistons and rings as fast as it is formed, carrying it round and round the oil system in the form of extremely fine dispersed particles, so fine that they can do no harm to the bearings.

PISTONS

The automobile piston, by a slow process of development, seems to have settled for two general types, the solid skirt and the split skirt, the solid skirt for the more highly rated engine where strength at operating temperature is at a premium, the split skirt for the less highly tuned engine in which such refinements as freedom from piston-slap are more important.

The top ring has always been the Achilles' heel of the automobile piston. The temperature at the centre of the piston crown under full load is about 250°C (480°F). The temperature of the top ring is not much less than this, even though about 85 per cent of all the heat passing into the crown of the piston is conducted to the cylinder walls through this single ring. Anything we can do to reduce the heat load of the top ring is good. Most piston designers provide a generous path from the crown to the lower rings in an attempt to divert heat from the top ring. One design of Diesel engine piston that the author calls to mind has a cast-iron insert in the form of a band around the top part of the piston. In this band is machined the top ring groove. The primary purpose of this insert is to reduce wear of the top and second-ring lands. The author believes an excellent design of piston for a sports car engine could be based on this principle. The poor conductivity of the cast iron and the temperature drop at the interface between the two metals would reduce the amount of heat flowing to the top ring, leaving a greater amount to pass out through the other rings.

It is customary to provide some form of heat barrier between the hot ring belt and the skirt. This permits a reduction in working clearance of the skirt with less likelihood of piston slap when cold. The heat barrier usually takes the form of slots or rows of holes between the two parts of the piston (see designs (a) and (b) in Figure 6.9). Sometimes the heat barrier is as complete as the slots shown in design (c).

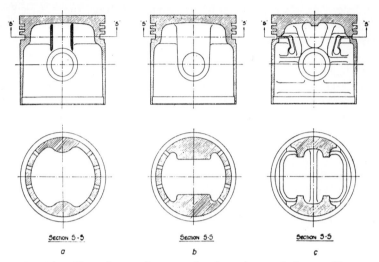

Fig. 6.9   Three forms of support for the gudgeon pin bosses. Note thermal barrier slots on Type C.

Oil control

We once thought that the manner in which a set of rings controls the passage of oil to the combustion chamber was by the cumulative action of successive piston rings scraping a little more oil off the cylinder walls until only a minute trace remained to lubricate the top ring. This small quantity escaping past the top ring was assumed to be lost and to represent the actual quantity burned in the combustion chamber. An experimental study carried out by Dr. P. de K. Dykes of Cambridge University completely upset this simple picture of ring behaviour and presented us with an entirely new concept. Dr Dykes showed that oil does in fact pass the rings *in both directions* and in large quantities. With a normal engine in good condition almost all the oil passing the rings on the downstroke is returned to the sump on the upstroke. Even if oil is added to the cylinder walls from above the rings, a good ring set will pass almost all the oil downwards to the sump, leaving only a negligible portion behind to be burned. Dr Dykes introduced two new words into the automobile engineer's vocabulary. A 'down-passing' ring or ring set is defined as 'one which when supplied with an ample amount of oil from both above and below, passes oil more rapidly downwards than upwards'. Conversely an 'up-passing' ring or ring set passes oil more rapidly towards the combustion chamber. The best ring sets are down-passing as a whole. If the lower rings are down-passing and the upper are not the oil consumption can still be high if the amount of oil passing the lower rings on the down-stroke is large. On the other hand, if the lower rings are up-passing and the upper rings are down-passing, a high oil consumption is inevitable since the up-passing lower rings cause a pressure to be built up between the rings which forces oil past the upper rings. When the whole ring set is down-passing the rate of oil consumption can, in some cases, be absolutely zero. This perfect condition will occur when all oil drops thrown into the combustion chamber can drain back to the cylinder walls. In general a few drops of oil get held back and are burned on the roof of the chamber or on the piston crown. Others are swept out with the exhaust gases.

Piston ring flutter

At high engine speeds a phenomenon sometimes occurs which is known as 'piston ring flutter'. It usually affects the top ring and in exceptional cases the second ring too. As long as a compression ring remains pressed against the lower face of its groove during the compression stroke, the pressure behind the ring is sensibly that in the combustion chamber. Near t.d.c., however, as the piston is decelerating, the inertia of the ring can make it move upwards against the upper face of the groove. When this happens, the ring acts as a valve, sealing the ring groove space against the cylinder pressure. The gas in the space behind the ring leaks away to the crankcase (or to the lower rings) and the ring collapses inwards under the action of cylinder pressure. Since this collapse occurs once every two revolutions of the engine with a recovery to normal diameter occurring when the cylinder pressure drops, the ring in effect 'flutters' at high speed and if the condition is allowed to persist, ring breakage is inevitable.

Ring inertia can be decreased by reducing the ring width. Using the recommended limits supplied by Messrs Hepworth and Grandage, the British piston manufactureres, we have calculated that a typical engine with a stroke of 80 mm would be limited to a maximum engine speed of 6,500 with a top ring width of 1.6 mm (1/16 in).

If then we provide this engine with valves and porting to run up to 7,000 or 8,000 r.p.m. we would have to use extremely narrow and fragile top rings. A more satisfactory engineering solution would be the use of a Dykes pattern of ring, an L-shaped ring in cross-section that is specially designed to maintain communication between the combustion chamber and the back of the ring at all

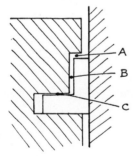

Fig. 6.10
Cross-section of Dykes ring for high-speed engine.

engine speeds. Figure 6.10 shows a cross-section through one type of Dykes ring. The side clearance at *A* is greater than at *C*. When the ring moves upwards under the action of the inertia force the gap *C* closes, but the gap *A* does not and the space *B* behind the upper part of the ring remains in communication with the combustion chamber. This ring then is free to move upwards under the action of maximum inertia forces, but the cylinder pressure is never cut off from the back face of the ring. The upper portion is usually made about twice as wide as the lower.

Chromium-plated top rings are in common use today. The bonded layer of chromium is only about 0.1 mm (0.004 in) thick, but its high resistance to corrosion and wear has been found to be of great value in this fiery zone where even boundary lubrication is difficult to maintain. On modern top rings both top and bottom edges are profiled as shown in Figure 6.11. This helps the ring to

Theoretical top ring profile

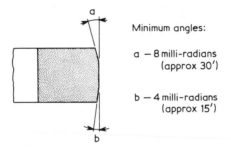

Minimum angles:

a — 8 milli-radians
    (approx 30′)

b — 4 milli-radians
    (approx 15′)

Average worn top ring profile

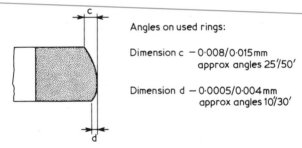

Angles on used rings:

Dimension c — 0·008/0·015mm
              approx angles 25′/50′

Dimension d — 0·0005/0·004mm
              approx angles 10′/30′

Fig. 6.11   Profile used for top ring to improve lubrication.

ride like a surf-board over the extremely thin oil film that exists in this zone without destroying it. When wear does eventually occur, the ring form is still effective.

COOLING

The amount of heat to be dissipated from a typical sports car engine cooling system is roughly equal to the heat equivalent of the power developed by the engine. As thermal efficiencies increase with the use of higher compression ratios the proportion of the total heat energy of the fuel passing out into the exhaust and cooling systems is correspondingly reduced. If we increase the power output by supercharging, however, we also increase the amount of waste heat to be dissipated. An increase of 20 per cent in b.h.p. by supercharging increases the heat given out to the water jackets by about 25 per cent, since a portion of the extra power developed in the combustion chamber is lost in driving the supercharger.

Air-cooling

If we are fortunate enough to be able to design an engine without prejudice or the dictates of a firm's established precedent we cannot avoid making a fundamental decision at the very beginning. Are we to cool the engine by air or water? The majority of experienced designers made up their minds on this issue a long time ago and the majority chose water. Yet Ferdinand Porsche with a wide experience of both types chose air-cooling when he began work on his ubiquitous People's Car. Today VW are making cars with water-cooled engines and Porsche recently introduced a new model with water-cooling, yet continue to air-cool their most expensive products. Obviously the decision is not an easy one.

In one sense we can say that all engines are cooled by air. What we call a water-cooled engine uses water as an intermediate fluid to pick up heat from the engine and transfer it to the air stream at the radiator. Air is a much less effective cooling medium than water. The specific heat of air is only one-quarter that of water and if we compare the two fluids on a volume basis it requires about 4,000 times the quantity of air to transfer an equal quantity of heat. Air being a less effective heat transfer medium it is necessary to increase the cooling surface on the outside of the cylinder by the provision of a multiplicity of deep cooling fins. There is a limit to the number of fins we can provide, since a spacing that is closer than about one-tenth of an inch brings the laminar layers on the fin surfaces so close that the efficiency begins to fall rapidly. There is also a limit to the depth of fin that can be effectively utilized. Thus we find that with the best system of cooling fins that modern manufacturing techniques can provide a greater temperature differential is still required to transmit the waste heat from the combustion chamber to the outside cooling medium when air is that medium. Air-cooled engines must always therefore run with higher cylinder head temperatures than water-cooled engines at the same specific power output. In the limit then, we cannot anticipate as high a specific power output from the air-cooled engine.

There is little doubt that the well-designed air-cooled engine can always be lighter than the water-cooled engine. The air-cooled engine requires a ducted fan and a system of ducts and baffles to guide the air around the heads and cylinder barrels, but these can be made of light-gauge metal. The finning on the cylinder heads and barrels adds substantially to the weight of the air-cooled engine, especially if the barrels are made of steel, but the weight of the radiator still tips the scales against the water-cooled engine.

We can briefly summarize the comparison in the table below:

Advantages of air-cooling

(1) Lightness.
(2) Compact dimensions.
(3) No water leaks, external or internal.
(4) No danger of frost damage.
(5) Quick warm-up.

Disadvantages of air-cooling

(1) More expensive construction.
(2) Higher operating temperatures.
(3) Slightly lower specific power output.
(4) More noise from combustion, pistons and fan.

Water cooling

The radiator

The resistance to the flow of heat from the water inside the radiator to the air outside can be considered largely in terms of two additive resistances, the water-film resistance and the air-film resistance. The relative sizes of these vary, but in general the air-film resistance is from four to six times that of the water-film resistance. The modern cellular radiator matrix is designed with this limitation in mind and the area of metal exposed to the air stream is much greater than that exposed to the water. This gives some measure of compensation for the disparity in film resistances. The rate of the dissipation to the air stream varies

directly as

(a) the effective area of the cooling surface,
(b) the mean temperature difference (strictly, the logarithmic mean) between the metal surface and the air stream,
(c) some power (approximately the 0.6 power) of the velocity,

and *inversely as*

(d) some power (approximately the 0.4 power) of the width of the air passages through the matrix.

For a radiator of small frontal area, therefore, the air passages through the matrix must be as small as possible. One limit to this is set by the danger of gradual blockage by insects and other debris. Another limit is set by the permissible air pressure drop across the block. If the resistance to flow through the matrix becomes too great the velocity through it will be seriously reduced. In practice the water walls of the matrix are seldom spaced any closer than 0.4 in. and the extended surface fins on the air side are spaced no closer than 0.2 in. The air velocity through the matrix depends, not only upon the speed of the car through the air but upon the shape and position of the entry duct or radiator cowl. This velocity is usually about 70 per cent of the external relative velocity. Thus if the road velocity of the car is 130 ft per sec and there is a following wind of 30 ft per sec the velocity through the radiator will only be 70 ft per sec.

At 100 m.p.h. the cooling-water horsepower (heat equivalent) to be dissipated will be more than four times that at 50 m.p.h. The cooling air velocity is only twice that at 50 m.p.h. (assuming zero wind velocity) and the increase in heat transfer coefficient, being approximately proportional to $V^{0.6}$ (where V is the air velocity through the matrix) is only about 50 per cent. This explains why the radiator temperature rises when we drive faster. This however is not the most exacting duty imposed on a radiator, since full power can be used in an intermediate gear when climbing a steep gradient. On a long alpine pass with hairpin bends, full power may be used for 80 per cent of the time at low cooling air velocities. The short distance between bends prevents the car attaining its ultimate speed for the particular gradient and with full power in use almost continuously at average speeds of only about 50 ft per sec a radiator designed for high-speed work only would prove inadequate.

The power absorbed by the fan at high engine speeds can be as much as 6 or 7 per cent of the gross power. This is a sheer waste of power and money since at high speeds there is no need to boost the air flow through the radiator. Many fan control systems have been tried and a popular design is driven by an electric motor which is only in action when the coolant temperature rises to a pre-determined level. The Datsun sports car is fitted with a viscous fan coupling which always slips at high speed, but has a variable point of engagement of the coupling depending upon the temperature of a thermostat built into the centre of the fan coupling (see Figure 6.12). Thus in hot weather the fan, which is driven from the front end of the water pump, operates at water pump speed up to about 2,500 r.p.m. At higher engine speeds the viscous coupling slips to hold the fan speed to this figure. In cold weather the coupling begins to slip at a much lower speed, down to a lower figure of about 1,600 r.p.m. The coiled bi-metal thermostat seen on the front face of the fan boss in Figure 6.12 is subjected to the temperature of the air leaving the rear of the radiator. As the coolant temperature rises and the air leaving the back of the radiator rises the bi-metal strip expands and opens the valve which admits silicon oil to the chamber that operates the clutch and puts the fan into operation. The Datsun system therefore not only saves power but it ensures rapid warm-up of the engine.

For the designer who is seeking to save weight and drag, two well tried methods are available, pressurizing and glycol cooling. Pressurizing the system to 0.82 bar (12 lbf/sq in) raises the boiling point to 117.5°C (243°F). This in turn raises the temperature difference between the water and the cooling air by 17.5°C (31.5°F). At the bottom of the radiator, this may even double the temperature difference. A saving of as much as 35 per cent in matrix weight has been achieved in this way. Ethylene Glycol, with a b.p. of 180°C (356°F) points the way to even greater reductions. To the author's knowledge, no designer of a sports/racing car has been bold enough yet to use 100 per cent ethylene glycol as a coolant. Apart from obvious disadvantages such as expense and the corrosive properties of the material (despite all efforts to find the perfect inhibitor) one disadvantage of using a higher exit radiator temperature would be the general increase in temperatures throughout the system. Water-jacket temperatures

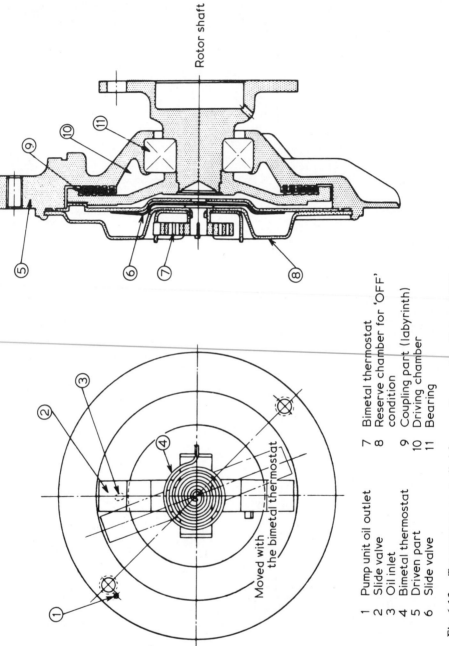

Rotor shaft

Moved with
the bimetal thermostat

1 Pump unit oil outlet
2 Slide valve
3 Oil inlet
4 Bimetal thermostat
5 Driven part
6 Slide valve

7 Bimetal thermostat
8 Reserve chamber for 'OFF'
   condition
9 Coupling part (labyrinth)
10 Driving chamber
11 Bearing

Fig. 6.12 Temperature controlled fan coupling used on Datsun 260Z sports car.

would also be much higher and the temperatures of the cylinder walls and rings would be higher. This is no light matter and on a high-output engine could mean the difference between trouble-free piston operation and piston failure.

The water pump

Without a pump the water velocity through the radiator is slow, depending as it does upon convection currents rising from the hotter parts of the cylinder head. The greatest objection to thermo-siphon cooling, however, is the erratic manner in which circulation is maintained. In certain hot-spots, such as exist around the exhaust valves, circulation is intermittent; vapour bubbles form at these points, momentarily blanketing the surface against effective heat transfer. When the bubbles break away from the surface and rise, relatively cool water is drawn in from the cylinder jackets to replace them. Thick cylinder head walls in these zones will assist in absorbing temperature fluctuations to a large extent, but there still remains the loss of cooling during the time the surface is blanketed by the steam. If the surface is blanketed with steam during 25 per cent of the time the effective cooling surface will be reduced by about 20 per cent.

When a pump is used, not only is good circulation promoted in the cylinder and head jackets but the increased velocity through the radiator matrix, to a smaller degree, increases the rate of heat transfer to the air stream. In some engines the pump does not circulate water through the cylinder jackets, only through the cylinder-head passages. In this way rapid warm-up is assisted. There are, of course, interconnecting passages between the cylinder and head jackets. The cooled water from the bottom tank of the radiator is led directly to the exhaust side of the cylinder head in such installations. Sometimes an internal tube is used, from which the water emerges in the form of high-velocity jets directed at the hottest zones behind the exhaust valve seats.

A cross-flow radiator is sometimes used in modern low-profile sports cars. Such a radiator can be made wide and shallow, with an inlet and outlet header tank on each side of the matrix. The top of the radiator unit is usually below the top of the cylinder-head level, but a make-up header tank is usually situated at a higher level on the engine bulkhead.

The design of an effective pump for a high-speed engine is not easy. The resistance of the cooling system to the flow of water remains fairly constant; the pressure of the pump to overcome this resistance varies as the speed of rotation. If the pump is designed to run at half-engine speed, circulation at 30 m.p.h. in top gear would probably be inadequate. If, however, the pump is designed to operate at engine speed, a phenomenon known as cavitation is liable to occur near maximum engine speed. Cavitation is caused by the creation of a high enough depression at the inlet to the impeller to flash off steam, thus causing suction at the impeller to break down completely. When this occurs, pumping ceases momentarily with, in some cases, spectacular and almost explosive boiling occurring at the cylinder head.

THE IGNITION SYSTEM

Magneto or coil

The early sports car engine almost invariably had magneto ignition, especially on the more highly developed engines giving peak power at speeds of 5,000 r.p.m. or higher. Such speeds were very near the limits of coil ignition, which, in its stage of development at the time, could not be depended upon to maintain a high enough voltage at these higher engine speeds. The early rotating armature magnetos were limited in speed by the centrifugal stresses in the windings. Nevertheless they could give reliable service at engine speeds of 6,000 r.p.m. in a 4-cylinder engine. Since those days there have been improvements in both magneto and coil ignition.

The magneto is a more efficient spark producer at high speed than at low. The coil, on the other hand, requires a certain time interval for the current to build up to its full value. This time is of the order of 0.01 sec. This current build-up can only occur during the time the contact breaker points are closed, and at speeds of about 6,000 r.p.m. on a 6-cylinder engine the sparking voltage on the old design of coil using the pre-war design of distributor would fall to about one-third of the low speed value. The builders of the more expensive sports cars in the 'thirties solved the problem of good ignition at both ends of the speed range by using two plugs per cylinder, one plug sparked by coil ignition, the other by magneto.

Coil ignition is still the choice today, but the spark is now triggered electronically on the latest designs. The mechanically operated contact breaker will soon be a 'vintage' memory. The Lucas electronic ignition is described later in the chapter.

Sparking plugs

Essentially a sparking plug is nothing more than a spark gap, but a spark gap that is asked to function under very arduous and dirty conditions. That it occasionally fails to operate is not really very surprising. For a plug to operate satisfactorily the nose of the insulator surrounding the central electrode must be at a temperature within the range 350-700°C (700-1300°F). If the temperature is too high, pre-ignition can occur. If the temperature is too low, the insulator will not keep clear of carbon. Since carbon is a good conductor of electricity it is an obvious necessity to keep the insulator nose clear of carbon deposits by maintaining it at a high enough temperature. A practical indication of this is given by the appearance of the nose when the plug is removed immediately after running at full power. A perfectly clean off-white insulator nose indicates too high an operating temperature. A light brown colour indicates a correct temperature and a plug blackened by 'lamp-black' type of carbon is running too cool. These indications are only relative and are influenced by other factors, such as mixture strength and the knock-rating of the fuel.

Plugs are made in a wide range of heat values (see Figure 6.13). Cool-running engines require 'hot' plugs, or 'soft' plugs as they are sometimes called. High

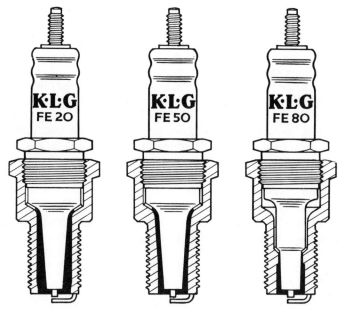

Fig. 6.13   A hot running plug usually has a greater distance from
the tip to the plug body. A very cool plug has a larger
diameter central electrode.

compression, high output engines developing high temperatures and pressures in
the combustion chamber require relatively 'cool' or 'hard' plugs for satisfactory
running. Some of the heat picked up by the insulator and central electrode from
the combustion gases is given to the relatively cool charge during the induction
and compression strokes. The major path for this heat, however, is outwards
through the body of the insulator to the copper seating in the plug body. For a
hot plug the distance from the nose of the insulator to this seating is made large.
For a cool plug the distance is much shorter. Although the maker's recommended plug or one of equivalent heat value is usually the one to be used, some
designs of engines are more sensitive in this respect than others and one
sometimes finds that plug types have to be varied to suit the driver rather than
the engine, a cool plug being required for the pole-position Grand Prix driver
and a hotter plug for the tyro in the back row.

To produce a spark across the sparking-plug points at the correct time in the
cycle calls for a voltage surge up to anything from 5,000 to 15,000 volts,
depending upon the size of the plug gap and the prevailing pressures inside the
cylinder. This is well within the capabilities of the modern conventional coil
ignition system under almost all conditions, except those of high-speed operation. It is this limitation that the spark begins to fail when we require a sparking
rate much higher than 400 per second that has led us at last into an era of
experimentation after a period of design stagnation lasting for more than a
quarter-century. Today we see transistorized ignition systems well established

and capacity discharge systems in an advanced stage of development. One of these will probably be the choice for the next quarter-century.

Wankel engines have presented a challenge to the plug manufacturers since the plug does not benefit from a cooling draught of mixture during an induction stroke or a compression stroke. The plug is in the firing line, so to speak, all the time since the same plug or pair of plugs are required to provide ignition for a succession of power strokes. Surface gap plugs have been developed for this arduous duty. Discharge occurs across the whole concentric area around the tip of the central electrode. These plugs have been found to function most effectively when used with the latest electronic ignitions where the voltage *rise-time* is very fast.

The conventional coil ignition system

The conventional circuit is shown in Figure 6.14. The cycle of operations begins when cam rotation causes the contacts to close and a current to flow through the primary windings, thus producing a magnetic field around the soft-iron core at

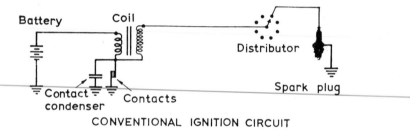

CONVENTIONAL IGNITION CIRCUIT

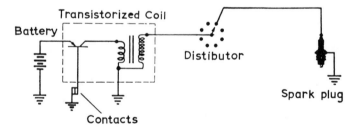

TRANSISTORIZED HIGH VOLTAGE IGNITION SYSTEM

Fig. 6.14

the centre of the coil. Breaking of the circuit as the contacts are opened causes a rapid collapse of the magnetic field which generates a transient voltage in the primary windings which can surge to a value of 200 to 300 volts. The primary windings consist of about 200 turns of covered wire. The purpose of the condenser is the storage of electrical energy when the points open. A clean break in the current would not be possible without this storage capacity and the points would suffer from the severe arcing. As soon as the induced current stops flowing, the condenser discharges back into the primary windings, this back flow helping to remove the remnants of the magnetic field around the core.

The secondary windings which are wound round the primary windings are made of extremely fine wire, about 20,000 turns in all. The two concentric coils thus constitute a transformer with a step-up ratio of 100 to 1. The more rapid the collapse of the magnetic field when the points open, the higher will be the voltage build-up in the secondary windings. The actual peak voltage reached is always that required to jump the plug gap. The larger the gap, the greater the voltage needed to jump it. Discharge of this secondary charge, lasting about a thousandth of a second, triggers an oscillating current in both primary and secondary circuits which persists until all the energy is dissipated. The contacts close again and the cycle is repeated. The purpose of the distributor is to channel the secondary current to each sparking plug in turn, depending upon the desired firing order. For a 6-cylinder engine running at 5,000 r.p.m. the time available for the whole sequence of events is about five thousandths of a second. The whole ignition story is told in Figure 6.15 by a typical trace from an ignition

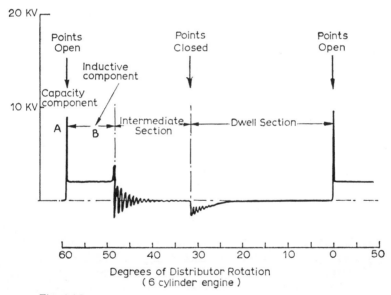

Fig. 6.15

oscilloscope. In this particular case the secondary voltage has risen to a voltage of about 9,000 before the plug gap has ionized sufficiently for the spark to jump. As soon as the gap has become conductive and for the rest of the 'inductive' part of the spark the voltage falls to a lower value to complete the discharge with a falling alternating current. The dwell section of Figure 6.15 is the period when the points are closed and the magnetic field is building up in the coil. If this period is inadequate, as it might well be at high engine speeds, the *available* voltage will fall in the manner shown in Figure 6.16. Fortunately the *required* secondary voltage also falls, since the falling volumetric efficiency at higher speeds results in lower cylinder pressures, which in turn require a lower voltage for a given spark gap to be bridged. The point of intersection of the 'available secondary voltage' and the 'required sparking voltage' lines is the limiting speed for reliable ignition. Thus in the case of the high-compression engine shown in Figure 6.16 occasional misfiring will begin to occur at about 7,000 r.p.m.

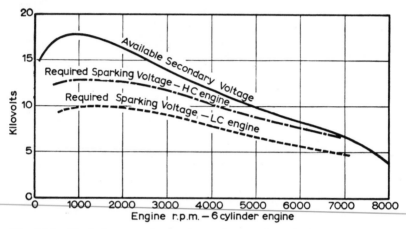

Fig. 6.16   Typical curves of secondary voltage and required sparking voltage with coil ignition.

The conventional coil ignition system has been working very close to its maximum capacity for many years and, with the trend to higher engine speeds, frequent maintenance has been required to keep it functioning in a reliable manner.

New ignition developments

Transistorized ignition systems have been available for several years and, when properly designed and with adequate cooling provided for the transistor, have been found to give reliable service with a marked increase in contact-breaker life. The majority of the American automobile manufacturers now offer a transistorized ignition system as an original equipment option. In these applications, the transistor simply serves as a relay switch to reduce the current carried by the contacts (see lower circuit of Figure 6.14). A very small current, almost one-quarter of an amp, is all that passes across the contacts in this system, and this current by the action of the crystals in the transistor, is stepped up to a current of about 7 amps to pass through the primary coil windings. No condenser is required and the life of the contacts is extended to at least 20,000 miles.

Transistors can be ruined by too high operating temperatures. They are usually mounted on a deeply finned block of aluminium, called a *heat sink*, but the location of this heat sink where too much heat is picked up from the surroundings can lead to transistor failure. Silicon transistors are most resistant to high temperature, but are more expensive than the popular germanium units.

The simple transistor-switching system can only be regarded as an interim stage in the development of the new ignition systems. For the system of the future we must look to the new 'breakerless' techniques developed over the last ten to fifteen years. The Lucas 'OPUS' system has been used on racing engines for more than ten years and in its latest production version is available for 4, 6, 8, and 12 cylinder engines.

The Mark 2 OPUS (Oscillating Pick-up System) is a contactless system and has a spark capability of 800 sparks per second, twice that of the best mechanical contact-breaker systems. Since the system will operate for very long periods without maintenance it has been of great benefit to British firms such as Jaguar and Triumph in meeting the stringent American anti-smog laws. The system is shown schematically in Figure 6.17. It comprises four main components, an amplifier unit, a ballast resistor unit, an ignition coil and a distributor.

The amplifier is a continuously operating fixed frequency (600kHz) oscillator, transformer-coupled to an amplifier stage and an output stage which is a power

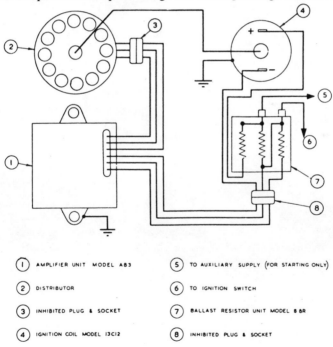

① AMPLIFIER UNIT MODEL A83	⑤ TO AUXILIARY SUPPLY (FOR STARTING ONLY)
② DISTRIBUTOR	⑥ TO IGNITION SWITCH
③ INHIBITED PLUG & SOCKET	⑦ BALLAST RESISTOR UNIT MODEL 8 8R
④ IGNITION COIL MODEL 13C12	⑧ INHIBITED PLUG & SOCKET

Fig. 6.17 Schematic arrangement of Lucas 'OPUS' Mark 2 ignition system.

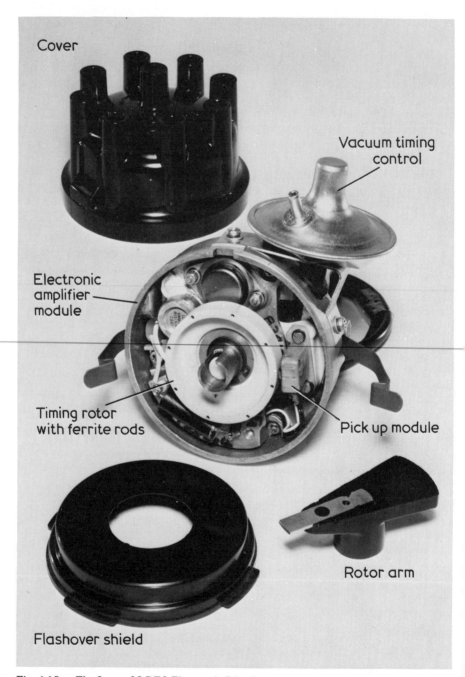

Cover

Vacuum timing control

Electronic amplifier module

Timing rotor with ferrite rods

Pick up module

Rotor arm

Flashover shield

Fig. 6.18 The Lucas 35 DE8 Electronic Distributor, one of a new range of 4, 6, 8 and 12 cylinder distributors designed to comply with increasingly stringent regulations governing emissions and service intervals.

transistor performing the function of the conventional contact-breaker. The amplifier unit is housed in a finned aluminium sink unit, since the power transistor must not be allowed to overheat.

The distributor (see Figure 6.18) resembles the conventional design externally, since the distributor cap performs the usually duty of distributing the high voltage current to the plug leads. Inside the cap one also finds the customary rotor arm. The familiar contact-breaker is replaced by the timing rotor which is a moulded fibre-glass-filled nylon disc with ferrite rods embedded in the periphery. The number of rods is equal to the number of cylinders in the engine. The pick-up module is an E-shaped transformer core. The outer limbs of the E carry input windings which are fed from the oscillator in the amplifier unit. The centre limb carries the output windings to drive the amplifier stage. By design the resultant magnetic flux in the centre limb is negligible and the output signal is consequently also negligible when one of the ferrite rods is not in line with the pick-up module. When a ferrite rod passes across the face of the E-core the magnetic circuits become unbalanced giving an increased signal voltage in the output coil. When fed to the amplifier this signal causes the output power transistor to be switched off. This breaks the primary circuit in the ignition coil (as in the case of a conventional contact-breaker). The voltage rise-time is very high and a high voltage is produced in the secondary windings to create the required spark at the plug.

A centrifugal advance mechanism is incorporated in the distributor and a normal vacuum unit adjusts the ignition timing under varying load conditions as in the conventional system.

7

Road-holding

'O what a flowery track lies spread before me, henceforth!
What dust clouds shall spring up behind me
as I speed on my reckless way!'

KENNETH GRAHAME

TYRES

Tyres were a source of great trouble to the early motorist, particularly when he raced. Figure 7.1 shows a competitor in the 1906 French Grand Prix struggling with a tyre-change at the side of the road while Vincenzo Lancia hurtles past in his 16-litre FIAT. The spare covers strapped to the back of Lancia's car suggests that he also anticipated tyre trouble.

To Dunlop and his generation his tyre was simply a means of absorbing the shocks that the rough roads of the period imparted to the bicycles and horseless carriages that travelled them. The pneumatic tyre's potential for clinging to the road surface to provide the incredible cornering power that the modern sports car driver takes for granted had to wait for two important things. First we had to have good hard-surfaced roads to give the tyre something to grip and secondly we had to wait for the tyre manufacturers to develop the teeth to give that grip, the modern tyre tread with its multiplicity of grooves and slits so designed to wipe away any film of water and to maintain a steady bite on the road surface.

The grip on the road

The only roads that existed for the early motorist were of crushed stone and these soon disintegrated until the surface became an unpredictable loose mixture of broken stones, smaller debris and dust. Even a modern tyre tread fails to get a grip on such a surface and the early motorist was forever haunted by what the motoring journals of the period called 'the dreaded side-slip'.

The grip of the tyres on the road is just as important during braking, when accelerating and when cornering. One might expect some relationship to exist between the limiting thrusts that a tyre can exert on the road surface, forwards,

Fig. 7.1 16-litre F.I.A.T. driven by Vincenzo Lancia in 1906 French Grand Prix. Note the need for frequent tyre changes. (Photography from the Cyril Posthumus collection).

backwards and sideways. An investigation by the Road Research Laboratory of D.S.I.R. showed that the same forces can be exerted by the contact patch of a tyre under identical surface conditions in any direction. Thus, if we are travelling on a good non-skid surface with a vertical load on the tyre of 500 lb and the limiting cornering side thrust per tyre is 400 lb, i.e. a centrifugal acceleration of 0.8 G, the limiting retardation and the limiting acceleration in a straight line will also be 0.8 G, or a thrust at the road surface of 400 lb. On the other hand if the surface is wet and the limiting side force is only 200 lb, the limiting straight-line acceleration and deceleration forces will also be about 200 lb.

The laws of friction are no longer regarded as a simple matter of applying a proportionality constant (called a coefficient of friction) to every pair of rubbing surfaces. We now know that the conditions at the surface are often more important than the nature of the materials themselves.

Five main types of friction are usually distinguished:

(*a*) *Smooth dry friction*. This is self-explanatory. It is seldom encountered on the public highway. Polished granite paving stones, still used on a few roads in the North of England, almost approach this condition.

(*b*) *Rough dry friction*. As in the first case the surfaces are in direct contact and are perfectly dry, but, owing to the uneven nature of one or both of the surfaces, projections on one cut through or lacerate portions of the other. This is encountered often when skidding on dry roads, particularly with an asphalt or tarred road with a rough surface. Under these conditions decelerations of 0.8 to 0.8 G are possible.

(*c*) *Loose dry friction*. When the two dry surfaces are held apart by a layer of loose particles such as sand or gravel, a sliding action takes place which is sometimes called a ball-bearing action. The more rounded the particles, the more they roll, the more angular, the more sliding and the less rolling takes place. The overall effect is a reduction of the coefficient of friction when compared with smooth dry surfaces in direct contact. This condition is frequently encountered on the road, especially near the road verge where loose gravel accumulates.

(*d*) *Lubricated friction*. This occurs when a liquid film completely separates the two surfaces, as in a well-lubricated bearing. This seldom occurs between the tyres and the road surface, except in the case of an icy road when a film of water can be maintained between the road surface and the contact patch of the tyre, in the same way as the film of water is formed by the pressure of the blade of a skate. The effect is very similar in both cases. Unfortunately the sliding motorist cannot turn his skates sideways in the manner of an expert skater! Occasionally wet granite paving stones give true lubricated friction, but in general a film of grit is present to modify the action.

(*e*) *Partially lubricated friction*. This occurs when separation by a liquid is not complete and the surfaces are in actual contact in places or, at the most, are only separated by a 'liquid' film of one or two molecules in thickness. This happens on wet roads and locked wheel decelerations of from 0.6 to 0.4 are

70 series

60 series

50 series

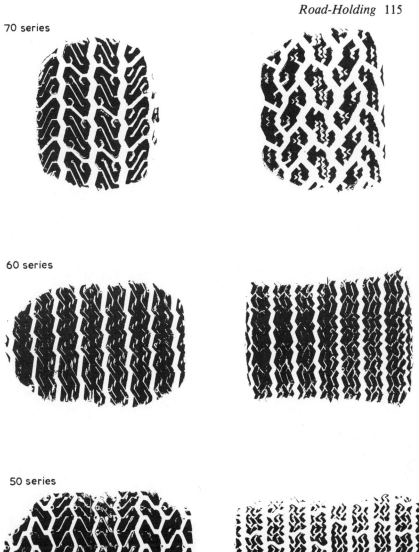

Fig. 7.2   Tyre footprints.

possible in these conditions. On muddy roads and particularly after a short shower of rain when the dry dust has been converted to a film of mud of such high viscosity that the squeegee action of the tyre treads fails to expel it completely from the surfaces in contact, conditions can again approach the fully lubricated state and locked wheel decelerations can be limited to values as low as 0.05 *G*. When acceleration or deceleration produces sufficient heat to melt the tar surface a condition of partial lubrication exists. When black streaks are produced in the road surface the limiting acceleration is usually only about 0.5 *G*.

The tyre footprints

Typical static tyre footprints are shown in Figure 7.2. These are static footprints or contact patches for tyres of various tread designs. For maximum traction and cornering on both dry and wet roads it is necessary to provide, not only circumferential grooves but a carefully evolved system of slots and 'sipes' that clings to the surface to give us the 'Graunchy Grippers' of the advertisements. An adequate drainage pattern to remove water from the contact patch as fast as it enters the leading edge is also necessary.

The dynamic behaviour of the footprint

Figure 7.3 shows the manner in which a tyre obtains a side thrust from the road surface to counter the centrifugal force when turning a corner or to prevent the car running into the ditch on a steeply cambered road. In Figure 7.3 the tyre is viewed from below as if running on a sheet of glass. This diagram shows that the plane of the wheel makes an angle, ϕ, with the path along which it is travelling. This is called the slip angle and the greater the side force required from the tyre,

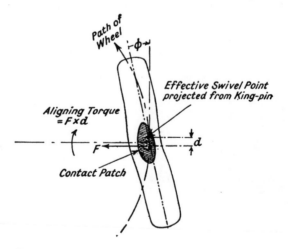

Fig. 7.3 Distortion of tyre centre-line at contact patch produces cornering force and self-aligning torque. (Distortion exaggerated).

the greater will be the slip angle up to the point at which it loses its grip on the road surface and skids. This is a similar condition to the stalling of an aeroplane wing when the critical angle of incidence is exceeded. The cornering force does not act at the centre of the contact patch, but slightly to the rear. This, plus the designed castor displacement of the steering layout, results in a turning moment, $F \times d$, called the self-aligning torque, which must be countered by the pull provided by the driver on the steering wheel. It is this torque, plus or minus any torque set up by the camber of the wheels, that goes to make the 'feel' of the steering in the driver's hands. This feel can sometimes be misleading, since it bears no relationship to the cornering power of the tyres.

Cornering power

The manner in which the tyre surface creates this cornering power is as follows:

Each portion of the tread as it approaches the contact patch must be pushed outwards and distorted from its natural shape to conform to the particular slip angle at which the tyre is operating. The rest of the tyre casing and tread must exert the force needed to distort the contact patch and it is this continuous process of distortion as each portion of the tread approaches the contact patch that contributes to the cornering power exerted on the vehicle. As each section of tread leaves the contact zone it recovers its original shape, but no work is done here, except a certain loss of energy, called hysteresis loss, which results in a heating up of the tyre.

The cornering power of a tyre is defined as the cornering force divided by the slip angle required to provide this force. The usual units are lb per degree. This cornering power under any given load can be measured on a special laboratory machine. Some companies, such as Dunlop, use a large rotating drum. Others prefer to use what is called a flat-bed rolling tyre tester. With these machines slip angles can be measured accurately under any combination of vertical loads and side loads to produce sets of curves of the type shown in Figure 7.4. With these machines it is possible to explore the influence of many factors that enter into the design of a tyre, such factors as tyre section width, tyre pressure and the influence of the angle at which the textile cords are set across the tyre centre line.

The following is a brief summary of these influences.

Inflation pressure. The introduction of ultra low profile tyres has accentuated the importance of tyre pressures. The aspect ratio (height to width ratio) of a tyre cross-section is variously expressed by tyre manufacturers as '70 Series' or '70 Profile' or by the aspect ratio incorporated after a 'stroke' in the tyre size, i.e., 185/70 VR 15; this indicating a tyre 185 mm wide with a 70 profile on a 15 inch diameter wheel and a VR speed rating — usually up to 150 m.p.h.

When tyre profiles were all at 100 percent the contact patch was very narrow and more heavily loaded. The actual tread profile (not profile ratio) presented to the road surface was very rounded and an increase in cornering power could usually be obtained by running at 10 or 15 per cent above the maker's recommended pressure. All this has changed now and with 70 or 60, and

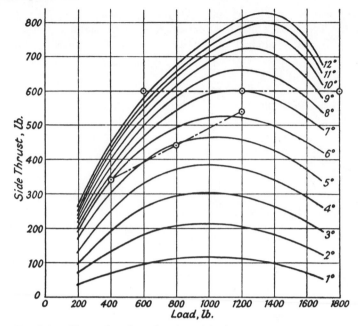

Fig. 7.4   Slip angles plotted against side thrust.

especially with the 50 Series tyre it is essential to maintain the correct tyre pressure, cornering power being reduced appreciably by a variation, either upwards or downwards, of more than 2 lb per sq in. The tread profile is very flat on these tyres and overpressure makes this slightly convex thus reducing the area of the contact patch. Conversely, a hollow centre part can be given to the contact patch with underinflation.

Grand Prix drivers using tyre profiles as low as 35 and even 30, are not only much concerned during the warming-up laps with the warming-up of their sticky tread compounds, but are also very finicky about tyre pressures, knowing that a slightly concave footprint is just as dangerous as a convex one. Most modern high speed road tyres are confined to the 70 and 60 Series although a few tyre manufacturers have ventured lower. Until tyre manufacturers can provide a tyre less sensitive to small changes in pressure this factor alone will provide a practical limit of about 50.

Camber. The influence of wheel camber on cornering power has become all-important in recent years since the introduction of ultra-low profile tyres. Racing car designers have even been turning in despair to thoughts of beam axles, a simple solution to the problem of keeping the wheels upright in a corner. With a profile of 50 or under there is a serious loss of cornering power when the camber angle exceeds about 3 degrees in either direction. De Dion suspension, as used by Aston Martin, is one solution to this problem since this is a sophisticated form of beam axle. Where independent suspension is used at both ends of the car a suspension geometry is usually chosen that maintains the outer wheels within about 2 degrees of vertical when cornering. Since the inner wheels are less lightly loaded when cornering near the limit, relatively larger changes in camber angle can be permitted without seriously reducing the overall cornering power.

Rim width. Wide tyres are less effective on narrow rims and a change to a lower profile tyre usually demands a change to a wider wheel.

Traction, braking and acceleration. Despite all the development work carried out on tread patterns one surprising fact always seems to emerge when tyres are tested. A tyre footprint will exert almost the same limiting force *in any*

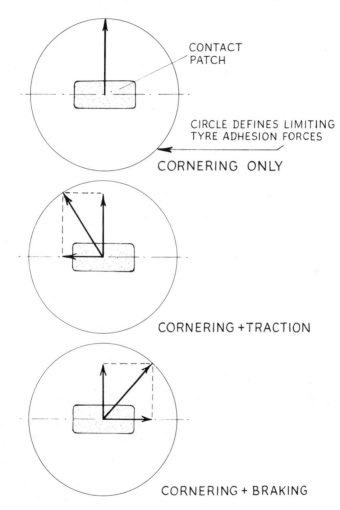

Fig. 7.5   The Circle of Forces: how available cornering force
is reduced during traction and braking.

direction. Thus if we apply traction or braking effort while the footprint is also subjected to a cornering force the limiting cornering force will be reduced. The 'Circle of Forces' shown in Figure 7.5 is a simple way to demonstrate this concept. Laboratory experiments carried out by the Ford Motor Company of America in the Sixties on a 9.00×14 tyre as used on a full-size sedan showed that traction or braking would reduce the limiting cornering force by as much as 30 per cent. Expressed another way one could say that with more moderate cornering the slip angle would have to be greater to exert the same cornering force when the car was braking or accelerating at the same time.

Load. The variation of cornering force with changes in the load carried by the wheel is best illustrated by Figure 7.4, which is a plot of side-thrust against load over a range of slip angles for a 6.00×16 tyre inflated to 28 lb per sq in. pressure. It should be noted that cornering force, not cornering power, has been plotted since the curves of cornering power against load would lie too much on top of each other for clarity. The influence of tyre load is seen to be small at small slip angles, but as the slip angle increases it becomes greater. When cornering near the limit, slip angles of 10° and in favourable circumstances even 14° are possible. In such conditions the transfer of load from the inner to the outer wheels by the rolling couple acting on the sprung mass begins to exercise an important influence on the cornering behaviour of the car. No transfer when cornering, a load of 800 lb on each wheel and a slip angle of 5° will give a side thrust of 440 lb per wheel for the tyre considered in Figure 7.4. But, in general, some transfer does occur and with a transfer of 400 lb from the inner to the outer wheels it is seen that a slip angle of $6\frac{1}{3}$° is now required to provide an average side thrust of 440 lb per wheel, i.e. 340 lb on the inner wheels and 540 lb on the outer wheels. From this we see that, all other things being equal, a car with a small roll angle on corners can corner slightly faster with safety than one with a large roll angle. The effect is most pronounced when the mean tyre load coincides with the peak of the side thrust/tyre load curve. Without load transfer a load of 1,200 lb and a side thrust of 600 lb would give a slip angle of 7° (see Figure 7.4). A load transfer of 50 per cent is quite moderate, but such a transfer would increase the slip angles to something greater than 12° which in many cases would result in a bad skid. The importance of choosing the tyre sizes to operate on the rising part of the thrust/load curve is thus emphasized.

Tyre construction

Twenty years ago we could divide tyre construction into two very distinctive types, *cross-ply* and *radial*. Since then the American tyre manufacturers, with large capital investments in plants to make cross-ply tyres, have shown ingenuity to combine the two types of tyre into *bias-belted* tyres and at the same time to make these with very little modification to their existing plants. On this side of the Atlantic there have also been many variations evolved on the original Michilin X steel-braced radial tyre.

The older design of tyre, the cross-ply, has the rubber carcase of the tyre reinforced by layers of bias-cut fabric which pass across the tyre from side to side being anchored to the bead wires on both sides. A conventional angle would be from 20 to 30 degrees to the circumferential centre-line. Cross-ply construction is shown in Figure 7.6. In this illustration the aspect ratio is 100 per cent.

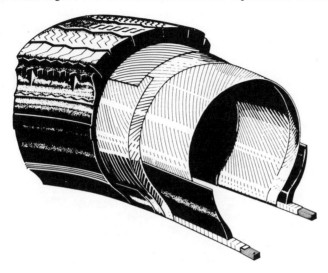

Fig. 7.6   Internal construction of cross-ply tyre.

Cross-ply construction is used, however, in racing tyres with profiles as extreme as 30 per cent. On such tyres the cord angle is decreased to about 20 degrees to resist centrifugal growth at high speed. This gives a very harsh uncomfortable ride.

Radial tyres, by definition, have the textile cords passing from bead to bead radially, i.e. at an angle of 90 degrees to the circumferential centre-line. This makes the side walls very flexible and with no attempt to stiffen the tread zone the natural cross-section would be circular and the unsupported tread would twist and squirm in all directions. In the original Michelin X tyre three-plies of steel mesh were placed below the tread to stiffen it and the effect was quite remarkable. Not only did it stabilise the tread in a way never achieved before on any cross-ply tyre but it reduced tread movement in the footprint area so much that tyre wear was reduced dramatically. Slip angles were lower for a given cornering force than on a cross-ply tyre and the limiting cornering forces were higher. The tyre crown was so resistant to sideways movement under high cornering forces that the gradual reduction in contact patch area that occurs on a cross-ply tyre as it reaches the limit was absent. This tended to give a rather sudden breakaway. Even so the original X tyres were, in their day, unsurpassed in the wet. Disadvantages were increased noise, a harsher ride and heavier steering.

Today after nearly thirty years of development the steel-braced tyre is a much more refined product and is in competition with a whole range of variants using combinations of many textile materials such as nylon and polyester to brace the tread zone. Typical of this modern generation of radials is the Dunlop SP Sport shown in cross-section in Figure 7.6. The same internal construction is used in the 60 Series SP Sport Super shown in Figure 7.8, but the tread bracing layers in this case are of steel. The SP Sport Super has a large block tread pattern with wide channels for water drainage. In the 70 Series it is fitted to the Jaguar XJ-S, and the Porsche 911. In the 60 Series it is used on the Lotus Elite.

Bias-belted tyres have been developed by the American tyre manufacturers

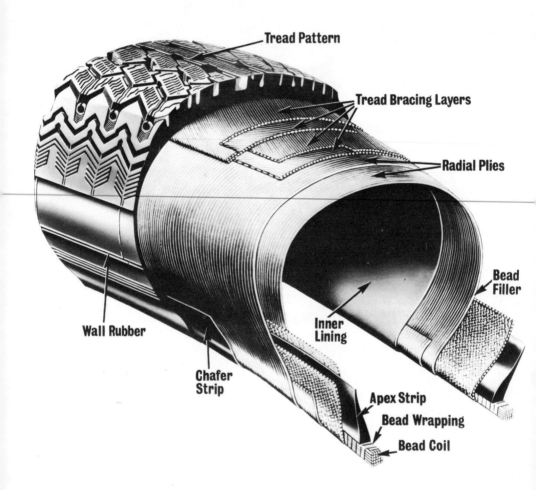

Fig. 7.7   Internal construction of Dunlop SP Sport steel-braced radial tyre.

Fig. 7.8   Dunlop SP Sport Super Tyre (60 Series) as used on Lotus Elite.

and are cross-ply tyres in general construction, but with the addition of a stiffening belt of steel mesh, nylon or polyester cord. As one would expect their general behaviour and performance falls somewhere between that of the old cross-ply and the best radials.

Tyre compounds

Natural rubber is rather soft, but has good flexibility even at low temperatures. Hardness can be increased by the degree of vulcanisation and by compounding with synthetic rubbers. It has poor resistance to oxidation and attack by atmospheric ozone.

Chloroprene copolymer (neoprene) is not as 'bouncy' as natural rubber, but is far superior in resistance to high temperature and ozone. It becomes very stiff at low temperatures.

Styrene butadiene copolymer (SBR), when compounded with reinforcing fillers, has physical and chemical properties very similar to natural rubber. It possesses high resistance to abrasion and has contributed largely to the much improved grip of modern tyres in the wet. Compounds using large additions of SBR are sometimes called 'high mu' compounds. Mu (μ) being the Greek letter used by tyre technologists for the coefficient of friction between the rubber and the road surface. Unfortunately, high mu compounds also exhibit high values of the property called 'hysteresis'. Hysteresis in this context means the amount of energy dissipated internally when the rubber is compressed and then released. This energy is converted into heat and high mu compounds, although suitable for wet-weather tyres, can become dangerously overheated when used on dry roads.

The choice of tyres at the start of a race is a headache for team managers, but we, happily, are not concerned with such matters in this book. For a sports car to be used every day of the week we need an all-weather tyre and the rubber is compounded to give a satisfactory compromise between wet and dry requirements and always with the need for excellent abrasion resistance in mind.

Aquaplaning

Aquaplaning (hydroplaning in America) is in effect high speed skating of the tyre on a film of water when travelling on wet roads. It was observed many years ago that aircraft landing on wet runways would occasionally suffer the loss of all braking effort. Investigation showed that the tyres could ride up on a wedge film of water in a manner that is closely related to the hydrodynamic wedge action of a lubricated bearing. The frictional coefficient becomes negligible and all braking and steering effort is lost. The same phenomenon can occur at speeds of 80 m.p.h. and over with standard automobile tyres. With a smooth tyre aquaplaning can occur at speeds as low as 60 m.p.h. — a reduction in the grip on the road can even occur at speeds as low as 35 m.p.h. Figure 7.9 shows photographs taken through a special glass section in a runway during experiments at the NASA Langley Field Center using 6.50 × 13 passenger car tyres. With a smooth tyre the contact patch completely disappears at 80 m.p.h. With a ribbed tyre the contact patch is reduced in area at 80 m.p.h. but is still making an effective enough contact for some braking effort to be applied to the road surface. At some unspecified higher speed even the ribbed tyre will lose all contact with the road surface and will slide as freely as on an icy surface.

The Dunlop Rubber Company developed the C41 tread to provide rapid effective drainage channels for the water film. This tyre has been shown to be about 15 per cent more effective on fully wetted surfaces than other tread designs. New patterns have since been developed which eject the water sideways along ducts moulded below the tread. The Dunlop SP Sport radial (79 Series) shown fitted to an E Type Jaguar in Figure 7.10 uses these water-clearing 'aqua-jets' to pump water away from the contact patch and is also given a central drainage groove, a technique learned by Dunlop to combat aquaplaning on their Formula 1 tyres.

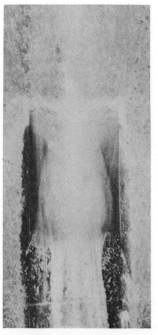

V = 46 m.p.h.

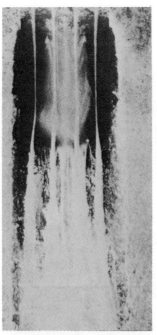

V = 79 m.p.h.

SMOOTH TREAD

V = 46 m.p.h.

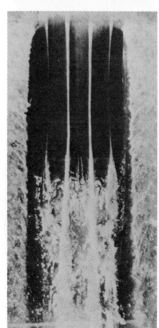

V = 80 m.p.h.

4- GROOVE RIB TREAD

Fig. 7.9   Aquaplaneing. Comparison of water flow under smooth and 4-groove rib tread tyres at speeds of 46 and approximately 80 m.p.h. Vertical load = 835lb; tyre pressure = 27 lb/in²; water depth = 0.02 inch.

Fig. 7.10   Dunlop SP Sport radial (70 Series) fitted to E-Type Jaguar.

CORNERING BEHAVIOUR

Oversteer and understeer

The stability of the motion of a car when travelling in a straight line on the highway at almost any speed is entirely a question of oversteer and understeer. Let us consider the case of a car travelling in a straight line on an uncambered road when the car is suddenly subjected to a small side thrust, such as might be caused by a gust of wind or a pot-hole. Under the action of the side thrust all four wheels will run at slip angles, ϕ_1 at the front and ϕ_2 at the rear. If ϕ_1 is less than ϕ_2 the car will steer towards the side force. The car is now following a curved path and the centrifugal force thus produced will augment the initial side force and ϕ_1 and ϕ_2 will both increase to new slip angles ϕ_1' and ϕ_2'. The increase in ϕ_2 will be greater than the increase in ϕ_1, thus increasing the centrifugal force still more. It is easy to see that the car is in an unstable condition and the situation will call for continual steering correction from the driver. This condition is known as *oversteer*.

The reverse effect is produced when ϕ_1 is greater than ϕ_2, since the car turns slightly away from the disturbing side force, producing a centrifugal force in the opposite direction that tends to cancel the initial disturbing force. This is a stable condition and means that many of the small disturbing forces are automatically damped out by the steering behaviour of the car itself without any action being required from the driver. This condition is called *understeer*. While opinions may differ as to the most desirable behaviour of a car when cornering, there is no doubt that every car should be set up to be in an understeering condition when running in a straight line. The amount of understeer need only be slight. The manner in which the designer arranges that the slip angle is always greater at the front is a complex subject. Some of the factors that influence understeer and oversteer will be considered later in the chapter.

Steering layout

The original Ackermann steering layout as used on the earliest horseless carriages was modified by Jeantend in 1878. On the older beam front axle the modified Ackermann geometry was given by inclining the links which connect the wheel steering pivots and the track-rod ends so that, if extended, they would intersect on the car centre-line about two-thirds of the wheel-base from the front. Only when making very slow turns, i.e. about 5 m.p.h., would a car turn about the Ackermann centre. Not only would the rear wheels be turning about a smaller radius than the front, but by turning about the Ackermann centre, the slip angles would be zero on all four wheels. It has already been demonstrated that a tyre must exert a side thrust when a car is cornering and this side thrust can only be exerted by the tyre running at a slip angle. It is reasonable to suppose that at moderate and high speeds the actual turning centre will be at some point further forward than the Ackermann centre. By turning about a centre such as *B* in Figure 7.11 the required slip angles are obtained.

It is now realized that the modified Ackermann layout is unsound for high-speed motoring. The outer wheel, the one taking most of the load, is given a smaller slip angle than the lightly loaded inner wheel. A negative Ackermann layout has been adopted by several modern designers since this allows the inner and outer wheels to operate much closer to their natural slip angles when cornering.

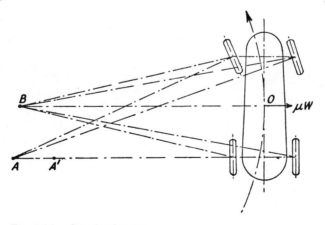

Fig. 7.11   Steering layout.

The car shown in Figure 7.11 is turning on a radius of 60 ft. (The drawing is not to scale.) Let us assume that the gross weight is 2,000 lb and that the slip angles, both front and rear, are 6½ degrees. If we simplify the problem by assuming tha the car does not roll, the load on each tyre will be identical and equal to 500 lb.

The centrifugal force resisted by each wheel,

$$F = \frac{Wv^2}{gr} = \frac{500v^2}{32 \cdot 2 \times 60} = 0 \cdot 26v^2$$

The side thrust per wheel with a vertical load of 500 lb and a slip angle of 6½ degrees we find from Figure 7.4 to be 400 lb for a tyre size of 6.00 × 16. This side thrust must of course equal the centrifugal force, i.e.

$$F = 400 = 0.26v^2$$
$$v = 56 \text{ ft per sec} = 38 \text{ m.p.h.}$$

If the car were travelling at a higher velocity, but still turning about a 60 ft radius the centrifugal loads would be higher, increasing as the square of the velocity, the required slip angles would be greater and the front wheels would be turned further into the corner so that the Ackermann centre would now be at some point A'. In practice the position B, the actual turning centre, will depend on the relative sizes of the slip angles on the front and rear wheels and the amount of tractive effort applied to the driving wheels. For an oversteering car, B will be further in since the slip angle on the rear wheels will be greater than on the front. For an understeering car, B will be further out.

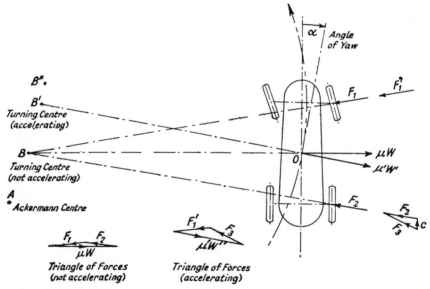

Fig. 7.12   Balance of cornering forces: rear wheel drive.

Rear wheel drive car

Let us first consider the simple case of a typical front-engined sports car with rear wheel drive and a fairly high power to weight ratio.

When an understeering car enters a corner at speed the driver finds that the front of the car must be pointed further into the corner than appears necessary from the actual curvature of the corner. This, of course, is caused by the need to generate cornering forces, i.e. the establishment of slip angles. Photographs of racing and sports cars which appear to be about to run into the inside verge on a corner are frequently shown in the motoring press. This effect is most noticeable on the 'drifting' racing car but it takes place, although to a less noticeable degree, on any car.

The four-wheel drift is a familiar sight to the race-going crowds, but the manner in which it works is not generally understood. Let us consider that the car in Figure 7.12 is a rear-wheel drive racing or sports car with a high power to weight ratio and that it is taking a corner at such a speed that the slip angles are high, let us say about 9° or 10°. The car is arranged by design to understeer on corners. With a slip angle of 10° on the front tyres, that on the rear tyres is only 8°. The effects of roll are neglected for simplicity. Taking first the simple case when the torque applied to the rear wheels is just sufficient to overcome the normal resistances of the road and the aerodynamic drag, i.e. the driver is going through the corner with his foot on the accelerator in the identical position it would occupy when travelling at the same velocity on the straight. On a long curve this would result in a steady drop in speed through the curve, since more power is required to maintain a given speed on a bend than on the straight. The centrifugal force, acting along the line BO, is equal to μW, where W is the gross weight of the car and μ is the value of the centrifugal force expressed in 'gravities'. If W equals 2,000 lb and μ equals 0.8 the centrifugal force will be 1,600 lb, or 400 lb per wheel.

To hold the car on its circle around point B the tyre cornering forces acting towards this point will be F_1 and F_2 as shown in the triangle of forces at the bottom of the figure.

Now let us suppose that the driver, wishing to maintain a constant speed throughout the bend, steps on the accelerator and applies an additional thrust at the rear tyre contact surface of 100 lb per wheel. The triangle of forces to the extreme right of the rear wheels indicates this force as C and the resultant thrust from the rear wheels is seen to be F_3. The immediate effect of this is to move the instantaneous turning centre from B to B'. The angle between F'_1 and $F3$, the resultant wheel thrusts when accelerating, is now greater than the angle between F_1 and F_2. This means that to counteract the same centrifugal acceleration, the slip angles must be greater when accelerating round a bend, since F'_1 and F_3 must be greater than F_1 and F_2 for the same value of μW.

One important effect of this additional thrust from the rear wheels is its effect on the 'attitude' or angle of yaw of the car to its path. The instantaneous direction of the car is at right angles to $B'O$, but the centre-line of the car is at an angle to this direction line. The yaw angle will vary in size with the extent of the acceleration. All the way round the bend the car is held at a yaw angle and if at any time the car gets dangerously near the verge the driver can either steer out or press harder on the accelerator. If he chooses to do the latter, the turning centre will move further forward from B' to B'' (see Figure 7.12), the angles between F'_1 and F_3 will increase still further and, to counteract the same centrifugal force, the slip angles at the back and front will have to increase. If the driver overdoes the acceleration, the front tyres will skid first, since the slip angles are greater at the front. This skidding of the front wheels automatically reduces the centrifugal force by increasing the radius of the turning circle. Provided there is room on the outside of the bend the loss of the true drift position in this way is not dangerous and the experienced driver soon recovers the correct yaw angle. Some drivers prefer to hold a constant throttle position on a bend and to make steering corrections to hold the drift. Techniques in starting the drift differ from driver to driver. A slow-motion film of Stirling Moss in action was once made by the Shell Film Unit. He started the drift with a sharp jab at the brake pedal and a flick of the steering wheel to catch the correct yaw angle. The car was held at the correct yaw angle by amazingly quick small steering corrections.

One of the characteristics of cornering near the limits of adhesion is the lack of feel at the steering wheel. Self-aligning torque usually increases up to a slip angle of 5°. At greater angles the torque falls off until at about 10° it becomes zero. In conditions where greater angles are possible the self-aligning torque can become negative. In other words, instead of the driver having to hold the steering wheel to prevent it flying back to the straight-forward position he finds it necessary to apply force in the opposite direction. To the inexperienced driver this can be disconcerting since the feel of the steering is contrary to his previous experience.

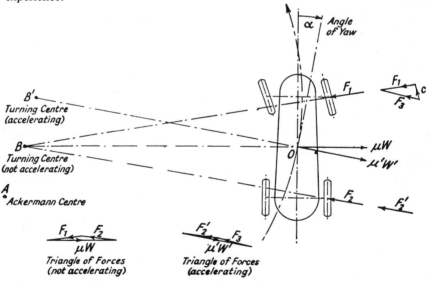

Fig. 7.13   Balance of forces: front wheel drive.

Front-wheel drive

The forces acting on a front-wheel-drive car when turning a corner are shown in Figure 7.13. When accelerating, the car travels at a yaw angle as in the case of the rear-wheel-drive car, but the line of action of the wheel thrusts, F'_2 and F_3, can come more into line with the centrifugal force $\mu'W'$ and can therefore be slightly smaller than in the non-accelerating case. This is the explanation of the oft-repeated saying that a front-wheel-drive car is 'more stable' when accelerating round a corner. It would be better to say that for a given limiting cornering thrust the F.W.D. car can corner faster when accelerating than when decelerating. Moreover, the *F.W.D. car is inherently faster round a corner than the R.W.D. car when the accelerating technique is used correctly.* From Figure 7.13 it will be seen that there is an optimum value for the acceleration. If C is too great, F_2 and F_3 will come out of line again. Here lies the danger in a front wheel drive racing car. When the optimum value is achieved the driver has reached a *point of no return.* Lifting the throttle, touching the brakes, even a slight variation in the line through the bend can result in a disastrous slide. Modern front wheel drive cars are very popular in Europe but the torque they can transmit to the front wheels when cornering is hardly enough to maintain a constant speed. Careful tuning of the suspension geometry and the strength of the anti-roll bars can give very forgiving handling on these underpowered family saloons. It is significant that no production sports cars are made today with front wheel drive.

Braking

The effect of braking on the position of the turning centre is exactly the opposite to the effect of acceleration. The deceleration thrusts at the road surface are of opposite sign, as shown in Figure 7.14 and the turning centre moves backwards to some point such as D. The immediate effect on the car is that it drifts towards the

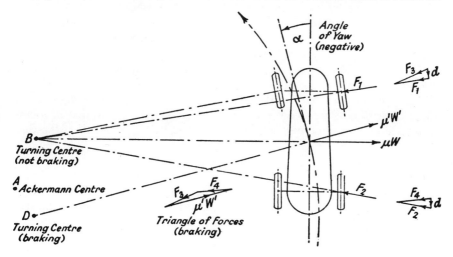

Fig. 7.14   Cornering forces during braking.

inner verge, since the yaw angle has reversed and if the driver does not correct this by immediately steering outwards the car will run into the verge. This is occasionally seen in racing when a driver is forced to brake to avoid a collision on the apex of a corner. Sometimes, however, savage braking on the soft-sprung modern sports car throws a greater load on the front wheels. Too great a cornering thrust is demanded from the front tyres and the car shoots off tangentially from its former turning circle.

The mid-engined sports car

Motoring writers sometimes state that the modern Grand Prix car is set up to oversteer. This is misleading, or at least an oversimplification. Formula 1 cars and turbocharged racing sports cars such as the Porsche 917 are capable in dry conditions of transmitting extremely high forces through their ultra-wide rear tyres. With a power to weight ratio of about 700 b.h.p. per ton the simple concept of 'the Circle of Forces' becomes of the utmost importance if we are to understand the behaviour of such a vehicle in a corner. If the driver puts his foot down harder in the middle of a corner the slip angles at the rear increase dramatically. If he eases the pressure they are decreased. The degree of oversteer is therefore under the control of the driver and in this sense the car may be said to be steered by the right foot. This bears little resemblance to the oversteer demonstrated by men like Gonzales on the 1½ litre supercharged BRM when he completed many corners with the steering on full opposite lock. This was very spectacular but only served to demonstrate a design deficiency.

The tread compounds and rounded tyre profiles of the racing tyres used in the early fifties were vastly inferior in performance by modern standards. Such notoriously oversteering monsters as the pre-war P-Wagen and the ill-fated original BRM could have been persuaded to handle in a most gentlemanly manner if modern tyre technology had been available at the time.

The Ferrari Dino, Lotus Esprit, Porsche Carrera and other mid-engined sports cars exploit the same cornering technique as the modern Grand Prix car, even to the use of wider tyres at the rear than the front. To a more modest extent, since the power to weight ratio is lower, the latest mid-engined sports cars can be controlled in a fast corner by the use of the accelerator. With the main masses of engine, transmission and passengers so disposed as to give a low polar moment of inertia the mid-engined car has a very quick steering response. Over-enthusiastic use of the accelerator when cornering is soon corrected by a quick flick of the very responsive steering.

Factors leading to understeer

The following factors all tend to produce understeer when cornering. Used singly or in combination almost any car can be made to understeer to the required degree:

(1) Re-distribution of the sprung weight so that a greater proportion is carried by the front wheels.

(2) Fitting larger tyres at the rear than at the front. This is much in evidence in Grand Prix racing.

(3) Arranging for the front wheels to have a greater outward camber than the rear wheels when the car rolls on a corner. This happens automatically on the most common suspension combination in use today, i.e. with wishbone I.F.S. and a beam or De Dion axle at the rear. When independent suspension of the wishbone type is used at both front and rear it is sometimes necessary to arrange the rear links in such a way that the camber when cornering is less at the rear than at the front. This can be achieved by making the lower links on the rear suspension disproportionately longer than the top links. This is sometimes referred to as providing a 'swing-axle effect' since a true swing axle gives a negative (inward) camber on a corner. The resulting camber, when longer bottom links are used at the rear, is still positive, but not as great as at the front for a given roll angle. This reduces the cornering powering of the front tyres relative to the rear and gives the desired understeer.

(4) Transferring more of the roll couple from the rear to the front. The rolling action of the sprung mass (body, frame, etc.) on a corner is resisted by the springs. An understeering tendency is given by making the front springs provide the major resistance to rolling. The anti-roll bar which is fitted to the front of many modern cars produces this effect.

Gyroscopic effects

A factor which is always present when cornering and which is often ignored is the gyroscopic reaction of the rotating mass of the engine components on the road wheels. This effect is well known to aircraft pilots and is unconsciously corrected by the experienced pilot. With the normal direction of engine rotation a left-hand turn produces a tendency for the nose to dip, i.e. a transfer of weight from the rear wheels to the front, a right-hand turn throws more weight on the rear wheels. On the level this effect is only noticeable in cars with very high power to weight ratios and at high engine speeds.

This gyroscopic torque should not be confused with the torque reaction which occurs during acceleration on cars with non-independent suspension at the rear. This causes a transfer of weight from the right-hand near wheel to the left-hand and is responsible for the smoking of the rear right-hand tyre when a big-engined car is accelerating from a standstill.

Roll centres

The relative positions of roll centres of the two ends of the car have a profound effect on the cornering behaviour and can explain the skittish manner in which some cars lift a wheel when cornering fast.

The roll centre may be defined as the point in the transverse plane of the front or rear suspension about which the sprung mass of the car rotates under the action of a side load, such as the centrifugal force when cornering. The sprung mass is of course all that part of the car mounted on the springs, i.e. body, frame, passengers, etc. In the case of a De Dion or independent rear suspension it includes the rear drive box. The position of the roll centre on several suspension systems is shown in Figures 7.15 to 7.22 and is indicated by *M*o in each case.

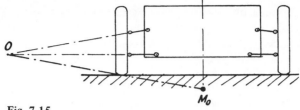

Fig. 7.15

Figure 7.15 is the popular unequal length wishbone system which is used at the front on the majority of cars and is also used at the rear on a few sports cars. To find the roll centre a line is drawn from the instantaneous link centre O, through the road wheel contact point to intersect the vertical centre line of the car. On a few older cars parallel wishbones are used in as Figure 7.16. Since in

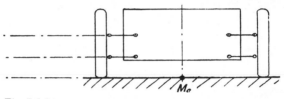

Fig. 7.16

this case the instantaneous link centre is at infinity M_0 must be at the road surface. The Morgan system (also used by Lancia on the early Aurelias) is shown diagrammatically in Figure 7.17. Here again the roll centre is at road level. The trailing link system, used by Porsche for so many years at both front and rear is simply another means of providing a parallel motion (parallel when viewed from the rear) to wheels on opposite sides. The roll centre for this system

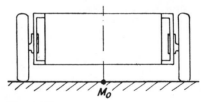

Fig. 7.17

too is at road level. A system that has become popular is the MacPherson or Chapman-strut system, as used on many former Lotus designs (see Figure 7.18). When used to provide independent rear suspension the wheel is located laterally by the fixed length drive shaft. Fore and aft location is provided by a two-piece radius arm. The action of the sliding strut, which is a combined damper and spring unit, and the joint action of the radius arm plus the lateral restraint of the flexibly-jointed drive shaft is very similar to an unequal length wishbone system, but with the upper wishbone inclined downwards, thus bringing the instantaneous link centre close to the plane of the wheel. Small changes in the forward location of the radius arm will change the roll centre height.

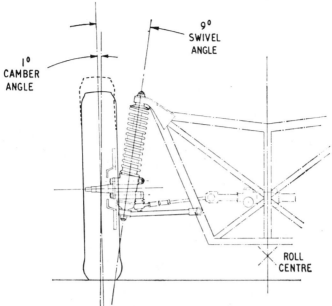

Fig. 7.18   Chapman strut on early Lotus sports car.

The roll centre on the beam axle, supported on semi-elliptic laminated springs, as used at both front and rear on pre-war sports cars (see Figure 7.19), is situated at a point between the axle centre-line and the spring shackles. To reduce the roll-centre height slightly the springs can be given a reverse camber,

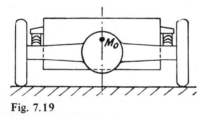

Fig. 7.19

thus lowering the position of the shackles. The D-Dion axle shown in Figure 7.20, is basically the same arrangement; the only difference being that the axle is not located by the springs. M_0 in this case lies at the pivot point of the axle as

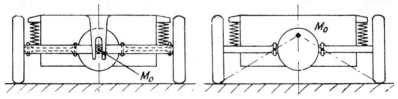

Fig. 7.20   **Fig. 7.21**

defined by the axle-locating links, shown here as a block sliding in vertical guides. Aston Martin use a Watt's parallel linkage.

Two types of swing axle have been used. The older basic design was used on the early Mercedes-Benz 300SL and is shown diagrammatically in Figure 7.21. The roll centre height is very high, higher even than that of the rigid beam axle. The 300SL Mercedes-Benz, fitted with unequal-length wishbones at the front (see Figure 7.15) and with normal swing-axle at the rear, thus had a very low roll centre at the front and a very high one at the rear. Despite the use of an anti-roll bar at the front the two systems were unbalanced and showed a marked roll-oversteer effect. The Daimler-Benz Company were not satisfied with the behaviour of the 300SL and evolved a low-pivot swing-axle system as shown in Figure 7.22. The rigid swinging arms were pivoted at a point below the rear-drive casing, thus giving a low roll centre to the sprung mass. To increase the roll resistance at the rear a 'compensating spring' is provided.

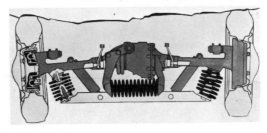

Fig. 7.22

Roll resistance

When the sprung mass of a car rolls under the action of a side force, a restraining couple tending to pull the whole sprung mass back towards its normal upright position is exerted by the suspension system. This is illustrated for the cases of a parallel wishbone system and a De Dion system in Figure 7.23. Let us take the case of a car for which the sprung mass, W_s, is acted upon by a centrifugal force of μ gravities. The side force will be μW_s and the rolling moment in the first case will be $\mu W_s h_1$ and in the second, $\mu W_s h_2$. This rolling moment is obviously greater in the first case. For a medium-sized sports car, h_1 might be about 15 in. and h_2 could be as little as 3 in. From this we see that case (a) in Figure 7.23 is at a disadvantage and will give large roll angles at speeds on corners. This lack of roll stiffness is usually compensated by the provision of an anti-roll bar at the front.

Wheel-lifting

An intriguing phenomenon is the trick exhibited by some cars of lifting a wheel when cornering fast. Sometimes it is a front wheel, sometimes a rear. The effect is a little disturbing to the onlooker in all cases.

When a mixed suspension system is used (with a high roll centre at one end and a low one at the other) the roll angle for a given rolling moment is roughly a

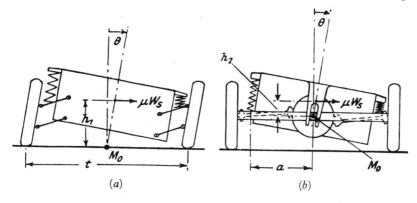

Fig. 7.23 (a) Rolling moment with I.F.S. (b) Rolling moment with De Dion axle.

mean of the angles that would be given by (*a*) a high roll centre at both ends and (*b*) a low roll centre at both ends. A typical arrangement might be parallel wishbones at the front and a De Dion axle at the rear. This would give zero roll contre height at the front and about 12 in. at the rear. The approximate height of the roll axis at the centre will be 6 in. and the side load will act at a height of about 15 in. (the C.G. of the sprung mass). The arm of the rolling moment at the centre of the car will therefore be 15 minus 6 in. = 9 in. This gives a rolling moment approximately three times that given when a beam axle is used at both ends.

This moment of magnitude $W \times 9$ is resisted by both front and rear springs and the resulting roll angle will be much greater than with the rigid-axle sports car. The spring deflections will also be greater and if these exceed a certain limit the load exerted by the inner spring at either front or rear will exceed the weight of the unsprung parts and this particular wheel will lift. It is customary to make the rear springs slightly stiffer than the front. In such cases it is the rear wheels that exert the greater portion of the restraining force and it is therefore a rear wheel that lifts first.

This can be prevented in three ways. The front spring rate can be increased; the rear spring rate can be decreased; an anti-roll bar or roll-stabilizer can be fitted at the front. The latter method has the advantage that the front spring stiffness to many types of wheel disturbance is not increased, the bar only being fully in torsion when one front wheel is in the maximum 'bump' position and the other in the maximum 're-bound' position. This is, of course, the position approached when cornering near the limit. The roll-stabilizer is a simple torsion bar, cranked at both ends and lying transversely across the frame. The outer cranked ends are attached to the wishbones at suitable points and as the outer wishbones rise and the inner ones fall under the rolling action induced by cornering, the ends of the bar are twisted in opposite directions.

Occasionally, but only when an unusual combination of springing systems is used, too much of the overturning moment is taken by the front suspension and it is one of the front wheels that lifts.

It is not suggested that the action of lifting a wheel is in itself dangerous, since most of the load is carried by the outside wheels when an independently sprung car is cornering near the limit. Anything we can do to raise the roll centres at both ends will make the inner wheels do a little more work in a corner and the slip angles on the outer wheels will be appreciably reduced. The phenomenon of wheel-lifting is a modern one. The older sports cars with beam axle front and rear and a high roll centre at both ends always skidded before the roll angle was at all critical.

The centre of gravity of the sprung mass

The importance of a low centre of gravity for the sprung mass of a sports car did not escape the attention of the early sports car designers, but there were those that hinted darkly at the dangers of *too low* a C.G. With the right C.G. height there would be a warning before the tyres lost their grip of the road surface (always the rear end in those days); with the C.G. too low the breakaway would be sudden and with no warning the driver might be too late to take steering correction. We now realize it was the absence of roll on corners when the C.G. of the sprung mass coincided with the roll centre that made such designs dangerous. Without roll the driver had no real indication of the centrifugal force he was asking the tyres to resist. The degree of indication was even less if the bucket seat had a good grip on his back. In these old cars the roll centres at both front and rear were high, being fairly close to wheel-centre height. Today with independent suspension at both front and rear, roll centres have been drastically lowered. As a consequence the designer is no longer afraid of a low centre of gravity. On the contrary he is for ever seeking ways to lower it.

The rear-engined sports car

The popularity of the rear-engined sports/racing car in recent years has led some people to make the claim that the rear-engined car can negotiate a given corner faster than a front-engined car. The author can find no convincing evidence to support this claim and, as demonstrated earlier in this chapter, the only layout with a fundamental advantage when accelerating in a bend is the front-wheel-drive car.

The popularity of the rear-engined car for circuit racing is well founded since there are several important advantages to be gained. These are:

(1) There is no propeller shaft in the way and the driver can be seated as low as possible, thus reducing the overall height and the frontal area of the car. (Only in a competition type of car with a 'one and a half seater' body does the propeller shaft tunnel intrude. On a sensible width of body there is ample space on either side of the tunnel for the seats.)

(2) There is a natural weight bias on the driven wheels since both engine and transmission is at this end. This reduces wheel spin. (This applies equally well to the front-wheel-drive car.)

(3) Weight transfer when accelerating increases the load on the rear wheels and improves traction. (In the f.w.d. car there is weight transfer away from the driven wheels.)

(4) Weight transfer to the front during braking tends to equalize the wheel loads and a brake distribution approaching 50/50 is possible. (On the f.w.d. front-engined car, the static weight bias to the front is accentuated and the front brakes are called upon to contribute most of the braking effort. This arrangement is more likely to lead to overheated front brakes.)

(5) When the front wheels are steered and the rear wheels are driven the engineering design problems associated with steering and driving *the same wheels* do not arise. It must be admitted that the latest designs of constant velocity universal joint have worked quite successfully on many small and medium powered saloon cars. Time alone will tell if equal success has been achieved when torques of 400 to 500 lb ft have to be transmitted through the front wheels.

(6) A good aerodynamic nose shape is easy to achieve on the body of a rear-engined car.

It is sometimes thought that a rear-engined car, with its inevitable weight bias to the rear, must of necessity be an oversteering car and perhaps even an unsafe car. This is not necessarily so. With the right combination of all the factors that contribute to understeer there is seldom any difficulty in taking the correct action to prevent oversteer. We have already mentioned the four major factors that influence understeer. The General Motors Research Laboratories have demonstrated that there are 27 interacting design parameters involved and now use this information in a computer programme to help them design the desired handling characteristics into their latest cars while still on the drawing board.

It is argued by some rear-engined car experts (Jim Hall who designed the Chaparrais is one of these) that a degree of oversteer when a car enters a corner is desirable. This is debatable, but the desirability of a gradual reduction in this oversteer as the centrifugal force in the corner increases seems to be generally accepted. Extreme cases of oversteer are now ancient history. To complete the final stages of a corner with full opposite lock is exhilarating to the driver and thrilling to the more naïve spectators, but it is never the fastest way through a bend.

The suspension

'Ye who borne about in chariots and sedans
Know no fatigue but that of idleness.

WILLIAM COWPER

Springs

It is always good to start at the beginning. Why then do we have springs? We could say we have them to isolate the occupants of the car from the up and down movements of the wheels as they run over an uneven surface. But is the word 'isolation' correct? If the road wheels pass over a 2-in. step in the road surface what happens to the passengers — do they rise 1 in., 2 in. or 4 in.? From experience we can say that they rise at least 2 in., often more. This can hardly be called 'isolation'.

Taking this as a concrete example, let us consider what happens when a car travelling at speed encounters a step in the road surface produced by running on to a newly tarred surface. The size of the step will be taken as 2 in. In Figure 8.1 the simplified car is seen to be suspended on trailing links and coil springs. The immediate effect of the front wheels mounting the ridge is a compression of the

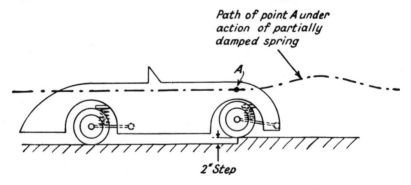

Path of point A under
action of partially
damped spring

A

2" Step

Fig. 8.1   Spring behaviour when negotiating step in road surface.

front springs by exactly 2 in. This is followed immediately by the recovery of the spring from this sudden compression. In the case of a partially damped system this spring recovery will lift the front of the car by an amount greater than 2 in. since the spring will overshoot its normal ride position. It is therefore seen that by fitting springs to the car we have magnified the road disturbance. Let us see, now, what happens if we dispense with springs altogether. The change of level of the front end of the car as the front wheels encountered the step would in this case be *instantaneous*. If we neglect the spring of the chassis and the upholstery and the natural spring of the driver's anatomy, the change in the driver's position is also instantaneous. This means an upward acceleration of *infinity!* This is of course impossible, but the practical implication, when allowance is made for the spring in the cushion, etc., is that the driver would be subjected to a most violent upward acceleration of several gravities which would jar his spine and project him out of his seat. Let us calculate now what the acceleration would be with a typical suspension system. A loaded spring always oscillates at a certain 'natural' frequency, depending, amongst other things, upon the size of the load. When all damping is neglected (including any damping inherent in the spring itself, such as the interleaf friction in a leaf spring) it oscillates with a simple harmonic motion. The time of a complete oscillation, in seconds, is

$$T = 2\pi\sqrt{(d/a)} \tag{1}$$

where d = the initial displacement of the spring under its static load W.

This displacement is measured in feet

a = the maximum acceleration, ft/sec². This will occur at the upper and lower extremities of the spring travel.

The frequency of a typical sprung mass can be taken as 90 oscillations per minute, i.e. $T = 0.67$

$$\therefore \text{Maximum acceleration} = (2\pi/T)^2 \times \text{displacement}$$
$$= (2\pi/T)^2 \times (2/12)$$
$$= 14.7 \text{ ft/sec}^2$$
$$= 0.45 \text{ gravities.}$$

It should be pointed out that T is dependent upon the load W acting on the spring. With the spring oscillating freely under the weight of the wheel and attendant unsprung parts, T will be much lower (i.e. the frequency will be higher) than when oscillating under the much greater weight of the sprung portion of the car.

The above acceleration of 0.45 G is the maximum to which the driver and passengers will be subjected and will occur at the top of 'the bounce', at a time interval of 0.33 seconds after the front wheels strike the step. This maximum acceleration and time interval will be the same whatever the speed of the car, *if the springs are undamped*. Shock absorbers modify the spring behaviour in such a way that the upward acceleration is increased the higher the speed. This will be discussed later.

When the rear wheels reach the step the behaviour of the rear sprung mass will be very much the same as described above. If the spring frequency is lower, i.e. T_r is greater than T_f, the acceleration will be reduced in the ratio $(T_f/T_r)^2$. We therefore see how desirable it is to have a low natural frequency for the springs, whether they be at the front or rear. Unfortunately a low frequency spring is a 'soft' spring. By 'soft' spring we mean one with a low rate. The spring rate being the load in lb required to produce a deflection of 1 in. This means that the initial deflection of the spring under its static load will be greater with a soft spring.

Table 8.1 shows how the spring frequency varies with initial spring deflection.

Table 8.1 Number of oscillations per minute for various initial spring deflections and the maximum accelerations given by a two-inch step in road surface

Initial spring deflection in.	No. of oscillations per minute	T Time of oscillation seconds	Max. acceleration given by two-inch step, gravities
1	188	0.32	2.00
2	133	0.45	1.00
3	108	0.56	0.67
4	94	0.64	0.50
5	83	0.72	0.39
6	77	0.78	0.34
7	71	0.85	0.28
8	66	0.91	0.25

An initial deflection greater than 6 in. is seldom possible in practice. With a 6-in. initial deflection the designed range between spring stops would be about 8 in. and this would be difficult to arrange in a low-built sports car. This, therefore, represents the absolute limit. The upward acceleration given by a 2-in. step would, with this spring frequency of 77, be as low as a third of a gravity, an upward acceleration so low that the occupants would experience no discomfort, especially when the spring impulse is conveyed to the person through a well-sprung seat. A lower frequency than 77 would be undesirable in a sports car, however, since the roll on corners would be excessive and the general behaviour much too spongy. In practice, with independent front suspension at the front and semi-elliptic springs at the rear, a frequency of about 80 is used at the front and 90-100 at the rear.

Now let us consider what takes place when a car passes over a ripple or similar depression in the road surface, as shown in Figure 8.2. For simplicity the following assumptions are made:

(a) the ripple affects both front wheels simultaneously and to the same extent;

(b) the ripple is sinusoidal in form;

(c) The car mass is divided into two parts, W_f and W_r, which are capable of up and down motion independently.

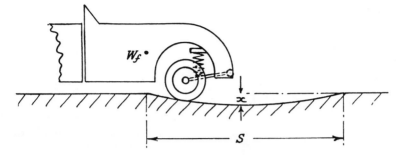

Fig. 8.2   Spring behaviour over ripple in road surface.

From the car designer's viewpoint we are interested in two things:

(1) How big must the depression be before a wheel loses contact with the road surface? (This is a most important factor, affecting as it does the road-holding of the car on rough roads.)

(2) What accelerations are produced on the sprung masses, W_f and W_r?

Let us take the natural front spring frequency, under the action of the sprung mass at the front, W_f, to be $1/T_f$, i.e. the oscillation period $= T_f$.

Under the action of the unsprung mass, i.e. the front wheel assembly, the natural period, t_f, therefore becomes $T_f\sqrt{(w_f/W_f)}$, where w_f is the mass of the front wheel assembly.

If the horizontal span of the ripple is s ft and the car velocity is v ft/sec, the time t, of the half oscillation induced by the ripple is s/v secs.

Contact of the tyre with the profile of the ripple is therefore maintained so long as s/v is greater than

$$\frac{T_f}{2}\sqrt{\left(\frac{w_f}{W_f}\right)}$$

i.e. in the limiting case,

$$t_f = T_f\sqrt{\left(\frac{w_f}{W_f}\right)} = \frac{2s}{v}$$

The minimum ripple length is therefore,

$$s = v\frac{T_f}{2}\sqrt{\left(\frac{w_f}{W_f}\right)} \qquad (2)$$

If we take typical values of

$$T_f = 0.67 \text{ sec.}$$
$$w_f = 100 \text{ lb}$$
$$W_f = 500 \text{ lb}$$
$$v = 44 \text{ ft/sec. (30 m.p.h.)}$$

$$s = \frac{44 \times 0.67}{2} \sqrt{\left(\frac{100}{500}\right)}$$

$$= 6.6 \text{ ft.}$$

At 60 m.p.h. the limiting length for contact will be 13.2 ft. (These calculations neglect such effects as the expansion of the tyre contact patch as the load is removed from the tyre and the movement of the sprung mass.)

The greatest depth of ripple that can be negotiated without loss of tyre contact is largely governed by the amount that the spring is already compressed under the weight of the car, i.e. the initial static spring deflection. If the initial deflection is 4 in. the load on the spring will be zero at the bottom of a 4-in depression of the 'correct' profile. The inertia of the unsprung mass will tend to carry the wheel to a slightly greater depth. For example, with no spring damping, if the wheel assembly weighs one-quarter of the sprung mass, the wheel will continue downwards for one-quarter of the initial deflection before starting to rebound. We can therefore say, as a rough guide, that the approximate maximum depth or height of ripple for limiting road contact is given by

$$x = d \left(1 + \frac{w_f}{W_f}\right) \tag{3}$$

where d = the initial static spring deflection.

Using equations (2) and (3) Table 8.2 shows the effect of changes of T_f and (w_f/W_f) on the 'ripple rideability' of a car travelling at 60 m.p.h. A value of 0.4 for T_f represents the case of the hard sprung vintage-type sports car. A value of 0.8 is approximately that of the Jaguar XJ-S front suspension. A value of one-quarter for w_f/W_f is typical for the front axle of a vintage car and a value of one-eighth is perhaps too high for the best type of modern front suspension but could be achieved by a modern independent rear suspension system.

We must not lose sight of the fact that several simplifying assumptions have been made. One factor, for instance, which we have neglected is the movement of the sprung mass itself. This will lag behind the wheel movement and at a

Table 8.2 Limiting ripple dimensions for tyre adhesion at 60 m.p.h.

T_f	$\dfrac{w_f}{W_f}$	Limiting ripple dimensions at 60 m.p.h.	
seconds		Length, s, ft	Depth, x, in.
0.4	$\frac{1}{4}$	8.8	1.9
0.4	$\frac{1}{8}$	6.2	1.7
0.8	$\frac{1}{4}$	17.6	7.8
0.8	$\frac{1}{8}$	12.4	7.0

speed of 60 m.p.h. the sprung mass will have hardly started to move downwards before the wheel has traversed the ripple. We therefore would not expect this particular assumption to invalidate the above figures. The natural frequency of the 'spring' in the tyre is much higher than that of the car springs; the static deflection is also relatively small and the overall effect of the tyres on the accuracy of the above calculations cannot be great.

Table 8.2 shows that when we are designing our suspension system with a view to maintaining tyre contact with the road at all times, the most important factor is spring frequency, $1/T$, which should be as low as possible. But what controls the practical lower limit for spring frequency?

The limit to spring frequency is obviously set by the mass of the wheel and the suspension unit, the unsprung mass. A low frequency means a low spring rate. If we were to use a low spring rate with a relatively high unsprung mass, the vertical wheel movements under the action of normal road undulations would be excessive. We therefore see that T_f is really controlled by w_f/W_f and that so far as this particular property of 'ripple rideability' is concerned this mass ratio must be as low as possible, i.e. for a given weight of car the unsprung weight should be as small as possible. This explains the steady decrease in wheel dimensions during the last thirty years. A small sports car in 1935, such as the M.G. Magnette, had 4.75×19 in. tyres. Its modern counterpart, the M.G. Midget has 145×13 tyres, giving a much lighter wheel. Unfortunately the advent of the low profile tyre fitted to a very wide wheel on the higher-powered sports cars has increased the weight of rubber in the tyre. To offset this it is now normal to use wheels of light alloy.

We have considered the effects of a ripple on wheel adhesion; it now remains to consider the effects of such a ripple on the sprung mass. What is the magnitude of the downward acceleration on the car itself and on what does it depend? This will first be considered for the general case where the spring frequency, $1/T_f$, does not coincide with the natural frequency of the undulations. In this case, from Newton's First Law, we see that the force P imparted by the wheel to the base of the spring will be transmitted through the spring to the sprung mass of the car itself. The acceleration of the wheel will be much higher than that of the sprung mass in the inverse ratio of the masses.

$$\text{Force} = \text{Mass} \times \text{Acceleration}$$

$$P = \frac{w_f}{G} \times a_f = \frac{W_f}{G} \times A_f$$

where a_f = the acceleration of the unsprung mass
A_f = the acceleration of the sprung mass

$$A_f = \frac{W_f}{w_f} \times a_f.$$

The vertical movements of the sprung mass will also be reduced in this same ratio, w_f/W_f.

For maximum passenger comfort and, what is of equal importance in the case of a sports car, minimum stress to sprung parts of chassis and body, it is necessary to keep w_f/W_f as low as possible.

Although called here 'the general case', this really only applies to a limited range of speeds over any given series of undulations in the road surface. In practice the vertical movements of the sprung mass can vary from as little as zero to as high as x, the depth of the depression itself. The first case, where the body movement is zero is well demonstrated by the corrugated dust roads so familiar to the motorists of Africa and Australia. If the frequency of the road undulations coincides with the natural frequency of the springing system when excited by the *unsprung* mass, the wheels and the lower ends of the springs will oscillate without transmitting any force to the upper ends of the springs and the car will travel along the corrugated road without a single tremor reaching the passengers. This ideal case is never quite achieved. Even where American sedans abound, spring frequencies of different models are not exactly alike and the corrugations are the *average* bounce period of the *average* car travelling at the *average* cruising speed. A vintage-type car would have to travel at about twice the cruising speed of the modern cars to 'get into the groove' and it would probably wreck itself before it got there!

If the length of the ripple from peak to bottom of depression is 10 feet a car with an average spring frequency of 80 per minute and a w_f/W_f ratio of ⅕ would travel most comfortable at a velocity of 59 ft per sec. or 40 m.p.h. (This comes directly from equation 2.) The initial corrugations in the dust roads were of course started by the natural spring oscillations of the first cars to go over them. Subsequent drivers chose the most comfortable cruising speeds to suit their particular spring frequencies and this served to dig the corrugations deeper and deeper.

The other extreme, that which gives the greatest movement to the body, occurs when the frequency of the road undulations coincides with the natural frequency of the springs when excited by the *sprung mass*. This frequency is of course much lower than the natural frequency of wheel bounce, as discussed in the previous paragraph.

In this case if

$$s = \tfrac{1}{2}(v T_f)$$
$$s = 30 \text{ ft and } T_f = 0.75$$
$$v = 80 \text{ ft per sec.}$$
$$\simeq 55 \text{ m.p.h.}$$

The natural reaction of a driver when he encounters a series of undulations of this character at the wrong speed is to take his foot off the accelerator. In some cases a more effective remedy would be to open the throttle more.

Pitching

One other common suspension phenomenon remains, that of pitching. Rolling may be regarded as a suspension phenomenon, but this has already been discussed in the previous chapter under the general question of 'Road-holding'.

In Figure 8.2 we treated our basic car as if it were two entirely separate parts, the front and the rear. This helped us to consider the problems of 'bounce' entirely divorced from that of 'pitch'. We cannot ignore pitching, however, since it happens to all cars to a greater or lesser extent. Pitching is best illustrated by jumping up and down on the bumpers of a modern car. The body will oscillate about the centre of gravity of the sprung mass. The time for a complete oscillation depends upon what is called 'the radius of gyration' (see Figure 8.3). This is in effect the radius at which the sprung mass could be considered to be concentrated in a single arc and still oscillate at the same frequency as the actual body.

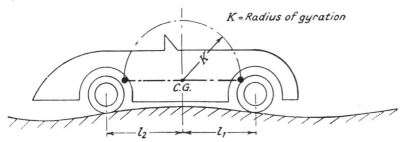

Fig. 8.3 Radius of gyration.

The bouncing period from equation (1) is

$$T = 2\pi\sqrt{(d/a)}$$

The pitching period is given by

$$t = 2\pi \sqrt{\left(\frac{d}{a} \times \frac{K^2}{l_1 \times l_2}\right)}$$

From this we see that if the C.G. is symmetrically placed, i.e. $l_1 = l_2$ and K, the radius of gyration $= l_1$,

$$T = t$$

In other words, the frequencies of pitching and bouncing are equal.

The customary layout of chassis components on a modern sports car gives an approximate value of $K^2/(l_1 \times l_2) = 0.9$. For the sports car of the thirties it was often as low as 0.7.

Pitching is, of course, induced by a depression or bump. As the front wheels drop into a pothole, the dip at the front end causes a rise at the rear and if this should coincide with the passage of the rear wheels over a bump in the road surface, the impulses, being additive, will produce bad pitching. It is apparent from this that a wavy road surface with a distance from bump to depression exactly equal to the wheel base will produce *resonance pitching*. If at the same time the car is driven over this road at such a speed as to produce *resonance bouncing*, interference between the two frequencies of bounce and pitch, $1/T$ and $1/t$, will produce a slow 'beat'. This objectional type of beat is occasionally encountered on the older arterial roads, where subsidence at the joints of the concrete sections has led to a wave formation. If $T = t$, the beat period becomes infinite, i.e. there is no beat.

On some of the older cars, with the engine set well back behind the front wheels and no overhang at the rear $K^2/(l_1 \times l_2)$ was sometimes as low as 0.7 and 'heterodyning' of these two simple harmonic motions would lead to the most disconcerting leaps in the air on occasions.

Summing up our discoveries so far, we would say that for good springing our fundamental needs are:

(*a*) a spring frequency as low as possible;

(b) unsprung masses, at both front and rear, as low as possible;

(c) disposition of the front and rear masses such that the period in pitch is as near as possible to that in bounce.

Independent suspension

All this has led us logically to the main reason for the introduction of independent springing about forty years ago. There were certain difficulties about its adoption for the rear wheels but almost all cars had changed to I.F.S. by the time the post-war models appeared. Independent springing, at front or rear, gives the lightest suspension system at present known. Moreover, the disappearance of the front axle has allowed the designer to move the engine forward, with obvious advantages in the case of the family saloon where

Table 8.3 Unsprung weights for front suspensions of 900 Kg (2000 lb) sports car

Suspension arrangement	Effective unsprung weight per wheel Kg (lb)	$\dfrac{W_f}{w_f}$
Wishbone or trailing link, with torsion bar or coil spring	36 (80)	6.2
Wishbone with transverse laminated spring	41 (90)	5.6
Front axle, with half-elliptic springs	54 (120)	4.2

passenger space is at a premium. A secondary advantage from this change which is of great importance to the sports car designer is the increase in the radius of gyration of the sprung mass, thus bringing the pitching period closer to the bouncing period.

Table 8.3 gives representative figures for the unsprung weights on a typical sports car of 2,000 lb kerb weight when different types of front suspension are used. Table 8.4 gives similar values for different designs of rear suspension. The De Dion axle is also included. It is not of course independent, since the

Table 8.4   Unsprung weight for rear suspensions of 900 kg (2000 lb) sports car

Suspension arrangement	Effective unsprung weight per wheel kg	(lb)	$\dfrac{W_f}{w_f}$
I.R.S. with torsion bar or coil spring; inboard brakes	30	(65)	7.7
I.R.S. with torsion bar or coil spring; outbroad brakes	41	(90)	5.6
Swing axle with coil springs	41	(90)	5.6
De Dion axle with torsion bar or coil spring; inboard brakes	34	(75)	6.7
De Dion axle with torsion bar or coil spring; outboard brakes	45	(100)	5.0
Live axle with trailing links and coil spring or to or torsion bar	50	(110)	4.5
Live axle, half elliptic springs	59	(130)	3.8

wheels are interconnected, but it is an attractive design, being both light and sturdy.

When we look at these two tables it is apparent that independent suspension offers the greatest saving in weight at the rear; a reduction of about one-third at the front and about one-half at the rear. Why then, we might ask, is I.R.S. not used as much as I.F.S.? Briefly, we can say that the complications which arise when we have to design an independent system for wheels that must be driven through two constant-velocity universal joints lead inevitably to more expense. Car manufacturers who wish to stay in business do not sanction expensive changes lightly. While I.F.S. offered so many advantages besides improved comfort, solving the old problems of tramp and shimmy, there are really only two major advantages to be gained by a change to I.R.S., a reduction in unsprung weight and an absence of transverse weight transfer during acceleration. This second advantage shows up most clearly on a sports car with a big

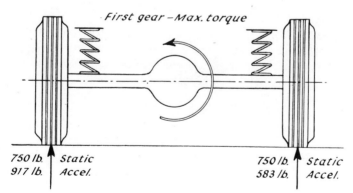

Fig. 8.4   Transfer of weight from right wheel to left wheel on a live rear axle during acceleration (1962 Corvette).

engine. Figure 8.4 shows how the static loads of 750 lb on each rear wheel of the non-independently sprung rear axle of the 1962 Corvette change to 917 lb on the left rear wheel and 583 lb on the right rear when the rear axle twists under the torque reaction as maximum engine torque is applied in bottom gear. Even on a good surface this results in bad wheel spin and loss of acceleration for the first ten yards or so. With a chassis-mounted rear-drive box on an I.R.S. installation the torque reaction is taken by the much greater sprung mass and results in a negligible weight transfer.

Shimmy and tramp

With the rigid front axle it was necessary to limit wheel movement with stiff springs and firm dampers or the tilting of the axle and both wheels as one wheel passed over a bump could introduce powerful gyroscopic forces that could cause the wheels to flap from side to side. The word 'shimmy' came from a popular dance of the 'twenties. The word 'tramp' was used to describe a rocking motion of the front axle, which in its most violent form would cause the front wheels to lift off the ground and 'patter' or 'tramp' on the road surface. There are several ways in which tramp or patter can be started on a beam front axle, but the primary cause of all the steering bothers was the high inertia of the whole front axle assembly with its heavy axle, brakes and wheels. The secondary cause was the interaction between wheel movements from side to side (see Figure 8.5).

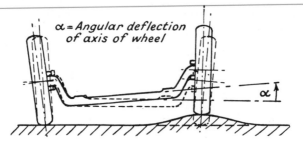

Fig. 8.5

Enough has been said to show why the designer was glad to be well rid of the front axle. The live rear axle, however, seems more or less innocuous. The steering effect of any bouncing or waggling it may do is not very noticeable and any sideways displacements may be discernible to rear seat passengers but these are a rarity in the case of the sports car. The live rear axle is not quite as innocuous as it seems. The unsprung weight is twice the weight it need be (see Table 8.4). This we have shown is undesirable if we wish to maintain contact of the rear wheels on the road surface on a bad road. The sports car with a live rear axle will therefore corner and brake just as well as the equivalent I.R.S. sports car so long as the road surface is as good as a billiard table. As soon as bad ripples appear in the road the independently sprung wheel comes into its own. Up to a point, if the ripples are small and within the road-holding capacity of the $w./W$. ratio of the beam-axle car, there will still be little difference in the cornering power, but with bad ripples the rigid axle car will corner at the limit in a succession of sideways hops, while the I.R.S. car performs a smooth well-controlled drift through the corner. Experience has confirmed that the De Dion axle, which is very little heavier than true I.R.S., gives a rear-end ride approaching that of the latter.

In recent years there have been many successful designs of I.R.S. on production sports cars of moderate price, the Corvette Stingray, the Datsun 280Z, the Lotus Elite and Esprit and at a lower price level still, the TVR and the whole range of Triumph models from TR2 to TR6. The latest TR7, however has a live rear axle.

There are problems associated with the design of a good system of independent suspension as an examination of a few modern examples will show.

REPRESENTATIVE DESIGNS

Jaguar

Double wishbone front suspension has been used on Jaguar sports cars for nearly thirty years. The E Type front suspension is shown in Figure 8.6. It was developed from the older XK design and used a fore and aft mounted torsion bar, built into the lower wishbone pivot, as the spring. Anti-dive geometry was given to the wishbone layout when the V-12 engine was installed in the E Type Chassis.

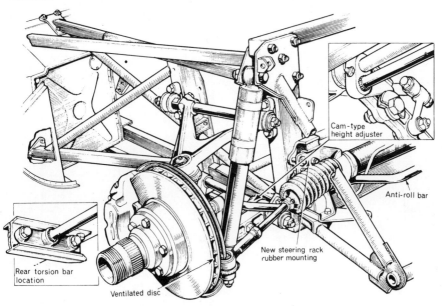

Fig. 8.6   Front suspension on the E Type Jaguar. With the later V-12 engined model the front suspension geometry was revised to give an anti-dive effect.

Anti-dive geometry is common practice on the softly suspended American cars. The method usually used is to cant the upper wishbone pivot axis upwards at the front and the lower pivot downwards. When braking, the kingposts react to the braking forces by attempting to rotate. This reaction is resisted by the wishbones and with the correct anti-dive angles an upward force is applied to the front of the chassis that is exactly equal to the inertia force that would otherwise make the front end of the car dip or 'dive'. Unfortunately, rotation of the kingposts also produces undesirable changes in castor angle. Jaguar

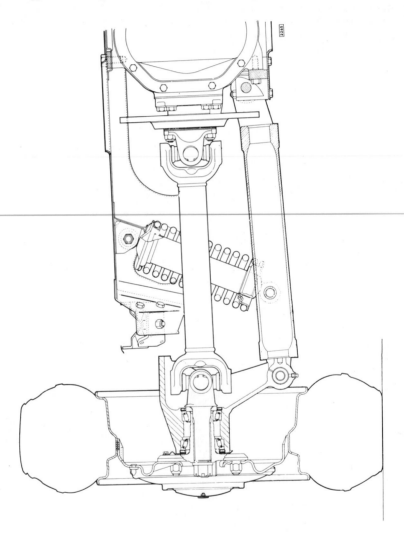

Fig. 8.7   Rear suspension on E Type Jaguar.

compromise by providing sufficient anti-dive to offset 50 per cent of the dive. This is given with an angle of 7½ degrees between upper and lower wishbone axes. The front suspension on the latest Jaguar, the SJ-S is similar in layout to that used on the V-12 engined E Type. Anti-dive geometry is again provided, but in this model the torsion bar is replaced by the more conventional coil spring.

The rear suspension on the XJ-S is almost identical to the well-tried IRS design used on the E Type (see Figure 8.7). Twin coil springs are placed in front and behind the lower suspension arms (only one can be seen in this cross-section). The universally-jointed drive shaft acts as the upper transverse suspension arm. Radius arms (not visible in the drawing) are attached to the hub carrier and serve to resist braking and accelerating torques.

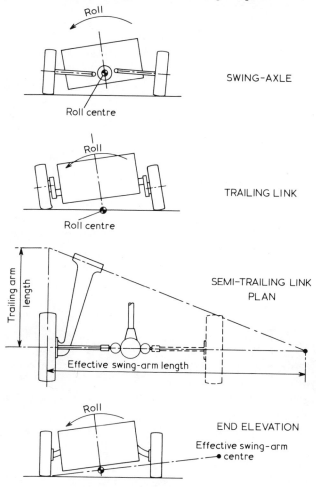

Fig. 8.8   Camber angle change under roll with swing-axle, trailing link and semi-trailing link suspensions.

Fig. 8.9 Swing-axle suspension is good — up to a point. 'Jacking action' caused by lifitng the throttle in the middle of a tight corner. (*Motor* photograph).

Porsche

The older Porsche trailing link suspension was very effective with narrow tyres with rounded sections, but a new system had to be devised as tyre sections became wider and flatter. Both front and rear suspensions on the modern Porsche are of the type described as 'semi-trailing link'. Many car designers are turning to this system in their new models. It is in effect a cross between trailing link, the old Porsche system and swing-axle, the system that Ferdinand Porsche Senior tried to tame before the war. Figure 8.8 serves to illustrate the problems associated with the two systems.

With a trailing link the wheel is constrained to move parallel to the body side. For single wheel movements that produce negligible body roll the full area of the contact patch is maintained. If the body rolls, however, the wheels change their camber angles to the same degree as the body roll. This of course is unacceptable with modern low profile tyres. Roll is inevitable since the roll centre is at ground level with a trailing link suspension. The roll-centre is much higher with swing-axle suspension and the tendency to roll is therefore much lower. Even so, when cornering near the limit the dreaded 'jacking action' can occur as demonstrated in Figure 8.9. When this occurs the body is jacked upwards under the action of centrifugal force and pivots about the only available flexible member in the drive system, the inboard universal joint on the heavily loaded side of the car. This can cause a dangerous loss of wheel adhesion since the camber change is so drastic. Camber change is also quite large for single-wheel

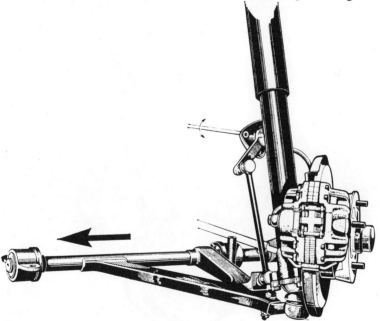

Fig. 8.10   Front suspension on Porsche Type 911.

bumps. The weakness of the swing-axle lies in the inherently short swing-axle length. Since the rear drive unit must occupy some of the available space the swing-axle length cannot be much more than 40 per cent of the total track width on a rear-drive design. Early Allards used swing-axle suspension at the front, but even with 50 per cent of the track available the cars still suffered from excessive camber change.

The semi-trailing link suspension extends the effective swing-axle length and thus reduces camber changes. Wheel movement is constrained to pivot about an inclined axis and the effective swing-axle length depends upon the angle chosen by the designer. When used on the driven end of the car it is necessary to provide a coupling with sliding splines on the drive shaft to accommodate the changes in drive shaft length introduced by the new pivots. This system can be given sufficient swing-axle length to remove all danger of jacking. The semi-trailing angle is chosen to strike the best compromise between the fully trailing link and the swing-axle. Since the trailing link gives *negative* wheel camber (the top of the wheel leaning outwards) on the outer wheel in a bend and the swing-axle gives *positive* wheel camber (except under jacking conditions) an angle close to 45 degrees will make the outer wheel stay very close to upright under most conditions of roll. This angle can be varied at the will of the designer to suit his particular requirements.

Typical examples of Porsche suspensions are given in Figures 8.10 and 8.11. This design is common, apart from small detail changes, to the Type 911, the Carrera and the Turbo. Damper struts and semi-trailing links are used at both

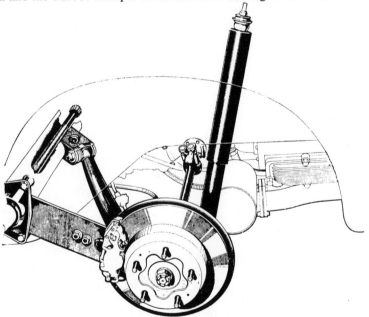

Fig. 8.11   Rear suspension on Porsche Type 911.

front and rear. The front suspension comprises a lower wishbone made from rectangular section tubes welded to a circular section tube housing the torsion bar. The damper strut is the only other suspension link. It must be one of the lightest suspension systems in use today. The rear suspension is similar in layout. In both cases the upper mounting of the MacPherson strut carries a rubber bush to permit a small degree of angular change as the wheel rises and falls.

Datsun

The Datsun 260Z and 280Z uses what may be called 'pure MacPherson' suspension at front and rear. Figure 8.12 gives a cross-section of the front

1	Strut mounting insulator	8	Wheel bearing
2	Thrust bearing	9	Suspension ball joint
3	Bound bumper rubber	10	Transverse link
4	Dust cover	11	Compression rod
5	Coil spring	12	Stabilizer bar
6	Strut assembly	13	Front suspension member
7	Front wheel hub		

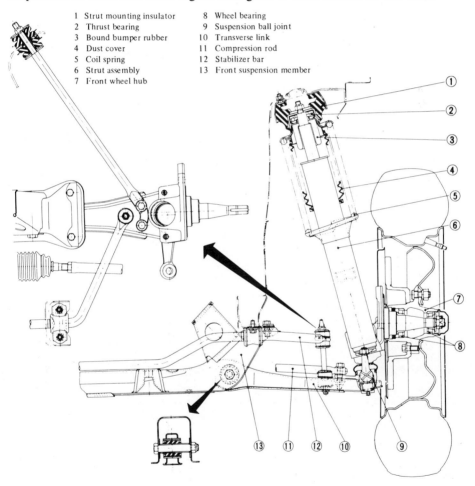

Fig. 8.12   Front suspension on Datsun 260Z.

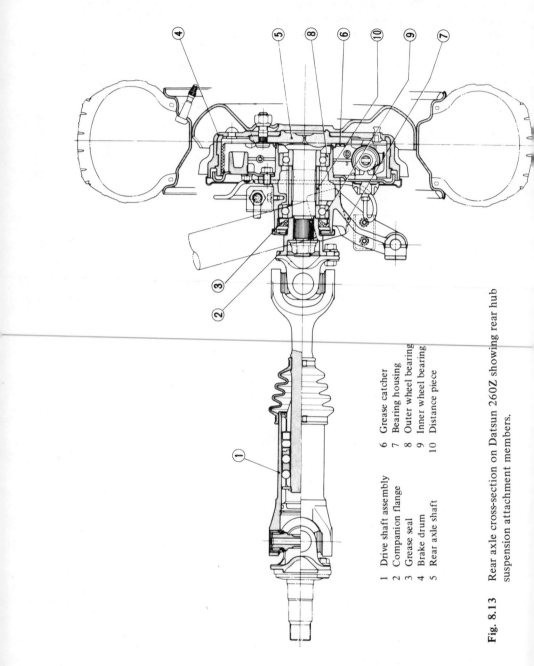

Fig. 8.13 Rear axle cross-section on Datsun 260Z showing rear hub suspension attachment members.

1 Drive shaft assembly
2 Companion flange
3 Grease seal
4 Brake drum
5 Rear axle shaft
6 Grease catcher
7 Bearing housing
8 Outer wheel bearing
9 Inner wheel bearing
10 Distance piece

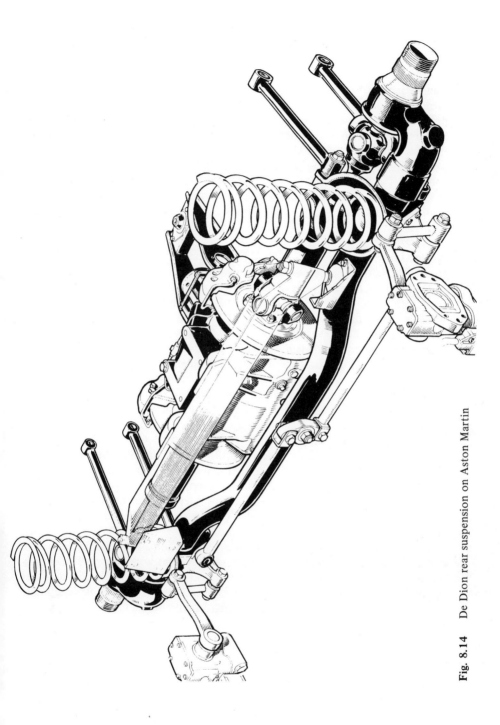

Fig. 8.14 De Dion rear suspension on Aston Martin

suspension with a plan view (upper left) to clarify the location of the compression rod and the stabiliser bar (parts 11 and 12 in the cross-section). The base of the MacPherson strut is located against transverse forces by part 10, the transverse link. Vertical wheel movements are controlled by the coil spring, part 5, and the damper unit incorporated in the strut. Fore and aft location is provided by the compression rod. The rear suspension uses a MacPherson stut inclined inwards at the upper end. The hub carrier is located by a strong transverse link. The drive shaft is universally-jointed at both ends and incorporates a sliding spline coupling, since the shaft length varies as the wheel rises and falls. The Datsun coupling uses hardened steel balls sliding in splines to give a low friction value, even under heavy torque. The coupling is filled with lubricant and sealed with a rubber bellow.

Aston Martin

Aston Martin use a conventional double wishbone and coil spring system at the front. It is in the rear suspension that we find our technical interest since the Aston Martin Company have used De Dion rear suspension for many years and have been happy to specify a similar system for their new 'space age' Lagonda which is not yet in production. Count De Dion first used the system at the end of the last century, but it was probably Harry Miller who first realised its excellent road-holding qualities when he adopted it for his front wheel drive racing cars in 1924. The De Dion axle uses a light rigid tube to connect the wheel hubs together. Separate drive shafts, each provided with two universal joints, take the drive from the final drive unit which is mounted on the chassis and is therefore not part of the unsprung weight. Since the distance between wheel centres remains constant as the wheels move up and down sliding splines are provided inside the inner universal joints.

The De Dion tube is located fore and aft by two parallel links on each side and transverse restraint is given by means of a Watt's linkage. This comprises two transverse links attached to the chassis at the outer ends and to a short rocking lever at their inner ends. The centre of the short lever is attached to the centre of the De Dion tube. This form of parallel motion was the brain-child of the great James Watt about two hundred years ago.

The De Dion system was used successfully in the past on racing cars. The control of camber change which is now so important with low profile tyres is admirably achieved when cornering hard with this system. Under single wheel bump there is some camber change however and this change, while acceptable on a sports car, would hardly give acceptable handling on a Grand Prix car with very low profile tyres.

THE SUSPENSION DAMPER

We have called it a shock absorber for so long that the habit is hard to break, but we have already demonstrated at the beginning of the chapter that it is the springs that are the shock absorbers. The devices used to damp out excessive oscillations in the springs are better described as dampers.

The laminated spring, even when anti-friction liners are used between the leaves, is never quite free from a small amount of internal damping, but the coil spring and the torsion bar possess no internal damping and if used on a car with no dampers at all would result in a car that was completely unsafe on the road unless driven at very low speeds, since it would bounce up and down without ceasing and would lean alarmingly on corners.

Hydraulic dampers were originally made to operate in one direction only, i.e. when the wheel lifted in passing over a bump. Today they work on rebound too. In America the word 'jounce' is used instead of 'bump'. The modern damper is usually set to give a greater degree of damping on rebound than on bump. Severe damping of the initial bump only results in greater vertical accelerations being applied to the sprung mass and it was shown earlier in the chapter that the reduction in these accelerations was the primary purpose of the suspension system. Our aim then is to damp out as quickly as possible each vertical impulse given by the road surface, without increasing unduly the maximum accelerations applied to the sprung mass. Perfect damping (neglecting the acceleration limitation) would mean that no bump could be followed by a rebound. With this there would be no possibility of residual oscillations from one impulse overlapping those of a subsequent impulse. Such overlapping impulses, if in phase, can lead to extremely high amplitudes with the springs crashing hard on their stops. The worst case with an undamped suspension is when the road impulses are of a regular character and their frequency coincides with the natural frequency of the springs.

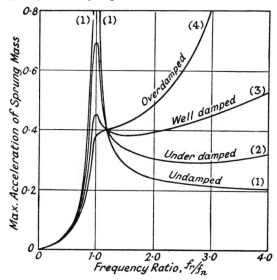

Fig. 8.15   Damping characteristics at different frequencies of road ripple.

Figure 8.15 shows the effect of various degrees of damping on the vertical accelerations experienced by the sprung mass.

f_r = the frequency of the road disturbances,
f_n = the natural frequency of the suspension.

With completely undamped springs, when $f_r = f_n$ the acceleration imparted to the sprung mass becomes infinite (Curve 1). Fortunately there is always some friction present to prevent this case arising. With a small degree of damping present, the chassis acceleration is still uncomfortably high when the frequencies resonate, but is low at f_r/f_n ratios of 1.5 or more (Curve 2). Curve 3 represents a well damped system. At resonance the vertical accelerations are low enough for comfort. At higher ratios of f_r/f_n, accelerations are higher than with the undamped system, but are still below the discomfort level. Curve 4 represents the case of an overdamped system. Below and at resonance the accelerations are very low but at high ratios of f_r/f_n, such as are encountered at high speeds, spring movement is so restricted by damping that the accelerations imparted to the chassis become impossibly high. Spring damping, we see then, is all a matter for compromise and the best final setting for any car in any given circumstances can only be decided by road-testing.

Early experiments with hydraulic dampers using simple jets to control the resistance to flow were found to give resistance/flow characteristics as shown in Figure 8.16. If one large jet was used the flow was turbulent over most of the operating range. If several small jets were used the flow through the jets became streamlined and the resistance to flow varied directly as the piston velocity. This

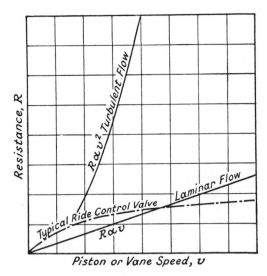

Fig. 8.16   Flow resistance characteristics of jets and ride-control valve.

approached the ideal resistance/flow curve for 'initial bump' damping, giving a resistance increasing linearly with car velocity for a given size of bump. For rebound and subsequent damping strokes a constant resistance is required at all car velocities for a given size of bump, since the time of recovery after the initial bump and for all subsequent half-oscillations is controlled by the spring periodicity, which is constant. For a small initial bump the time of recovery is exactly the same as for a large initial bump. The fluid velocity through the jets during rebound is therefore directly proportional to the size of the bump and, to a large extent, to the amount of energy to be absorbed. If the resistance to oil flow varies directly as the vertical velocity we therefore have ideal rebound damping. Unfortunately a very large number of small holes would be required to achieve laminar flow and the danger of choking with dirt would be great.

The modern 'ride-control' valve is a spring-loaded valve which opens to a greater or less extent with increase or decrease of fluid velocity. It gives what is, in effect, a variable size jet and by variation in spring strength and port shape a wide range of resistance/flow curves can be obtained. The principle is illustrated

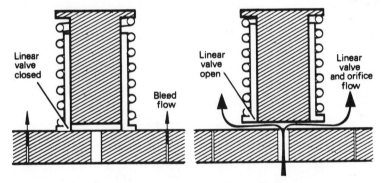

Fig. 8.17 The principle of the 'ride-control' or 'linear' valve.

in Figure 8.17. Typical flow characteristics given by this type of valve are given in Figure 8.18. The other function of the ride-control valve is to provide a measure of compensation for variations in viscosity. An oil with a high viscosity index is always used in hydraulic dampers, but the variation in viscosity over the working temperature range can still be 2 to 1 and a valve that gives a larger effective area as the viscosity increases can help to reduce the 'hardening' of the dampers in cold weather and the 'softening up' as the fluid temperature rises on a journey.

Very high frequency movements (*circa* 300 reversals per second) of small magnitude, such as those induced by travelling over a well-maintained British paved road at, say, 40 m.p.h., are largely absorbed by the tyres. A Continental pavé in poor condition will produce larger amplitudes, still of a frequency of 100 reversals per second or more, and the inertia of the spring-loaded ride-control or 'pressure' valves is too great to allow fluid movement to keep pace with the extremely rapid realtively small movements of the suspension. To cope with

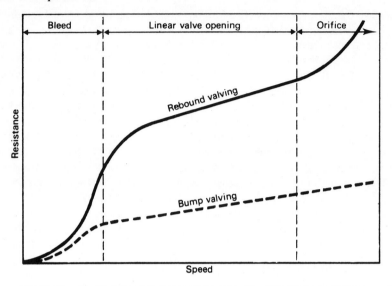

Fig. 8.18   Typical flow characteristics given by bleed flow and linear valve flow.

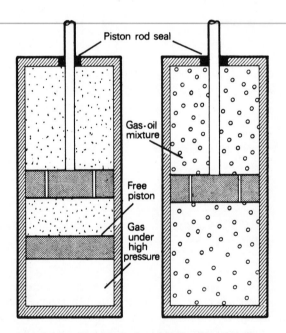

Fig. 8.19   `The De Carbon (Girling Monitube) principle and the Woodhead Monotube principle.

these high frequency low amplitude movements a bleed is provided which by-passes the ride-control valve.

The double-tube damper

Modern sports cars are fitted with dampers of the direct acting telescopic type. These are now made in two patterns. The older, double-tube design, uses two chambers in the form of concentric tubes. The inner tube is the working cylinder containing the piston and the space between this tube and the larger diameter tube is the oil reservoir. The need for this reservoir or recuperation cylinder is apparent when we see that the effective area of the piston is greater on the down-stroke by an amount equal to the cross-sectional area of the piston rod (see Figure 8.20). Liquids are of course *almost* incompressible. Since the

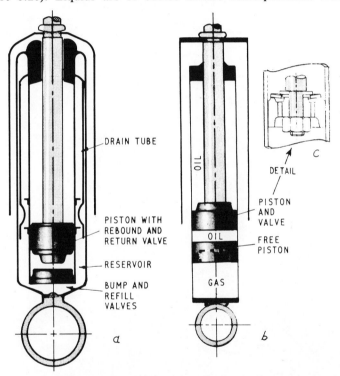

DRAIN TUBE

OIL

DETAIL *c*

PISTON AND VALVE

PISTON WITH REBOUND AND RETURN VALVE

OIL

FREE PISTON

RESERVOIR

BUMP AND REFILL VALVES

GAS

a

b

Fig. 8.20 Damper details (a) twin-tube, (b) single-tube, (c) double-acting Belville valve used as ride-control valve.

working cylinder is full of oil the excess oil pumped through the bleed holes ride control valves on the down-stroke must go somewhere. It passes into the annular chamber. On the return stroke the flow is reversed. This flow of oil is a considerable amount and calls for a large recuperator valve with unrestricted passages if aeration is not to take place when riding over rough roads.

Aeration can still be a problem in all types of hydraulic damper. Since room for expansion is necessary in the recuperation chamber the oil surface is always in contact with the air. Over rough roads the oil surges badly, producing aeration throughout the bulk of the oil. In the telescopic damper the high flow backwards and forwards through the recuperator valve aggravates this condition. Very few older designs of damper are entirely free from aeration on long journeys over rough roads. Careful design can prevent serious loss of damper efficiency from this cause.

A typical modern direct-acting damper of very robust construction is the Dutch made Koni, shown in Figure 8.21. The piston rod has two upper drillings

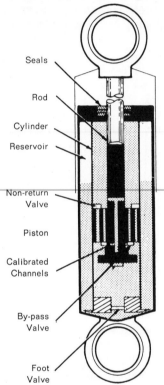

Seals

Rod

Cylinder

Reservoir

Non-return
Valve

Piston

Calibrated
Channels

By-pass
Valve

Foot
Valve

Fig. 8.21   Cutaway view of Koni damper, showing arrangement of valves and passageways.

that connect radially with a concentric drilling that permits the passage of oil into the centre of the rod. The central passage is closed at the base by a lock-bolt. The final connection between the upper and lower portions of the cylinder is made by two calibrated radial holes on opposite sides of the rod, the left one being slightly higher than the right. This slight difference in height is part of the Koni system of adjustment, since by turning the adjusting nut so that it screws further on to the externally threaded end of the piston rod, first the right-hand hole can be gradually covered, then the left-hand. In this way the damping action in bump or 'jounce' is increased.

When the damper is compressed under bump action the fluid below the piston becomes compressed and begins to flow through the calibrated holes. At the same time, if the rate at which the damper has been compressed is rapid enough, the return valve will also open against the action of the dished control spring. Thus for low-speed bumps only the calibrated holes are open for the flow of oil. For more rapid movements under bump action the additional passage through the return valve is open. Since the fluid displacement below the piston is greater than above, an excess of fluid must be passed into the reservoir through the base valve.

On the rebound stroke the fluid in the upper part of the cylinder is compressed. With relatively slow movement all the fluid can be passed through the two calibrated radial holes above the adjusting nut. If the rebound speed is greater, pressure will build up to a high enough value for the by-pass valve to open. This valve is controlled by a conical coil spring seated around the adjusting nut.

To increase the damper settings in both bump and rebound the damper should be completely collapsed until the slot in the base of the adjusting nut engages a slot in the base valve body. The adjusting nut can now be screwed further into the base of the piston. The first half-turn will begin to close off the lower of the two radial calibrated holes. Two-and-a-half more turns will completely block the first hole and partially block the second. It is recommended that changes of no more than one complete turn be made between road tests.

It should be noted that inward rotation of the adjusting nut also compresses the conical coil spring which controls the by-pass valve and thus also increases the resistance to fluid flow on rebound.

The single-tube damper

The principle used in the Girling monitube damper is shown in Figures 8.19 and 8.20. This principle was first used on the De Carbon dampers many years ago. With modern shaft-sealing techniques very successful applications of this old principle have been evolved. The recuperation cylinder is replaced by an extension to the working cylinder containing gas under high pressure. This chamber is separated from the working cylinder by a free piston made of glass-reinforced nylon. Movement of this low-inertia free piston accommodates the oil flow caused by the differences in swept volume on the two sides of the working piston. Valving for both bump and rebound flow is incorporated in the piston.

The development engineers at Woodhead-Munroe showed much ingenuity when they designed the new generation damper for their company. As an example of what is sometimes called 'lateral thinking' they solved the problem of aeration by designing constant aeration into the system. Their single-tube damper is charged with a finely emulsified mixture of oil and gas under pressure. This Woodhead Monotube damper shown in Figure 8.22 absorbs variations in displacement by compressing or expanding the gas bubbles. Since the valving is designed to suit a gas/liquid mixture there is little change in

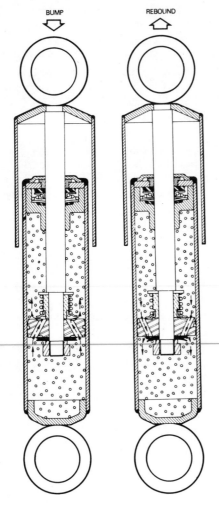

Fig. 8.22   Woodhead-Munroe
Monotube damper.

damper effectiveness as the fluid heats up after prolonged use on rough roads.
The problem of aeration no longer exists since the fluid is always aerated! 'If
you can't lick 'em, join 'em,' is a dubious policy for a politician but it
sometimes works for engineers.

The chassis, frame and body

'The Admiralty opposes the building of ironclads
because iron is heavier than wood and will sink.'
SIR FRANCIS BARING
(First Lord of the Admiralty, 1850)

Materials

When Lotus Cars were asked to provide a submarine version of the Elite for the latest James Bond film the problem of buoyancy was no doubt a new experience, but the normal considerations in the mind of a car designer when choosing his materials of construction are strength, stiffness and resistance to wear and corrosion. Not all designers are in agreement on the most suitable materials. The vintage design in which a steel ladder-type frame supports an ash body panelled in aluminium now only survives in a few vintage replicas and in that appealing hand-made product of the Morgan Motor Company at Malvern. Even they now make certain concessions in the design of the frame to increase the torsional stiffness.

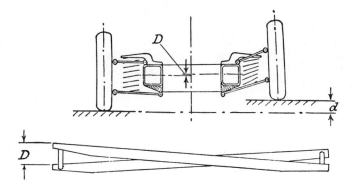

Fig. 9.1   Torsional deflection of frame (much exaggerated).

Torsional stiffness

When one wheel of a car travels over a bump in the road surface the spring attached to this wheel is compressed and the spring load is transmitted to the frame and the frame is deflected (see Figure 9.1). If the spring rate is c lb/in. and the deflection produced on the spring by the bump is d inches, the load transmitted to the frame is cd lb. If the torsional stiffness of the frame is C lb/in., the torsional deflection of the chassis, D, will be cd/C in. Let us consider a case of a spring rate of 100 lb/in. and a road wheel deflection of 4 in. If we wish to limit the frame deflection to 1/32 in. the torsional stiffness of the frame will need to be $(100 \times 4) \div 1/32 = 12{,}800$ lb/in. or 230 Kg/mm.

To the older motorist with experience of the wood-framed coach-built body, a high degree of torsional stiffness is very desirable. The creaking of timber and squeaking of joints was all too much in evidence on many of the older cars and if one carelessly parked the car with one wheel on the grass verge and the other three on the road, it was not unusual to find one of the doors jammed by the twisting of the frame. Yet the chassis frame usually had a battleship solidity in appearance and weighed at least twice as much as modern designs. We saw in Chapter Eight that the most important factor contributing to the smoothness of the ride is the weight of the unsprung parts. The change to independent suspension at the front and the decrease in wheel sizes all round has reduced the unsprung weight by about one-half and roughly doubled the ability of the wheels to cling to the ripples in the road surface. In the same manner the vertical impulse given to the frame when a car travels over a bump is directly proportional to the unsprung weight. This explains, in part, why the older non-independently sprung chassis, despite its apparent robustness, suffered more under shocks of a rough road than the modern chassis. Nevertheless, this is not the whole explanation. The older chassis designer used a lot of metal in his frame, but he put it in the wrong places. To understand what is meant by this let us consider the stiffness of the simple sheet of metal in Figure 9.2. The torsional stiffness of this thin plate is very low, as shown at (*a*); the resistance to a force such as X in (*b*) is obviously high. If the reader doubts this let him take a piece of 18 gauge mild steel (about 1/20 in. thick) about 2 in. wide and 6 in. long, clamp

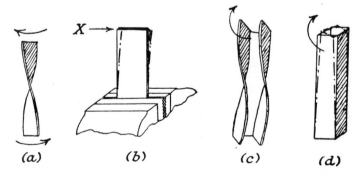

Fig. 9.2   (a), (b), (c) and (d) Torsional stiffness.

it in a vice and try to push it in the manner of Figure 9.2(*b*). The first case (*a*) we shall call 'flat-plate stiffness', the second (*b*) 'lozenge stiffness'.

Since welding had not yet become a production technique the vintage car designer used riveting and his basic structural material was the rolled steel section. The channel section was found to be the most convenient and the cheapest (Bugatti, who loved to be different, once used a sandwich section with steel plate on the outside and wood in the middle, but the method was expensive). The channel section has no lozenge stiffness (see Figure 9.2(*c*)). Each of the three sides twist in the manner of Figure 9.2 (*a*). However, as soon as we close in the fourth side we find that 'flat-plate' twisting is now almost completely prevented and the manner in which the box section twists is now by lozenging. The stiffness from lozenging is so much greater than that from flat plate twisting that the latter may be neglected. If we compare two similar sections using the same weight of steel, the first of channel section, the second of box section, the torsional stiffness of the second will be about 500 times that of the first. The torsional stiffness of a similar weight of circular section tubing would be of the same order.

One might ask at this stage: if the designer wanted increased torsional stiffness, why did it take him thirty years to realize that the channel section was so weak in torsion? The answer is that many designers believed that a certain amount of flexibility was required to improve road-holding.

The flexible chassis contributed in no small way to the effective spring rate to single wheel movement, without affecting appreciably the spring rate when both front or both rear wheels passed over a bump. In this way wheel adhesion on a bumpy corner was much improved since the double bump, affecting both front wheels or both rear wheels simultaneously, is not as common as the single bump. What then is the price paid for this additional 'frame springing'? If we consider the case of a typical 'flexible' frame, we might expect, when a front wheel passes over a 4-in. bump at the same time as the opposite rear wheel passes over a similar bump, that the frame deflection at each end might be as much as ¼ in. In the case of a beam front axle, this twisting of the frame has no effect at all on the camber angle of the wheels, which is controlled entirely by the movement of the axle. This movement, however, is severe enough in itself. If the bump is 4 in. and the track 48 in., the tangent of camber angle change is $4/48 = 0.083$ and the camber angle change is $4° 42'$. This means that with a level road camber angle of $2° 30'$ the camber angles when passing over the bump become $7° 12'$ for one front wheel and $-2° 12'$ for the other. The gyroscopic torque from such a camber change will be high and will demand instant steering correction from the driver if the car is not to change its course.

With independent front suspension, however, the camber angle is controlled largely by the geometry of the suspension linkages, i.e. if double wishbones are used, and the frame does not twist, the designer can choose the ratio of top to bottom linkage lengths to give him the camber angles he wishes at all positions of bump and rebound. If the frame twists the camber angles change and this is one reason why the designer prefers, nay, insists upon, the stiffest possible frame. Having achieved an almost perfect control over such important factors as camber and castor angle, he cannot have his plans upset by a frame that twists and weaves as the car travels along a rough road.

The tubular frame

The use of steel tubing welded into a strong light frame is an attractive solution, the expense varying with the complexity of the design. Examples vary, from the straight-forward space-frame construction that Lotus used with such success in their early sports and racing cars to the spaghetti-like 'bird-cage' frame of the Maserati Type 61.

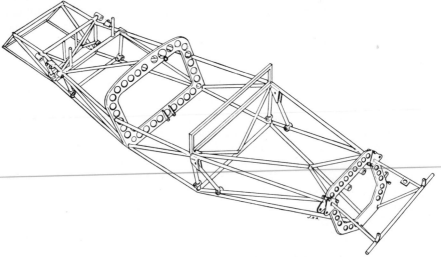

Fig. 9.3   Space frame for rear-engined sports car: Lotus Nineteen.

Figure 9.3 shows the Lotus Nineteen frame. Behind the radiator there are two tubular bulkheads arranged to be in line with the front and rear arms of the front suspension wishbones. Amidships is a scuttle bulkhead, formed from sheet steel with suitable lightening holes. It will be noted that diagonal bracing is used throughout the frame, with the exception of the two-sheet steel bulkheads, which have sufficient depth of section to resist lozenging. The engine bulkhead, immediately behind the seats, is a rectangular cross-braced tubular structure. The parallel radius arms, used to provide fore-and-aft location for the rear wheel hubs, are attached to brackets on the sides of this bulkhead. The upper ends of the coil spring/damper units for the rear suspension system are attached to brackets at the top corners of the rear bulkhead. The complete frame, with all brackets, weighed 32 kg (70 lb).

Unitary body-chassis construction

Logically it would seem that the final answer must be a successful merging of the chassis and body into one unit. This unit would provide the necessary outer protective envelope that is normally provided by the body and at the same time would be a structural framework to house the engine, transmission, fuel tank, seats, etc. Such an integrated unit would be designed to withstand the maximum loads imposed by the suspension system and would distribute them to the structure in such a way that no undue vibration or noise is transmitted to the occupants.

This type of integrated body/chassis is in common use throughout the world. The very complexity of the structure, made up of innumerable welded box sections, ribbed panels, arches, door openings, etc., makes it impossible for a perfectly engineered structure ever to be achieved. Inevitably, however carefully the separate sections that make the whole are designed, some of them will be more heavily stressed. Despite this criticism, the inherent superiority of the unitary construction over the use of a separate body and chassis is still overwhelming. In one aspect only does it still create a problem. With a separate body we are free to mount it on special shock-absorbing mountings that help to isolate the occupants from road shocks. With a unitary construction this is not possible. One solution is to use special rubber mountings where the suspension links are attached to the frame.

A typical unitary design is the Datsun 260Z shown in Figure 9.4. There must be at least a hundred different pressings in this structure, yet the pressing of the basic components employs very little labour. The major work content has been in the welding together of all these components and many large-scale manufacturers have now started to automate this operation. This is all in direct contrast to the hand-built vintage car involving many hours of panel beating and very little welding. Needless to say the modern car is held together by spot welds or series of stitch welds. Continuous welding would be far too expensive and would create alignment problems from distortion.

The backbone chassis

In the Elan the Lotus Company reverted to an older conception, using a welded sheet steel backbone to carry a moulded fibre-glass body that is partially stressed. The idea is reminiscent of the R Type M.G. chassis which was an advanced design for 1935, in which a backbone chassis was supported on four independently sprung wheels. The Elan had an immensely stiff backbone (see Figure 9.5), the torsional stiffness between the wheel planes being about 700 kg m per degree (5000 lb-ft per degree). The centre section, about 60 cm (24 in) long, was a welded mild steel box, 15 cm (6 in) wide and 27 cm (11 in) deep. Forward of this section the frame forked to pass on each side of the gearbox and engine. At the rear, similar forks terminated in rectangular vertical pillars that provided upper mountings for the Chapman-struts.

Since they evolved the Elan, the Lotus engineers have concentrated on building increased strength into the fibre-glass body shell and the result has been a body/chassis structure that can meet all the US Federal and European safety requirements. The Lotus body is now injection moulded, using fibre-glass

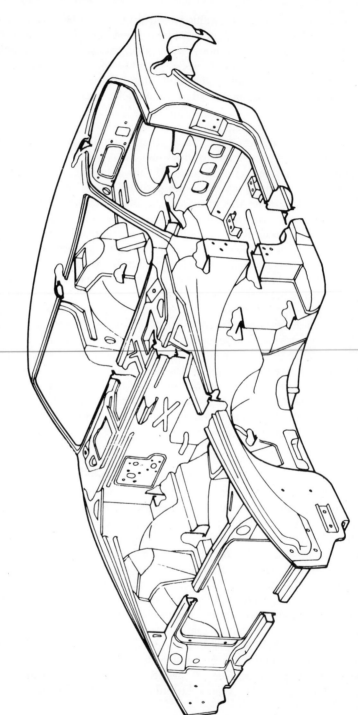

Fig. 9.4 Typical unitary body-chassis construction. The Datsun 260Z sports car. Broken sections show the shape of several box sections. Note how the simple lesson of Figure 9.2 is applied effectively.

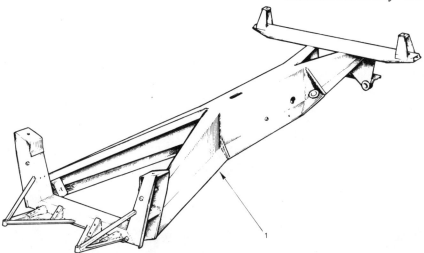

Fig. 9.5 Backbone chassis used on the Lotus Elite and Eclat.

moulds to take the place of the steel moulds one would use when injection moulding small plastic components. Not only is the surface finish as perfect as one would wish but the control of section thickness is very precise. Lotus have also used a process of paint application in which *the mould* is sprayed with paint before it is filled with fibre-glass mats and injected with resin. The penetration of the paint gives a well-bonded effective paint film of about 1 mm (0.040 in).

On the Elite the bifurcated section at the rear of the chassis carries a cross-member which supports the final drive unit, rear suspension mountings and fuel tank. The torsional stiffness of this steel backbone alone is 250 kgm per degree (1800 lb-ft per degree). The latest design of Lotus fibre-glass body now contributes much more to the overall torsional resistance than was the case with the Elan. A steel roll-over bar passes across the roof behind the front doors and the door locks engage striker-plates fixed to this member. The door locks are built into the steel girder that is used to stiffen the door to meet the U.S. Federal side impact regulations. An interesting feature of the door lock design to prevent 'bursting' of the lock under side impact is that the striker-plate is designed to bend in such a way that the door lock and striker-plate remain in reasonable alignment and do not separate even when the centre of the door has been pushed inwards as much as 12 inches. The Federal requirements are that the centre of the door should not be pushed inwards more than 12 inches when rammed by a pole under a force of 3500 lbf (1600 kg). The Lotus doors meet this requirement with a good margin in hand. To meet the 30 m.p.h. frontal crash test requirements it was necessary to design the body structure from the bumper backwards as a deformable structure. Exceptional strength in the structure, would, of course, reduce damage to the car but would subject the occupants to dangerous decelerations. In the Federal test front-seated dummies wearing seat belts carry G-meters to register the maximum decelerations reached during the 30 m.p.h. crash test.

On all Lotus models a deformable box-section of moulded fibre-glass encloses each pop-up headlamp and transmits the crash load from the bumper backwards to the double-skinned front wheel arches. Behind these further hollow beams carry the crash loads back to the double-skinned door sills and into the main structure. The bumpers are constructed of a fibre-glass outer shell filled with polyurethane foam. This is necessary to comply with the 5 m.p.h. crash test which all bumpers are required to absorb without damage.

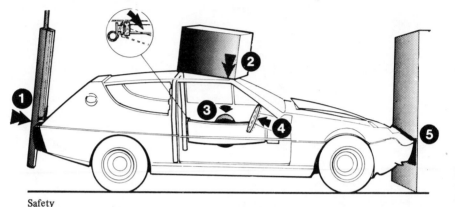

Safety

The Elite meets all Federal and European safety requirements with generous margins.

1   5 mph Federal bumpers (for cars sold in the States only). Car withstands 5 mph barrier collision and 5 mph pendulum striker impact without sustaining damage. No contact with pendulum except on impact surface – therefore no damage to bodywork.

2   Roof crush resistance. Maximum allowable deflection of 5in when subjected to static load of 1½ times vehicle weight. Elite deflected only 3 in.

3   Side impact resistance. Pole-shaped former pushed into door with body clamped rigidly in place.

	Requirements	Elite Performance
Average force to deflect door by 6in	2250 lb	3400 lb
Average force to deflect door by 12 in	3500 lb	4700 lb
Peak force	4774 lb	8200 lb

Steel door beam acts in tension for large deflections giving high strength. Door lock hoop is fixed to plate attached to roll-over bar. Plate bends (see insert) during deflection of door maintaining two halves of lock in alignment and thus integrity of system.

4   Steering wheel displacement in 30 mph barrier collision. Maximum permissible: 5in. For Elite: ½in.

5   30 mph crash test; Exceptionally low decelerations and forces on onstrumented dummies wearing seatbelts.

Fig. 9.6   How the Lotus Elite meets U.S. Federal and European safety requirements.

Figure 9.6 gives a summary of the Federal and European safety requirements. The gradual collapse of the fibre-glass box sections in the Lotus body in the 30 m.p.h. crash test is also illustrated.

THE SHAPE OF THE BODY

There is always a conflict of requirements when designing an automobile body. The family motorist is probably the most difficult to please, since he demands a large seating capacity and luggage accommodation all within modest overall dimensions and at the same time expects the stylist to provide something with extravagant sweeping lines. The sports car owner is more interested in performance and will sacrifice some body space in the interests of aerodynamic efficiency. The typical pre-war motor car wasted a lot of power in pushing a flat-fronted angular body through the air at a typical top speed of 60 to 70 m.p.h. The 1¼-litre M.G. saloon, post-war design, was typical of these earlier cars, with a rather square body, a flat windscreen, square upright radiator and separate headlamps mounted between the radiator and the wings. To propel such a car at 60 m.p.h. required about 32 b.h.p. at the road wheels. The Porsche 911 with a body developed by extensive wind tunnel testing requires less than 20 b.h.p. to propel it at the same speed. To reach a speed of 100 m.p.h. the 1¼-litre M.G. saloon would have required an engine producing about 150 b.h.p. The Porsche requires only half this power to cruise at 100 m.p.h.

Drag coefficients

The resistance to forward motion of any body in its passage through the air can be considered to consist of two types of drag. *Form drag*, expressed simply, is the work done by the body in pushing the air out of the way. The less streamlined the body, the greater the form drag for a given frontal area. A flat plate represents the ultimate in poor streamlining since its passage through the air at the speeds under consideration produces eddies in the air over a much wider area than that of the actual plate. The perfect streamline form only disturbs the air in its own vicinity. *Friction drag* is the resistance to motion set up by the layers of air adjacent to the surface of the body. The replacement of an older square-type body by a modern streamlined design, while decreasing the form drag, will sometimes increase the friction drag, since the total surface of the streamlined design tends to be greater.

The drag coefficient is a useful value by which the aerodynamic efficiencies of body shapes can be compared. The appropriate formula in self-consistent units is:

$$F = C_d \, A \, V^2$$

where F is the drag (force units)

C_d is the drag coefficient

A is the maximum cross-sectional area

V is the velocity.

Expressed in the popular motoring units of V in mph, A in square feet and force in lbf, the formula becomes:

$$F = \frac{C_d \, A \, V^2}{391}$$

The power to overcome this drag is given by:

$$\text{Drag horsepower} = \frac{C_d\,A.v^3}{146,000}$$

where C_d = drag coefficient (dimensionless)
A = frontal area in sq ft.
v = airspeed, m.p.h.

For an automobile we have another resistance to add, the road resistance. This will vary with tyre design, with road surface, with tyre pressure and with load. As an indication of the size of this resistance Figure 9.7 is given. Road

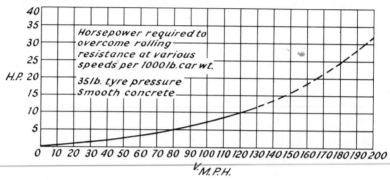

Fig. 9.7   Horsepower used in overcoming road resistance.

resistance here is given in terms of horsepower per 1,000 lb of car weight. The power consumption increases approximately as the square of the speed. Since aerodynamic drag horsepower increases as the cube of the speed, the road resistance becomes a small percentage of the total power loss at speeds above 100 m.p.h.

In Chapter Twelve we will examine the performance of several modern sports cars and make estimates of their drag coefficients from their maximum speeds. Values of C_d are here found to vary between a lower limit of 0.31 for the Lotus Esprit to 0.74 for the Lotus Seven.

An open cockpit and an erect windscreen completely spoil the airflow pattern over a sports car and a higher maximum speed is always given with a hard top fitted and the side windows closed. The provision of a metal cover over the passenger's seat on a Triumph TR2, a single aero-screen for the driver and spats over the rear wheel openings, reduced the drag coefficient by 10 per cent and the frontal area by about 20 per cent, a total saving in drag horsepower of about 28 per cent.

Wind-tunnel tests on scale models of cars have shown that the behaviour of the air flowing round a car body adjacent to a flat surface, i.e. the road surface, is vastly different from the flow pattern around the same body in free air. There is a build-up of pressure underneath the car which can lead to steering lightness at speed. On a high-speed car it is sometimes necessary to modify the upper surfaces at the front end, even moving away from the true streamline shape, in order to produce a downward thrust on the nose of the car. The laminar, or streamline, nature of the flow does not persist for long on the upper and side surfaces of the body. The flow underneath, even when an undershield is fitted, is turbulent over almost the whole length of the car. Early streamlined cars had very long tails in an attempt to conform to the basic streamline form for the maximum speed. The early break-up of the laminar flow, however, produced by the presence of the road surface and the eddies induced by such unavoidable excrescences as the windscreen, mirror, exhaust system, wheel arches, etc., makes it impossible to derive any benefit from the use of a long tail. The flow over the tail is fully turbulent, even with a good design of body, and the use of a long tail only leads to excessive friction drag. The modern high speed tail is therefore no tail at all, usually having the appearance of being chopped of with a knife. Dr. W.I.E. Kamm of Germany was the first to apply this knowledge to the design of streamlined automobiles. These were not a commercial success, since the motorist has a prejudice against anything that he considers to be 'unstreamlined'. In competition there was not the same prejudice, particularly when it was realized that the Kamm tail also lightened the vehicle (see Figure 9.11).

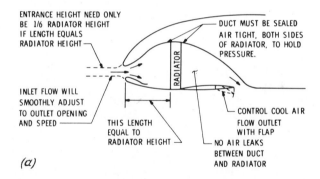

(a)

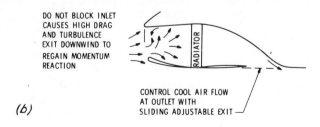

(b)

Fig. 9.8 (a), (b) The design of radiator ducts.

The internal air resistance of a car is almost as important as the external. Air must pass into the car to cool the radiator (or the cylinders on an air-cooled engine), to cool the brakes and to ventilate the cockpit. Air must also be taken to the carburettors. All this air must leave the body again (even the carburetted air must leave in the form of exhaust gas) and the positions chosen for these exits, if badly chosen, can seriously upset the airflow round the body. If the air is exhausted into a pressure area the flow through the duct can be reduced or even stopped. Internal ducting for the radiator and brakes must be designed to reduce turbulence to a minimum and to have as few bends as possible. The power to move this air through the ducts must be provided by the engine. Figure 9.8 (*a*) shows how the inlet to a radiator cooling duct for a sports/racing car need only have about one-sixth of the actual radiator area to give adequate cooling. Figure 9.8 (*b*) shows how a blanking plate across the inlet can cause excessive turbulence and power loss.

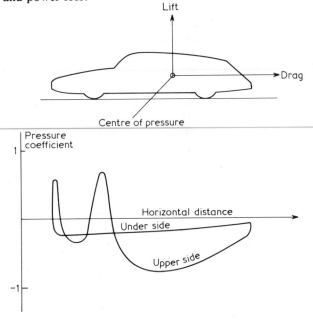

Fig. 9.9   Pressure distribution, lift and drag on a typical body.

Lift at high speed

The side profile of a typical car is unsymmetrical, being relatively flat at the base and curved on the top, a little like the cross-section of a thick aeroplane wing. It is not surprising then that lift can be produced at high speed. On a typical sports car a lift of about 150 lb is produced at 100 m.p.h., most of this being applied to the rear end. At higher speeds the lift increases and can seriously affect the stability and controllability of the car. In the colourful words of Hap Sharp, of the Chaparral racing team, 'You're blasting down the straight ... and then you begin to hear this kind of high-pitched whine, a kind of whirring noise, and everything begins to go soft on you. And you better believe you are trying to fly.' The Chaparral was fitted with an uptilted flap at the rear end of the body, a 'spoiler' in aeronautical terminology, to create a downward thrust on the rear wheels to counteract the induced lift and the handling of the car at high speed became much less hazardous.

In the 1967 Chaparral the spoiler concept was developed into an adjustable aerofoil mounted on struts at the rear of the car. By moving a lever the driver could dip the leading edge of the aerofoil to produce the desired downthrust at high speed, to reduce wheel spin during acceleration or increase cornering power in fast bends.

The followers of Motor Sport will know what a plethora of flimsy, even dangerous, aerofoils appeared on Grand Prix cars in the following years. The FIA safety committee have now got the situation under control and the spin-off from this intensive experimentation over the last ten years has been the application of this aerodynamic knowledge to the design of high-speed sports cars. Figure 9.9 shows a typical pressure distribution from front to rear on a typical sports car body. Areas of positive pressure exist, as one might expect, at the front of the car and in front of the windscreen. Overall, however, the mean pressure from front to rear is negative. As the speed increases so does the magnitude of this lift. The centre of pressure, which is to *pressure* what a centre of gravity is to *mass*, i.e. an effective point at which the summation of all the individual pressure zones may be considered to act, has a tendency to move forwards as the speed increases. Hence the need for an aerodynamic device to create a downthrust at the rear of the car if the car is to handle in a stable manner at speed. A typical aerofoil or rear spoiler as fitted to the Porsche Turbo is seen in Figure 9.10.

Fig. 9.10   The Porsche Turbo body, showing the aerofoil to prevent rear-end lightness at speed.

The air dam

Even when a designer provides a smooth underfloor to his car, with an exhaust system effectively buried in a tunnel and very little else exposed to the airstream but the suspension components and the brake discs, the turbulent condition of the air that passes underneath the car contributes considerably to the overall drag loss. We can, however, by confining our design to sensible limits on ground clearance, attempt to deflect the air stream approaching the front of the car so that a proportion no longer passes under the car but is directed outwards and upwards to flow along the sides. With the help of the wind tunnel the designer can angle this front spoiler or air dam to create a measure of downthrust in the manner of the rear spoiler.

Many modern high-speed cars are fitted with air dams and tests have shown in a few cases that they help to reduce fuel consumption.

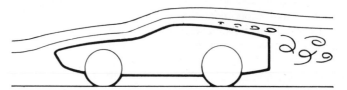

Fig. 9.11   Kamm tail profile, showing separation of boundary layer and break-up into vortices.

Directional stability at high speed

A body should be designed so that the air forces acting all round it will tend to heat it into the direction the nose is pointed in the manner of a flighted dart. The fins fitted to the tails of land-speed record cars act like the feathers on a dart, providing a powerful side-thrust to the rear end to bring it back into line if the car should veer from its true course. Designers of modern sports cars try to

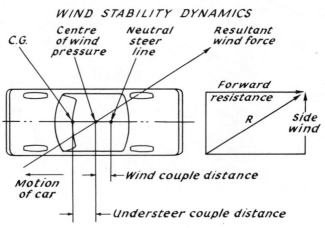

Fig. 9.12   Stability under cross-wind.

introducing the additional drag that stabilizing fins always inflict and try to achieve the same effect from the shape of the rear section of the body itself (Figure 9.11). How this instability arises can be understood by referring to Figure 9.12, which shows the relative positions of the centre of gravity and the centre of pressure in a car which has aerodynamic stability. The centre of gravity is the point at which we could balance the mass on the point of a pin. In the same way, the centre of pressure is the point at which the forces produced by the air pressure, both positive and negative, acting all round the body, may be considered to be concentrated. In the case shown, the air pressures tend to hold the car in stable equilibrium. If the car should be deflected from its straight path by a bump in the road or a sudden gust of wind against the side, the pressure on the side of the car towards which the rear end turns will increase and the turning moment about the centre of gravity will bring the car on a straight path again. The forces from the tyres tending to produce under or oversteer (see Chapter Seven) are superimposed on the above forces.

As the car travels at higher and higher speeds the positive air pressures at the front increase at a greater rate than the negative ones at the rear and the centre of pressure moves forward. With the usual modern body shape, at speeds above 120 m.p.h. the centre of pressure moves in front of the centre of gravity and a state of unstable equilibrium is reached in which any swing from the true course brings into action a turning moment about the centre of gravity which tends to increase the swing still further. This calls for extremely quick and frequent steering corrections from the driver. A palliative used in certain cases is to increase the slip angles of the front tyres relative to the rear, thus bringing into play greater understeering forces from the tyres. If overdone, this can lead to excessive understeer at low speeds. The remedy adopted by many aerodynamicists

Fig. 9.13   One-eighth scale model used in wind tunnel tests of Jaguar XJ-S.

Fig. 9.14   Stabilising 'fins' at rear of Jaguar XJ-S body.

is to incorporate additional vertical surfaces at the rear end of the car. Rear and mid-engined cars present no problem here since the body sides tend to be high at the rear to accommodate the bulk of the engine and its auxiliaries.

Fig. 9.15   Wind tunnel testing of XJ-S at MIRA laboratories. Note use of wool-tufts and white smoke to indicate flow lines and degree of turbulence

Wind tunnel tests on the model of the prototype Jaguar XJ-S made by the late Malcolm Sayer led him to incorporate curving side fins at the rear quarters. These can be seen on the one-eighth scale model (Figure 9.13) and more distinctly in the three-quarter rear view of the production XJ-S (Figure 9.14). The rear of the car is also seen to have a cut-off tail, a much less drastic treatment than the full 'Kamm tail' shown earlier in Figure 9.11.

Many techniques have been used to study the flow lines around a car body, but the old wool-tuft method is still popular. Figure 9.15 shows the method in use on the prototype XJ-S. Each tuft is glued to the body at one end. The extent of eddy formation (turbulence) in any zone can be recorded by still photography and, more effectively, by the movie camera, since the speed of the tuft agitation can be seen in this way. As shown in this photograph white smoke, introduced at the tunnel inlet, can also help the aerodynamicist to study the general flow pattern. The air dam on the XJ-S can be clearly seen below the front bumper.

10

The transmission

'Consider that men will do the same things nevertheless,
even though thou shouldst burst.'

MARCUS AURELIUS

Torque multiplication

Unlike the steam engine, the petrol engine is characterized by a lack of flexibility in its torque range. At tick-over speeds of 500-700 r.p.m., or thereabouts, on the modern car engine all the power produced in the combustion chamber is absorbed in overcoming the internal resistance of the engine. With the throttle almost closed, at tick-over, however, satisfactory carburation is achieved. If the clutch is engaged and the throttle opened wider the experienced driver knows that the engine speed must rise to 1000-1500 r.p.m. before the clutch is fully engaged or the torque transmitted will be insufficient and the engine will stall. The lack of torque at low engine speeds and large throttle openings is entirely a question of carburettor limitations. Large throttle openings at low speeds cause a breakdown in carburation since the air velocity in the induction tract becomes too low to carry the fuel droplets in suspension. With the relatively large choke sizes used on sports cars this effect is aggravated.

The limiting torque range on a typical 125 m.p.h. sports car might be 1500 to 6000 r.p.m. If the driver were clever enough to start in top gear, then he would be required to slip the clutch until the car speed was more than 30 m.p.h. before he could risk full engagement. Full engagement below this speed would mean a stalled engine. Apart from the difficulty of such sensitive clutch operation, few clutches would withstand such a high degree of slip for long. This is one reason for having a gearbox. The other is the need for 'torque multiplication' between the engine and the road wheels. Acceleration takes place when the torque transmitted to the driving wheels exceeds the torque necessary to overcome the tractive resistance, the combined rolling and air resistances; the greater the excess torque, the greater the acceleration. If we wish, then to achieve maximum acceleration over the whole speed range of the car, the overall gear ratio between the engine and the road wheels must be varied in such a way that the engine is always running at the speed which gives the maximum torque at the road wheels.* This is the ideal and can only be given by an infinitely variable speed gear. The automatic transmission is a combination of a limited range torque converter and a self-change gearbox. Unfortunately the torque converter is not as efficient as a gear train, despite improvements in recent years. Even so there is a gradual drift in the minds of many designers towards the acceptance of automatic transmissions for sports cars.

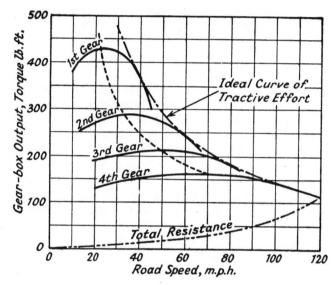

Fig. 10.1   Gearbox torque/speed curves.

The manual gearbox is a compromise (see Figure 10.1), giving, as it does, 3, 4 or 5 definite changes in ratio at intervals in the speed range of the car. In this way, when accelerating through the gears the engine speed varies in turn in each gear between approximately maximum torque engine speed and maximum power engine speed, thus giving no great drop in torque at either limit. The engine designer may have chosen his valve timing, carburettor choke sizes, etc., with the sole object of producing a flat torque curve over the operating range. In this case the design of a suitable gearbox is easy. Unfortunately, if the designer's aim has been to win as much power as possible from his engine, then the torque at low speed is poor and careful choice of gear ratios is necessary if acceleration is not to suffer. This is precisely the position with some sports cars today and has led to the adoption of a five-speed gearbox in some cases.

*At first sight, one would expect this to be the speed giving maximum engine torque. The torque curve falls off slowly, however, and by using a bigger overall speed reduction ratio, more torque is given at the road wheels at higher engine speeds, and in fact, for a given road speed, the greatest torque is given to the road wheels at maximum power engine speed.

The gear ratios

It requires no great gift for mathematics to see that to achieve the maximum rate of acceleration through the whole speed range the step-up ratio between adjacent gears must form a geometric progression, i.e.

$$\frac{\text{1st ratio}}{\text{2nd ratio}} = \frac{\text{2nd ratio}}{\text{3rd ratio}} = \frac{\text{3rd ratio}}{\text{4th ratio}}$$

If the step-up ratio between the gears is, say, 1.5 and the final ratio is 4.0, the gear ratios would be as follows:

$$13.5 \ : \ 9.0 \ : \ 6.0 \ : \ 4.0$$

With this set of ratios and a perfect driver, i.e. one who changes gear at the right engine speed each time, the same speed range of the torque curve will be used in each gear as he accelerates from a standstill up to speed.

The typical European car driver spends much of his time changing backwards and forwards between top and third gear. A change down to second is made less frequently. Often, in the typical European terrain, a gradient is encountered which calls for a step-up ratio, not as much as 1.5, but something less drastic, say, 1.3. This type of box with a small step-up ratio between top and third and a large step-up ratio between third and second and an equally large step-up ratio between second and first was popular for many years and is still used on some popular cars. A more logical set of gear ratios is given when the step-up ratio is gradually reduced when travelling through the gears from low to high. A typical set of gears would be:

Gear ratio	13.5	:	7.8	:	5.2	:	4.0
Step-up ratio		1.7		1.5		1.3	

Compare this with the set of gears above, which cover the same range but with *geometric progression*.

The overdrive

Many British sports cars are fitted with the Laycock de Normanville overdrive unit. Not only does this lead to an improvement in fuel economy at high cruising speeds but it gives all the advantages of a 5- or even a 6-speed gearbox with the additional advantage of fingertip gear selection in the higher ratios. Some designers prefer to use the overdrive on top gear only, giving in effect a 5-speed gearbox. Others prefer to make it opeative on both top and third, so that overdrive third gear is an intermediate step between direct third and direct top.

Essentially, the Laycock de Normanville overdrive is an epicyclic gear train. This gear train being brought into operation by means of a hydraulically actuated cone clutch. This clutch locks the sun wheel to the outer casing and releases the internally toothed annulus. When overdrive is engaged the input shaft rotates the carrier holding the three planet wheels around the stationary sun wheel to drive the annulus, which is connected to the output shaft, at a higher speed (from 22 to 32 per cent higher — depending upon the model).

Hydraulic pressure is supplied from a hydraulic accumulator and a plunger-type pump, cam-operated from the input shaft. Selection of overdrive is controlled by a small switch, conveniently placed near the driver's hand, a relay and a solenoid-operated hydraulic valve. An over-riding gearbox switch is used to make the overdrive inoperative in the appropriate lower gears and in reverse gear.

In direct drive, the sliding cone clutch releases the sun wheel from the friction lining on the outside of the clutch and locks it by its inner friction lining to the annulus. This renders the epicyclic train inoperative. Engine power is transmitted directly through a uni-directional clutch unit which couples the input and output shafts. This clutch resembles the old Rover free-wheel device in that a set of hardened steel rollers slides up ramps on the inner clutch member to engage claws on the outer member. On the over-run the rollers slide inwards down the ramps releasing the claws and allowing the outer member to free-wheel. This free-wheeling clutch is required so that the annulus can disengage from the input shaft and rotate at a higher speed when overdrive is in operation.

An outstanding feature of this clever design is that engine braking is given at all times. In direct drive the sun wheel and annulus are locked together by the cone clutch and engine braking is obtained through the locked train. In overdrive, the sun wheel is locked to the outer casing and rotation of the annulus in the reverse direction is resisted by rotation of the planet carrier against the engine.

Synchromesh

The baulk-ring (called blocker synchro in America) type of synchromesh has now replaced the older constant-load type of synchromesh on all quality cars. It was invented by Professor Ferdinand Porsche and first used on his 1947 Cisitalia racing car. In this system it is physically impossible to engage the gear dogs until synchronization is achieved. There have been many versions of baulk-ring synchromesh since the Porsche original and they all work on the same basic principle whereby a slotted ring is caused to rotate several degrees under the action of the torque created at the mating surfaces of the cones. This small amount of rotation of the baulk ring moves the slot (or slots) in the ring so that they block the further movement of the sliding clutch member. When the speeds become synchronized there is no longer a torque applied to the baulk ring and it returns to its original position. The slots in the ring now line up with the pins or keys in the sliding clutch member and the dog clutch is now free to move into full engagement with the external driving dogs at the side of the gear wheel. It is obvious from this that the dogs cannot clash since it is impossible for them to be engaged until the cones are perfectly synchronized.

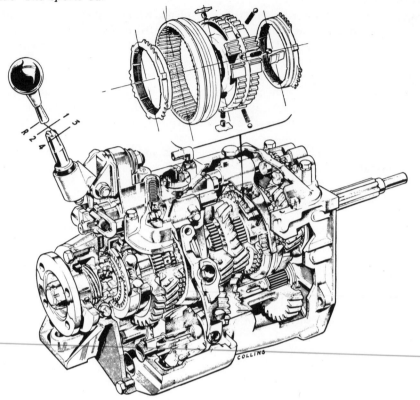

Fig. 10.2　The Jaguar gearbox with details of baulk-ring synchromesh.

The clutch

The single-plate diaphragm clutch is used on many British sports cars (see Figure 10.3). The Datsun 260Z clutch is very similar in design, but in this case a ball-bearing design of clutch release is used instead of the older carbon-faced ring. In the diaphragm clutch the ring of coil springs that were formerly used to hold the pressure plate in contact with the driven plate are replaced with a single dished spring consisting of an outer rim and a number of integral fingers radiating inwards from this rim. The clutch release bearing moves the inner ends of these fingers to release the load on the pressure plate and free the driven plate from the flywheel face. With large engines, requiring the 10 or 11 in. diameter clutch, the centrifugal loading on this design of clutch becomes so great that it is not advisable to use it for engine speeds above 6,500 r.p.m. For higher engine speeds on competition engines a more reliable dlutch would be the multi-plate clutch that Borg and Beck developed specially for this arduous duty.

The automatic transmission

The automatic transmission is the norm in America; it has been developed to a

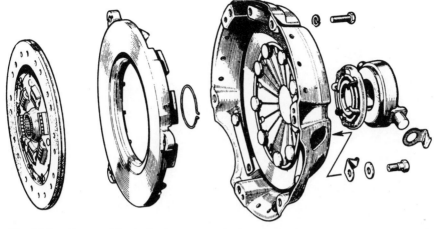

Fig. 10.3 Borg and Beck diaphragm clutch.

high degree of reliability and is only about 8 per cent less efficient than the manual gearbox in terms of overall fuel consumption. The ZF Company of Germany have developed a new type of automatic gearbox that is more attractive to the sporting motorist and this is the basis of the 'Sportomatic' gearbox that is currently available on Porsche cars.

The ZF philosophy is based on a realisation that a simple plate clutch is one of the most abused and overworked components fitted to the modern motor car when one considers the number of engagements and disengagements made in a short suburban journey during the rush hour. It could be argued that this is not the milieu intended for the sports car, but the typical owner does, unwillingly, spend many hours of his motoring life under these tedious conditions. Friends in the motor trade assure me that the average life of a clutch today in city traffic is less than 40,000, yet the engine is still in excellent condition after twice this mileage.

The WSK transmission, first shown by ZF at the Frankfurt Show, comprises a three-element torque converter with automatic lock-up and a free-wheel to give engine braking effect. The torque converter is connected by a single-plate clutch to a standard ZF synchromesh gearbox with 3, 4 or even 5 ratios. On the Porsche 3 ratios are provided. There is a weight penalty of about 12 per cent when compared with a simple manual gearbox and single-plate clutch, but the additional expense is recovered by the inherent long-life of the transmission.

On the Porsche an induction vacuum-operated control system has been devised to operate the clutch, which is never used to take up full torque, but is only used to lock-up the drive to eliminate converter losses when the car is on the move. The wear and tear on the clutch surfaces is therefore minimal. With the converter in lock-up normal gearchanges can be carried out by the driver without the use of a clutch pedal. It is a simple two-pedal system as in the popular American automatic transmission, but there is no possibility of an

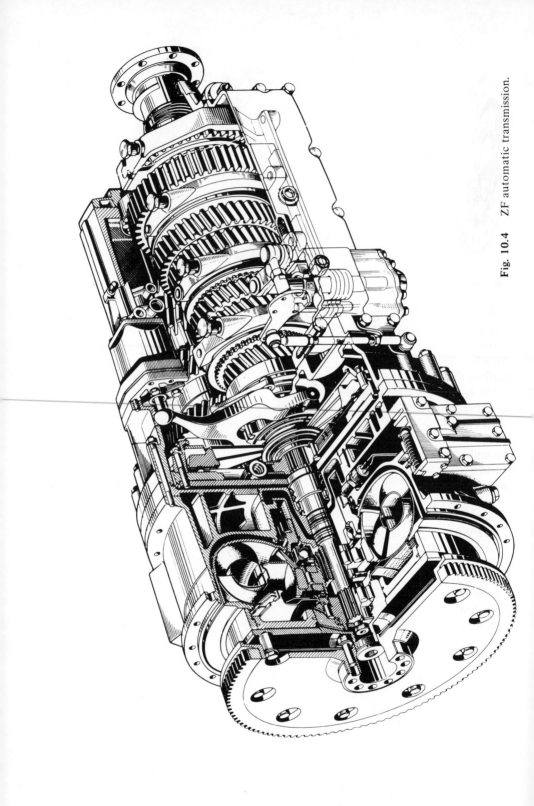

Fig. 10.4   ZF automatic transmission.

unexpected change into a higher gear if the accelerator is released momentarily and the driver is always in full control of the gearbox. In heavy traffic the driver can let the torque converter take over, thus reducing the number of operations of the lock-up clutch to about one-tenth the number that would occur with a normal clutch and manual gearbox.

The cross-section of the transmission shown in Figure 10.4 shows the main elements of the WSK system. This is not the Porsche automatic transmission but it serves to illustrate the principle.

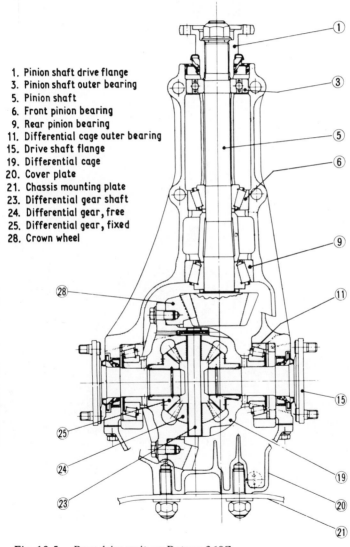

1. Pinion shaft drive flange
3. Pinion shaft outer bearing
5. Pinion shaft
6. Front pinion bearing
9. Rear pinion bearing
11. Differential cage outer bearing
15. Drive shaft flange
19. Differential cage
20. Cover plate
21. Chassis mounting plate
23. Differential gear shaft
24. Differential gear, free
25. Differential gear, fixed
28. Crown wheel

Fig. 10.5   Rear drive unit on Datsun 260Z.

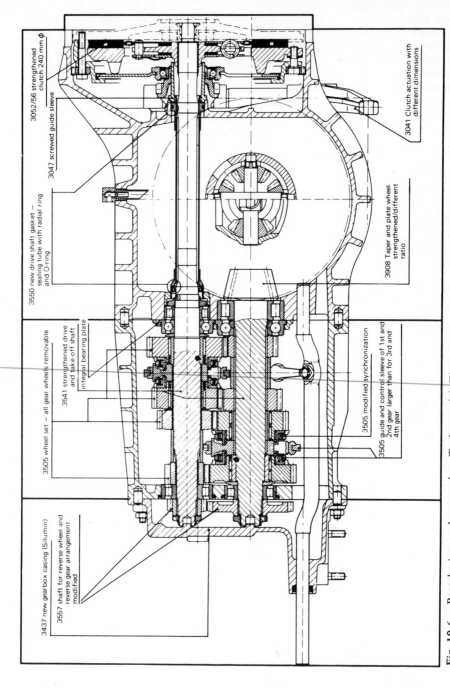

3052/56 strengthened clutch 240 mm φ

3047 screwed guide sleeve

3041 Clutch actuation with different dimensions

3550 new drive shaft gasket – sealing tube with radial ring and O-ring

3908 Taper and plate wheel – strengthened/different ratio

3505 wheel set – all gear wheels removable

3541 strengthened drive and take-off shaft integral bearing plate

3505 modified synchronization

3505 guide and control sleeve of 1st and 2nd gear larger than for 3rd and 4th gear

3437 new gearbox casing (Silumin)

3557 shaft for reverse wheel and reverse gear arrangement modified

Fig. 10.6 Porsche transaxle as used on Turbo model. The notes on the drawing refer to modifications made to the 1976 model.

The final drive

The bevel drive, and its popular variant, the off-set bevel or hypoid drive, have been with us so long that we take their quiet reliability for granted giving no thought to the long history of development behind them.

Originally introduced with great zest by the gear specialists to please the body stylists (whose desire to provide a low floor-line for the rear-seated duchess was very commendable), the hypoid gear is now almost universal and is in use on many sports cars that do not have rear seats.

The name 'hypoid' is an abbreviation for 'hyperboloid of revolution', since this is the form of the envelope traced out by the pitch surfaces of this particular gear tooth profile. The pitch surfaces of a spiral bevel and pinion, however, lie on cones with a common apex. A discussion of hypoid tooth forms is beyond the scope fo a book of this kind. It is enough to state that the hypoid gains fractionally from the greater number of teeth in mesh and the load-carrying capacity is a little greater. Nevertheless there is a serious disadvantage. The spiral bevel gives a pure rolling contact. With the hypoid gears a certain amount of sliding occurs between the mating teeth. Much research has been carried out by the oil companies and special hypoid oils have been developed which prevent scuffing of the tooth surfaces under this sliding action.

A good example of the rear drive unit on a front-engined sports car with IRS is shown in Figure 10.5. This is a broken section on the Datsun 260Z, the cross-section being on two levels since, with a hypoid gear set, the pinion is situated at a lower level in this plan view than the centre-line of the crown wheel. The pinion shaft is carried in one ball bearing and two tapered roller bearings which are preloaded during assembly. This is common modern practice.

Cars with rear or mid-engine location usually have a combined gearbox and final drive assembly called a *transaxle*. An excellent example is the latest Porsche Type 930 transaxle as used on the Turbo model. In this case, it will be seen that the spiral bevel gear set is not a hypoid, i.e. the pinion shaft centre-line intercepts that of the crown wheel. Porsche obviously prefer to use large enough gears rather than accept the undesirable scuffing action of the hypoid gears. The single-plate clutch, seen on the right of Figure 10.6, transmits engine torque via the drive shaft across the top of the differential cage to the gearbox at the rear. The four forward gears are contained in the main casting, which is of silicon aluminium alloy. The reverse gears are behind the rear bearings in a separate compartment. The gear selector shaft can be seen at the bottom of the housing.

Porsche have a policy of incorporating improvements and modifications on a continuous basis, not at the behest of 'Motor Show'-conscious sales managers. Figure 10.6 is a drawing issued by the Porsche Service Department to indicate new features on the 1975/76 Turbo model.

Universal joints

If it is true that 'necessity is the mother of invention', it is also true that the period of gestation is unpredictable. The need for a good reliable *constant-velocity* universal joint existed for two decades or more before Rzeppa found the answer. The lack of a good constant-velocity universal joint led to the failure or 'limited success' of several front wheel drive cars in the past. Today we have the Rzeppa and the Weiss joint, both using balls located in matching half-grooves in the two halves of the joint and both providing a constant velocity action.

Let us explain what we mean by *constant velocity*. The majority of the older universal joints operated in the manner of a simple Hooke's joint, two of which are shown in Figure 10.7. If the two shafts are at an angle and the driving shaft

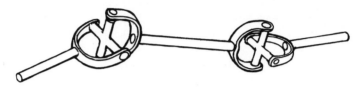

Fig. 10.7   Double Hooke's joint.

is rotating at a constant angular velocity, the angular velocity of the driven shaft goes through a cyclical variation every 90 degrees, being slower than the driving shaft at first, then faster, the *mean* velocity over each quarter revolution being, of course, equal. For an angular displacement of 8 degrees between driven and driving shafts, the maximum velocity variation is only 2 per cent, but if the angle between the shafts is trebled to 24 degrees the velocity variation is increased nine-fold to 18 per cent, which is a serious variation.

The use of two Hooke's joints, 90 degrees out-of-phase, as shown in Figure 10.7, is one way to transmit a constant velocity, but the centre shaft still goes through a cyclical velocity variation and this in itself can transmit unpleasant vibrations to the whole assembly and to the car itself if shaft angles of 20 degrees are exceeded. For a front wheel drive car, angles of 40 degrees or more are necessary.

The Rzeppa joint and the British equivalent, the Birfield-Rzeppa which is used on the Leyland front wheel drive cars, are shown in cross-section in

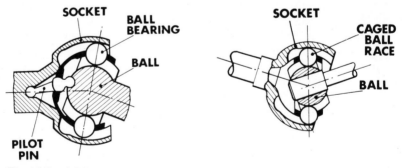

Fig. 10.8   (a) Rzeppa constant-velocity joint. (b) Birfield-Rzeppa constant-velocity joint.

Figure 10.8. The drive is transmitted through the six hardened steel balls which roll in grooved raceways in the two halves of the joint. Constant velocity is achieved by the geometry of the ball grooves which maintains the six balls and their locating cage in a half-angle position at all times. That is to say that the six balls and their cage always lie in the same place, this being the plane which bisects the angle between the driving and the driven shaft — whatever that angle may be. This is illustrated in Figure 10.9. The driven shaft rotates at exactly the

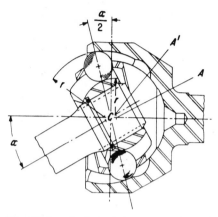

Fig. 10.9 Action of the Rzeppa joint.

same angular velocity as the driving shaft at all times. The Rzeppa uses a circular contour for the ball grooves. The Birfield-Rzeppa uses an elliptical contour giving a two-point contact with each ball instead of a line. Both designs are quiet and cool running and will give long life if not loaded beyond their designed capacity.

A good example of modern front wheel drive transmission using constant velocity universal joints is the Lancia Beta shown in Figure 10.10.

The limited slip differential

If one wheel loses traction on a normal differential no torque can be applied to the opposite wheel. This is an obvious disadvantage when driving in snow and ice and can also be found to reduce acceleration on good road surfaces, particularly when the driven wheels are not independently sprung and load transference can occur between the driven wheels, as discussed in Chapter Eight and illustrated in Figure 8.4. An early solution to the problem of excessive one-wheel spin was to provide a ready means for locking the differential. This was a drastic solution since we still would like the benefits of the differential when turning corners. The solution that is used today is a device which allows the differential to operate, but limits the relative speeds at which the two driven wheels can rotate. In other words, slip is limited. A good modern example is the Thornton *Power-Lok*, made by the Dana Corporation in America and Salisbury Transmission in England and fitted to the XJ-S Jaguar. In this design multi-disc

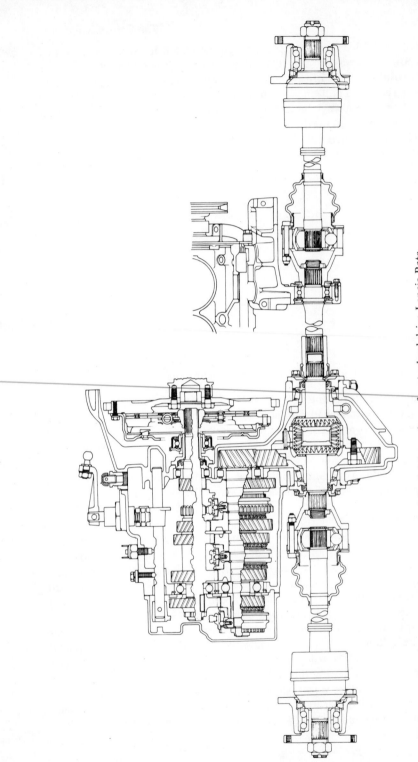

Fig. 10.10   Transverse section of gearbox and final drive unit on front-wheel drive Lancia Beta.

clutches are fitted on the outside of each differential side gear. Each clutch unit comprises four discs loaded by a Belleville (cone spring) washer. When one wheel starts to spin, axial thrust produces a cam action between the wedge-shaped ends of the pinion shafts and corresponding wedge-sided holes cut in the differential carrier. The differential carrier is split and is permitted outward axial movement. This outward movement occurs under the cam action from the pinion shaft ends and puts pressure on the clutches, automatically restricting rotation of the differential carrier. Anyone who has driven in the wet in one of the older 3.8-litre Jaguars with non-independent suspension at the rear and with no limited slip differential will appreciate how much this device can contribute to road safety.

11

The brakes

'Let it make no difference to thee
whether thou art cold or warm,
if thou art doing thy duty.'

MARCUS AURELIUS

The grip on the road

Whatever power we may apply to the brake shoes, whatever we may do to try to keep the drums cool, our final limitation on the rate of retardation is the grip of the tyres on the road surface. Locked wheels are of little use on a slippery surface as many of us have learned from experience of winter motoring.

In Table 11.1 are given average stopping distances from 30 m.p.h. on several typical surfaces. The values were obtained with smooth tyres; improved figures could, of course, be obtained with a good tread.

Table 11.1   Average stopping distance from 30 m.p.h. with smooth tyres

	ft
Clean dry surface (without ruts)	30-35
Clean dry surface with tar melting	40-60
Dry surface with loose sand	60-70
Wet 'non-skid surface	30-35
Average wet surface	50-60
Wet surface with loose sand	70-90
Icy surface	150-250
Wet surface with poor skid resistance	200-250

Experiments by the Road Research Laboratory have shown that locked-wheel stopping distances of the order of 30 to 40 ft from 30 m.p.h. can be obtained under the best conditions on the following surfaces:

(a) concrete;

(b) macadam;

(c) hot-rolled asphalt with precoated chippings;

(d) hot-rolled asphalt without precoated chippings, but with stone in the mix;

(e) dense tar surfacing;

(f) fine-texture asphalt.

Stone setts, wood blocks, cast-iron paving, rubber blocks and rock and mastic asphalts without precoated chippings all give stopping distances of 50 ft or more in the most favourable conditions. These experiments, however, showed that a wide range of stopping distances are given by all surfaces. Concrete, for example, over 70 tests showed a range of 34 to 130 ft. The best figures were given by dense tar surfacing and rock asphalt with precoated chippings for which the ranges were 32 to 64 and 44 to 60 ft respectively. Rock asphalt gave in one test a stopping distance from 30 m.p.h. of 495 ft — a truly magnificent skid! Since the above surfaces were chosen at random throughout the British Isles, one shudders to think of the consequences of a pedestrian crossing placed on one of the worst of these.

One aspect of road surfacing which must not be neglected is the abnormal wear that can be produced on the tyres of a high-speed car when abnormally large chippings are used to provide a non-skid surface. Since a surface with the same non-skid properties can be made with a relatively smooth finish which is less injurious to the tyres the continued use of such abrasive surfaces only increases the cost of motoring.

Braking forces

The above is a broad picture of the limitations set by the frictional forces between the tyres and the road surface. However great the braking forces we are able to apply to the brake drums, the upper limit on the rate of retardation is always set by the grip of the tyres on the road. There is no need to stress how much depends upon the driver's ability to recognize road surfaces and to drive accordingly. The designer nevertheless must provide adequate braking for the best conditions where decelerations of 1.0 to 1.3G are possible. Since a certain falling off in braking efficiency is inevitable between overhauls, it is advisable to increase this slightly and provide braking forces to give a maximum retardation of 1.5G.

Weight transfer under braking

Under hard braking the load on the front wheels is increased considerably, that on the rear wheels correspondingly reduced. We usually call this 'weight transfer'. Pedants could object to this, since the pull of gravity is not changed. It is really a transfer of force, not weight, but our interest is in the loads on the tyres, since this helps the designer to determine relative areas of the brake pads or brake linings at front and rear.

In Figure 11.1 it is seen that under a braking effort of 1G, the moment Wx is resisted by the couple $W_b l$, where W_b is the load transferred from rear to front.

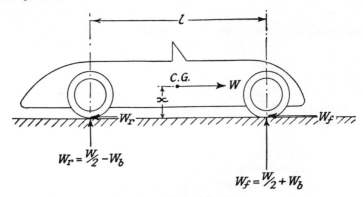

Fig. 11.1   Weight transfer under braking.

If we take:

$$x = 1.5 \text{ ft}, W = 2000 \text{ lb}, l = 8 \text{ ft}.$$

$$W_b = \frac{1.5 \times 2000}{8} = 375 \text{ lb}.$$

$$\therefore W_f = \frac{W}{2} + W_b = 1375 \text{ lb}.$$

$$W_r = \frac{W}{2} - W_b = 625 \text{ lb}.$$

This therefore calls for a braking distribution of approximately 70/30. If we were to design on this figure what would happen if, on a wet road surface we found the limiting deceleration to be only 0.2 G? The braking transfer couple would become

$$W_b = \frac{0.2 \times 1.5 \times 2,000}{8} = 75 \text{ lb}.$$

$$\therefore W_f = 1075 \text{ lb}.$$
$$W_r = 925 \text{ lb}.$$

With a brake actuation giving a 70/30 distribution, the retarding force at the road surface at the rear would be

$$0.2 \times 2000 \times 0.3 = 120 \text{ lb}$$

and at the front,

$$0.2 \times 2000 \times 0.7 = 280 \text{ lb}.$$

With the actual loads at the front and rear with this low rate of deceleration, the forces at the rear tyre will tend to give a deceleration of

$$\frac{120}{925} = 0.13\ G$$

and at the front,

$$\frac{280}{1075} = 0.26\ G$$

Since the limiting deceleration on the wet road surface is 0.2 *G*, the front wheels will slide and the rear wheels will still be turning.

We are now faced with a problem. Is it better to choose a 70/30 distribution which will lock the front wheels on wet roads or a 55/45 distribution which will lock the rear wheels when braking hard on dry roads?

Experiments all over the world, beginning as far back as Darwin and Burton's work on 'Side slip on motor cars', reported in *Engineering*, September 1904, have confirmed the following:

Locking the rear wheels only, produced a condition which resulted in partial or complete loss of control of the vehicle. This state was very unstable and the car could easily go into a spin.

Locking the front wheels only, produced a stable condition in which the vehicle travelled in a straight line. In this condition there was almost complete loss of steering control.

Locking all four wheels produced a condition which was fairly stable, resulting in the car travelling in a straight line. If the wheels on one side encountered a higher coefficient of friction than those on the other side, the car would turn towards the side with the higher drag. (A good example of this would be braking hard on a road with a loose surface near the verge. The loose 'ball-bearing' friction on the near-side would offer the least resistance to a locked wheel and the car would gradually turn towards the crown of the road, the back end sliding more and more into the ditch. If on the other hand the road were icy, with a lower coefficient of friction near the centre of the road than on the gravelled surface near the verge, the car would tend to dive nose first into the ditch.)

From all this we see that if we must lock any pair of wheels, it is safer to lock the front ones, since this ensures a stable straight line ditch-free halt. This has led to the adoption of a 60/40 distribution in general and a 65/35 distribution for racing cars and sports cars. There is no doubt that an easy adjustment of the braking distribution operated from the driver's seat would be invaluable to the keen motorist and especially to the rally competitor.

Brake fade

This phenomenon has led to a revolution in brake design in which the disc brake has gradually replaced the drum brake on the front wheels of nearly every car sold in Europe with any pretensions to high performance. In a few more years the changeover will be complete at the rear end too.

Brake fade is caused in two ways. The first cause is the drop in the coefficient of friction that can occur rather suddenly when the temperature of the brake lining rises above some critical temperature, usually about 400°C (750°F). Attempts to combat fade on drum brakes by using a hard lining were not too successful since the second cause of fade is the loss of 'bedding' of the linings when the drums expand away from the linings. Since the curvature of the expanded drum no longer conforms to the curvature of the linings there is a serious loss of effective brake area when rigid unyielding linings are used — and linings that retain a high coefficient of friction at high temperatures are inevitably hard linings. Coefficients measured on hard and soft Mintex linings are shown in Figure 11.2

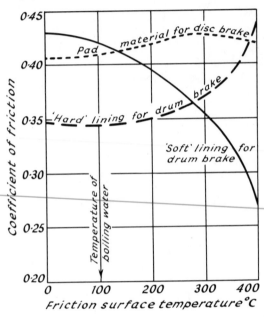

Fig. 11.2　Variation of coefficient of friction with rising temperatures on several Mintex lining materials.

When we brake a medium-sized sports car from 100 to 30 m.p.h. using the brakes to the full, we generate enough heat in the brakes to bring a 2-quart size kettle of water to the boil and all in about five seconds.

There is little hope that we could ever dissipate it as fast as it is generated. The temperature of the linings, the shoes and the drums rise during braking and fall again during the intervals between brake applications. On a twisty road taken at speed, the brake applications follow in quick succession and the heat from one application has not been fully dissipated before the next one occurs. In these circumstances the temperature of the linings can rise towards the dangerous critical point at which fade begins. With certain poor designs with full disc wheels and enclosed wings with spats, the temperature can rise to 500°C

(930°F). The effect of this on the coefficient of friction varies from lining to lining, but in most cases it results in a serious falling off in the braking effort.

To expose the wheel again to the full blast of the air stream as on the older sports cars would be a simple solution but the attendant drag from the wheel and suspension system becomes formidable at speeds above 120 m.p.h. and this solution, except in certain special cases, cannot be entertained.

DISC BRAKES

Disc brakes proved to be the answer to the problem of brake fade. The idea was not new. Dr F. Lanchester took out a British patent on a type of disc brake in 1902 and it was used for the first time on the 1906 25 h.p. Lanchester car. The Lanchester brake used calipers to grip both sides of a thin disc. Operation was mechanical and was not outstandingly efficient, even by 1906 standards.

During the war the Aviation Division of the Dunlop Rubber Company produced a successful aircraft disc brake. In 1949 they began to apply this experience to the automobile field. In this first experimental automobile design a ¾-in. thick, 12-in. diameter cast-iron disc, mounted on the wheel hub and rotating with the wheel, was straddled by a heavy U-section caliper member containing three pairs of circular friction pads. Braking was achieved by the three pairs of pads gripping the sides of the disc when hydraulic pressure was applied to three pairs of pistons behind the pads. Instead of the normal hydraulic system a hydraulic servo system was used in which pedal pressure controlled the output of a hydraulic pump driven from the gearbox mainshaft. Racing experience with these brakes in 1952 led to their appearance in modified form on the 1953 Jaguars at Le Mans. The effect was electrifying, especially at the end of the 160 m.p.h. Mulsanne Straight, where the Jaguar drivers could delay the application of their brakes to a point 300 yards nearer the hairpin than their Continental rivals. There is little doubt that these new brakes won the race that day. This form of brake was later used on the 'D'-Type Jaguar, three pairs of pads being used on each front wheel and two pairs on each rear wheel.

Experience of disc brakes suggested at first that they were the complete and final answer to the problem of brake fade. Improvements in tread compounds and the arrival of low profile tyres have made it possible to use even higher rates of deceleration and it has now become necessary on racing cars to use ventilated disc brakes. These are hollow discs with the passage in the central section designed like a shrouded impellor or fan to produce a radial air flow. Ventilated disc brakes are now being used on some of the faster production sports cars, such as the Ferrari and Porsche.

The freedom from fade we associate with the disc brake comes in the main from its direct exposure to a blast of cooling air. The use of a cooling fan on a drum brake will draw cooling air over the inner surface of the drum, but the direct air-blast cooling of the disc brake is far superior. Even when the temperature of the disc and the pads rises under the action of fierce and frequent brake applications the effects of differential expansion are negligible since the mating area of the two surfaces suffers no distortion. In the case of the drum brake, differential expansion can change the relative radii of curvature and seriously reduce the effective mating area. Another problem associated with drum brakes is the accumulation of dust in the drums — dust produced by wear of the lining material. Erratic braking can sometimes be caused when the leading edges of the linings fail to wipe the drum surfaces clean. Such debris cannot collect on the exposed surface of a disc brake and the pads are presented at all times with a clean braking surface. Wetting of the disc with rain gives no appreciable loss of braking effort since the pressures applied to the relatively small pads are far greater than those applied between the linings and drums on conventional brakes and the film of water is completely removed by the wiping action of the pads.

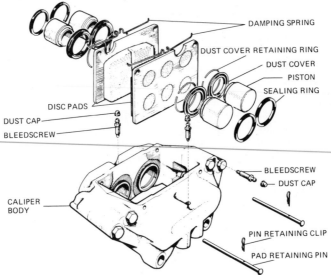

Fig. 11.3   Girling disc brake caliper — exploded view.

It is important to stress that the disc brake does not provide any greater rate of retardation than the drum brake. This limiting deceleration is set by the grip of the tyres on the road and it is not difficult to design drum brakes to provide this value *for one brake application*. The unique feature of the disc brake is its ability to provide this braking effort time and time again without any decrease in effectiveness.

An exploded view of a typical Girling disc brake caliper is shown in Figure 11.3. The action of the disc brake is simple. When the brake pedal is depressed, hydraulic fluid under pressure from the master cylinder forces the pistons towards the disc until the friction pads grip the disc from their respective sides, under full hydraulic line pressure. Many of us have experienced how effective the method can be on the ordinary bicycle. The heat generated in the disc is continuously removed by the airstream, since about 80 per cent of the disc area is subjected to a blast of cooling air. This is a much more effective cooling system than that available to the drum brake where the heat must first pass through the metal drum itself before it reaches the air stream. The limiting rate of heat input to a drum brake is about 2.5 b.h.p. per sq in of lining area. For a disc brake this limit is about 8 b.h.p. per sq in of pad area.

Girling Ltd (who absorbed Dunlop's disc brake division some years ago) developed a caliper brake that incorporates hydraulic operation from the foot brake and mechanical operation from the hand brake. This design is shown in Figure 11.4. It consists of a caliper body that straddles the disc, two opposed

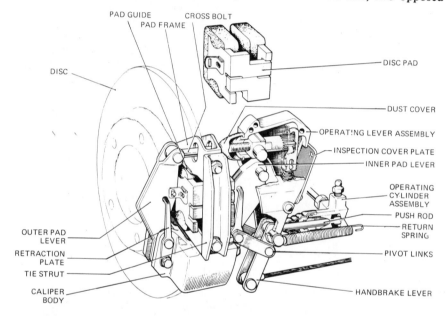

Fig. 11.4 Girling rear brakes with cable handbrake operation.

friction pad levers and an operating lever. The pad levers are mounted on fulcrum pins attached to the caliper and linked by an adjustable cross bolt. One end of the cross bolt is pinned to the outer pad lever and the opposite end is secured to the nut of the self-adjusting mechanism housed in the operating lever. Connected to the other end of the operating lever are the handbrake cable and the operating cylinder assembly. The friction pad assemblies are housed within a steel frame bolted to the caliper. Any tendency for the pads to tilt is resisted by the right-angled backing plates moulded to the friction material.

After each brake application the retraction plates withdraw the pads off the disc to maintain a constant small clearance between the pads and the disc. The operating lever incorporates a ratchet mechanism that automatically adjusts the pad clearance as the friction material wears.

Disc brakes for the high-speed sports cars

The disc brakes on the 'D'-type Jaguars used a hydraulic servo pump driven by the gearbox to step up the pressures in the system to a much higher level than in a normal hydraulic system. Disc brakes have been successfully applied to small light European sports cars without recourse to servo mechanisms or special pumps. The larger European sports or G.T. cars such as the Aston Martin, the Jaguar and the Ferrari, now use a vacuum servo mechanism to boost operating pressures on 4-wheel disc brake systems. When Zora Arkus-Duntov decided the time had come to fit disc brakes to the Corvette he decided to design a system that would stop this 1600 kg (3500 lb) car effectively without any servo assistance of any kind. The brakes were developed by the Delco Moraine Division of General Motors and are notable for the use of a ventilated disc. In this way the effective cooling area of the disc is doubled. The better cooling afforded by the vented disc is shown by the curves of Figure 11.5. The left-hand

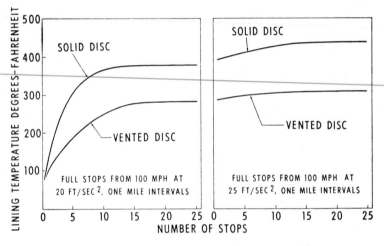

Fig. 11.5   Improved cooling of pad material with vented disc.

curves are the lining temperatures during 25 repeat stops of 0.62 *G* deceleration at one mile intervals. The right-hand curves show how the lining temperatures rise to new higher levels when the deceleration rate is stepped up to 0.77 *G*. The final temperature of the vented disc was 130°F (72°C) lower than the solid disc.

The development work that led up to the ventilated disc brakes on the fabulous turbocharged Type 917/10 Can-Am Championship-winning Porsche is a fine example of recent practice in racing sports car design. With such experience behind them no one who buys a production Porsche in the future need fear that the performance of the car will be allowed to outstrip its ability to stop! The earlier unsupercharged Type 917s were unofficially timed on the

Fig. 11.6 Porsche-designed front brake of Type 917/10 Can-Am car.

Mulsanne Straight at Le Mans in 1971 at 240 m.p.h. The development engineers were well aware by 1969 that the solid disc brake had reached the limits of its heat dissipating capacity. In the Daytona 24-Hour Race in 1970 they used a ventilated disc fabricated from an aluminium alloy spider that formed the fan blades with copper-chromium alloy discs rivetted on each side. They still experienced brake fade.

The solution, which has proved adequate for the 850-950 b.h.p. turbocharged racing cars is shown in Figure 11.6. For lightness the ventilated disc is attached to the steel wheel hub via an aluminium alloy conical member (distinguished by the larger lightening holes in the photograph). The disc itself is in cast-iron with curved vanes inside the two flanges. Drilling of the disc flanges (the 'Gruyère' design in the factory jargon) was originally undertaken to reduce unsprung weight. It was found that the modification improved pad cooling and maintained a high coefficient of friction of almost constant value over a very wide temperature range. Water and mud could be cleaned from the surface much more effectively and the wear pattern on the pads was much more regular.

Ventilated disc brakes now feature as standard equipment on the Carrera and the Turbo model Porsches.

Pad materials

Makers of brake-lining materials are now able to produce a formulation for the brake pads that will maintain a fairly constant coefficient of friction of about 0.4 up to a temperature of at least 500°C (930°F) and over a wide range of pedal pressures. The new materials have much longer life than the earlier pads and do not give any undue wear or scoring of the discs. Brake squeal is usually caused by vibrations set up in the calipers. It can be reduced by a change in pad material, but a permanent cure can only be made by a redesign of the caliper.

To achieve these results conventional brake-lining materials are still used, these being asbestos fibre, mineral or metallic oxide fillers and an organic bonding agent. Sintered metal pads of identical material to the drum-type linings that have worked so well under racing conditions on drum brakes did not perform well on disc brakes. Durability was poor and the high thermal conductivity caused them to conduct too much heat to the brake fluid, thus introducing a danger of vapour lock from vaporized brake fluid, which of course can lead to a complete loss of brake effort. Much research is still to be done in this new field.

12

Performance

'Often think of the rapidity with which
things pass and disappear.'

MARCUS AURELIUS

Standards of performance

Standards are changing all the time, in the way we live, in our morals, in our automobiles and in the performance we expect from them. Many a seemingly modest young lady will appear in public today in clothes that would have led to her arrest for indecent exposure fifty years ago. And so it is with the speed and acceleration of our cars. When the author, as a young schoolboy, first crashed through the magical one-mile-a-minute barrier as he crouched down in the passenger's seat of his father's Studebaker tourer, he experienced not only a great sense of achievement but a certain feeling of guilt. Was it right to travel at this speed on the public highway, even without another car in sight? Today this same middle-aged schoolboy has to move over in to the slow lane if he wishes to dawdle at 60 m.p.h.

It is intriguing to compare the fabulous performances of the giants of the past with those of today. Fifty years ago the 4½ litre Bentley, representing the best in British sports car design would accelerate from zero to 60 m.p.h. in about 15 seconds. Today, a perfectly ordinary family car of only one-third the engine capacity of the Bentley will reach 60 m.p.h. from zero in about the same time. Larger engined sports cars, such as the Aston Martin, the Maserati Bora and the Ferrari Dino will reach 60 m.p.h. in about 6 seconds. The mind boggles when we turn to the acceleration potential of modern racing machinery. The following figures were calculated by the factory computer for the Porsche turbocharged Type 917/10 Group 7 racing car with the turbocharger controls set to produce maximum power (about 950 b.h.p. DIN):

> 0 to 60 m.p.h. (96 k.p.h.) ....2.1 seconds
> 0 to 100 m.p.h. (161 k.p.h.) ....3.9 seconds
> 0 to 200 m.p.h. (322 k.p.h.) ....13.4 seconds.

These figures were supplied by Dr Fuhrmann, Porsche's Managing and Technical Director and we have no reason not to believe them. No driver would indulge in such fireworks in a race since the tyre wear would be unacceptable. It is interesting to note however that this fantastic Porsche would reach 200 m.p.h. before the old Bentley had reached 60 m.p.h.!

The meaning of power

Before considering the performance of modern sports cars we must refer briefly to that pampered and rather sluggish horse that contributes to the measurement of the 'SAE gross horsepower.' Corrupted by a horse-power race in the sixties the American motor manufacturers were content to quote horsepowers in the Press using an SAE approved method in which power was measured on the dynamometer with the dynamo and cooling fan disconnected, the exhaust front pipe exhausting into an underground ducting maintained at a pressure slightly below atmospheric pressure and the ignition timing set to give maximum power, with no regard to the actual ignition advance curve dictated normally by the distributor. The final cheat was the application of a correction in which the engine was motored over with water and oil at normal operating temperatures to measure the power absorbed by internal friction and pumping losses. This friction horsepower was then *added* to the previously measured value to give the completely fictitious figure called the '*gross* SAE horsepower.'

This sort of chicanery allowed claims of 400 'horsepower' for engines that gave little more than 300 b.h.p. at the flywheel when fitted into the car. Several European manufacturers used the same methods for many years.

There is an air of realism abroad in Detroit now and the net SAE horsepowers they quote today are very close to the values measured on British, French, German and Italian test-beds. The Deutsche Industrie Norm (DIN) horsepower has always been a fair one and the author has adopted this one in this chapter when the value is available. The International Standards Organisation (ISO) have set up another slightly different procedure and one can only hope that this will eventually be adopted by all countries.

ACCELERATION

What determines a given rate of acceleration? Is it power to weight ratio — is it torque to weight ratio — or is it a mixture of the two? It will be useful, before we look further into this question, to clarify our ideas on horsepower and torque. Horsepower is a *rate* of doing work, i.e. the time element is involved. It is measured in units of work per unit time. Torque, on the other hand, is a twisting moment, simply a force times a distance. If a rear wheel is 12 inches radius and is exerting a force of 400 lb at the road surface to propel the vehicle forwards, the torque transmitted is 4,800 lb in. or 400 lb ft. If the wheel is turning at a speed of 500 r.p.m. the number of radians turned through in a minute while the torque is acting will be $2\pi \times 500$. The rate of doing work is, therefore, $2\pi \times 500 \times 400$ ft lb per minute. The horsepower per wheel is therefore

$$\frac{2\pi \times torque \times r.p.m.}{33,000}$$

$$= \frac{2\pi \times 400 \times 500}{33,000}$$

$$= 38.1 \; b.h.p.$$

If the same torque of 400 lb ft were transmitted to the road surface by the 2-ft diameter wheel at twice the speed, i.e. 1,000 r.p.m., the power transmitted would be double, or 76.2 b.h.p.

Let us now consider what happens to the power of the engine on its way from the flywheel to the driving wheels. In top gear one would not expect to lose much of the power in the gearbox, but the churning of the oil can still absorb a little power, as can be verified by feeling the rise in temperature of the gearbox-casting after a long run. The transmission efficiency of the hypoid gear in the rear axle will be 94-95 per cent and in all about 7 per cent of the power leaving the flywheel will disappear in the form of heat and noise before it reaches the road wheels. In the intermediate gears about 88-90 per cent of the engine power will perform useful work.

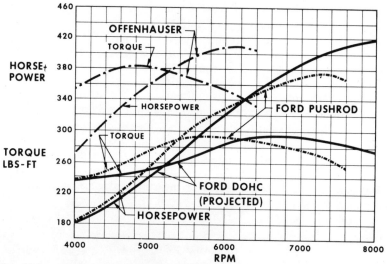

Fig. 12.1 Comparative power and torque curves of Indianapolis engines. The Ford engines were used later in the Lotus 30 competition sports car and the G.T. Fords.

Figure 12.1 gives two examples of the power and torque curves for the highly tuned V-8 engines developed specially by the Ford Motor Company for the 1963 and 1964 Indianapolis Lotus-Fords and used later in the Lotus 30 and the Ford G.T. sports cars. It is of interest to compare the performance of these short stroke, medium bore V-8s, one with push-rod operated valves, the other with a twin o.h.c. head to each bank and 4 valves to each cylinder, and the near-culmination of the Meyer Drake Company's development of the big-bore, long-stroke 4-cylinder Offenhauser engine. The bore and stroke of the Ford V-8 is 95.6 mm × 73 mm, of the Offenhauser 109 mm × 111 mm. The push-rod Ford gave slightly less power, the d.o.h.c. Ford slightly more power than the 1963 Offenhauser, but the big 4-cylinder Offenhauser develops peak power at a much lower speed and the torque is much superior. Such an engine will give greater acceleration, for acceleration is dependent on torque, as we shall demonstrate later in this chapter.

It was shown in our companion volume *Design of Racing Sports Cars* that a good approximation to the mathematical relationship between bhp and the cylinder dimensions is

$$\text{Max. b.h.p.} \propto d^{1 \cdot 65} s^{0 \cdot 5}$$

where *d* is the cylinder bore
       s is the stroke.

When the stoke/bore ratio is constant,

$$\text{b.h.p.} \propto d^{2 \cdot 15}$$

or approximately,

$$\text{b.h.p.} \propto \text{piston area.}$$

The torque, however, with a given fuel and cylinder head design and compression ratio is directly proportional to the swept volume.

With a constant stroke/bore ratio

$$\text{torque} \propto d^3.$$

For our purpose it is more convenient to measure engine size in terms of the swept volume, *V*.

In terms of this then,

$$\text{b.h.p.} \propto V^{\frac{2}{3}}$$
$$\text{torque} \propto V.$$

Based on this relationship we would expect a series of DOHC engines as used in modern sports cars to give the values for maximum power and torque given in Table 12.1.

The 6-litre engine is seen to have three times the torque of the 2-litre, but only slightly more than twice the power. Every engine tuner looks for higher 'revs' if he wants more power. In this manner some engine tuners obtain quite impressive increases in power from otherwise standard engines. The torque,

Table 12.1 Approximate variation of power and torque in high-performance sports car engines

Engine litres	capacity cu in	Net power bhp	kW	Net torque lb ft	Nm
2	122	180	134	140	190
3	183	240	179	210	284
4	244	290	216	280	380
5	304	335	250	350	475
6	365	380	283	420	569

however, does not benefit from increased r.p.m. as such, but only from the improved breathing that has led to the higher engine speeds. Putting this another way, an increase in volumetric efficiency from the use of larger inlet valves, may increase the maximum torque by, say, 10 per cent. The power curve will now peak at 15-20 per cent higher r.p.m. and the overall effect will be an increase in maximum power of as much as 30 per cent.

When engines are designed for different basic duties it is possible for two engines to have the same power output but very different torques. The pre-war American engine was designed for the lazy driver who wanted to get into top gear as soon as possible and to stay there, only using the lower gears on steep hills and when brought to a standstill at traffic lights. A single small choke carburettor was always used and the inlet valves were correspondingly small. Good torque at low speeds was obtained at the expense of maximum power. The power curve peaked at about 3,500 r.p.m. A typical 4-litre engine of the period would develop 100 b.h.p. with a maximum torque of 190 lb ft. A modern 1½-litre sports engine could deliver 100 b.h.p., but the torque would probably not exceed 90 lb ft. If we took two similar cars with similar bodies and installed the two engines, the 4-litre American engine and the 1½-litre sports car engine, in such a way that the kerb weights were identical, they would give identical top speeds, provided that the right rear axle ratios were chosen. The American engined car however would out-accelerate the sports car engined car, and would cut the acceleration times of the latter car by two.

Acceleration times for 0-60 m.p.h.

It would be of value, especially to the 'special' designer, if we could estimate the probable acceleration to be expected from a given specification of car. For general road conditions the most important acceleration range is 0-60 m.p.h. Let us then see if we can devise an empirical formula giving a fair approximation to the time taken to accelerate through the gears to 60 m.p.h. on any given car.

The basic acceleration formula, from simple mechanics, is in self-consistent units

$$P = Mf$$

where P = the force producing acceleration,

M = the mass to be accelerated,

f = the acceleration.

The force to produce acceleration, in our case, is directly proportional to the excess torque; the excess torque being the torque remaining when we deduct from the total torque the torque absorbed in overcoming road resistance and air resistance. Over the speed range of 0-60 m.p.h. only a small percentage of the total torque is absorbed in overcoming the resistance to motion. At 60 m.p.h. on a typical sports car rolling resistance will be about 30-40 lb; the air resistance about 70-80 lb — a total of about 110 lb. If we take a typical engine torque of 120 lb ft and a second gear ratio, overall, of 8 to 1, a transmission efficiency of 90 per cent and a tyre diameter of 26 inches, the propelling thrust at the rear tyres is

$$\frac{120 \times 0.9 \times 8 \times 12}{13} = 800 \text{ lb.}$$

The excess thrust is therefore 800—110 = 690 lb or 86 per cent of the total.

At 30 m.p.h. the total resistance will be about 30 lb. The excess thrust is therefore 800—30 = 770 lb or 96 per cent of the total.

With a bigger engined car the excess torque will be a higher percentage of the total. For a car like the Aston Martin it will rise to about 95 per cent of the total over this speed range and for a smaller engined car such as the M.G.B. it will fall to about 80 per cent. In general, however, it seems reasonable to take P into the formula as being proportional to T, the total engine torque.

$$f \propto \frac{P}{M} \propto \frac{T}{M}$$

where T is the maximum engine torque, lb. ft.

Our formula then becomes:

Time in seconds, 0-60 m.p.h. $\propto M/T$

or, if we take the car test weight in lb = W

$$t_{0\text{-}60} = KW/T \quad (1)$$

However, when we try to apply this formula, it is soon apparent that something has been neglected. Let us test it by choosing a value of $K = 0.4$ to give agreement with the road-test value for the modest powered Alfa Sud. As we use this value to estimate the performance of higher powered sports cars the error increases with each increase in power to weight ratio. The table opposite illustrates this.

Errors of this magnitude cannot be dismissed as the effects of wheel-spin. It is in fact caused by making no allowance for the losses from *internal* accelerations, the torque absorbed in accelerating the rotating and reciprocating components in the engine, the rotating parts of the clutch, gearbox and final drive. Even the

Make and Type	Time to accelerate 0 to 60 mph		Deviation from formula
	by road-test	*by formula*	
Alfa Sud L	14.1	14.1	0
Lotus 7	8.8	7.1	19%
MGB GT V-8	7.7	5.8	25%
Maserati Bora	6.5	4.5	31%
Porsche 917 (1971 Le Mans specification)	3.7	1.7	54%

wheels and tyres must be accelerated in a rotary sense as well as a linear sense. In the case of a high-powered sports/racing car such as the Porsche Type 917 approximately 50 per cent of the total torque that would be available in steady motion is lost in rotational accelerations, leaving only about 50 per cent for linear acceleration of the car's mass.

The concept of effective mass

Our simple Newtonian formula of $P = Mf$ must be replaced by a more sophisticated concept if we are to make an accurate estimate of the acceleration potential of any new design of sports car at the drawing board stage, especially if the projected specification is for a high-performance vehicle.

The author is indebted to J.L. Koffman (*Automobile Engineer*, December, 1955) for the concept of effective mass. In the simple Newtonian acceleration formula M is replaced by M', where

$$M' = M(1 + \alpha + \beta)$$

α is a correction factor for the polar moment of inertia of the engine. (This correction factor is dependent upon the overall gear ratio, being higher in 1st gear than in top gear.)

β is a correction factor for the polar moment of inertia of the road wheels.

The polar moment of inertia of the gearbox, propeller shaft and final drive gears are all very small and can be neglected.

To apply the Koffman formula to any vehicle we need the following information:

(1) the net torque curve for the engine,
(2) the gear ratios,
(3) the rolling radius of the driving wheels (this increases with speed),
(4) the rolling resistance of the car (the road resistance plus the air resistance),
(5) the test weight of the car,
(6) an approximate value for the polar moment of inertia of the engine, flywheel and clutch.

The author was able to collect the above data for a Jaguar XK150S and to calculate the acceleration times through the gears from 10 m.p.h. to 120 m.p.h.

The calculated values give remarkably close agreement with the road test values taken from *The Autocar* test of September 18, 1959. The influence of the polar moment of inertia of the rotating masses on the performance of this car can be judged from the following figures. The true mass of the XK150S, the test weight, was 3,590 lb. The effective mass in each gear was calculated to be:

	lb
M' in first gear	= 5,060
M' in second gear	= 4,130
M' in third gear	= 3,880
M' in fourth gear	= 3,840
M' in overdrive	= 3,770

The effective mass in first gear is 141 per cent of the true mass. Thus in first gear about one-third of the torque developed at the crankshaft is absorbed in accelerating the engine, the clutch and all the rotating masses, even the road wheels. The actual polar moment of inertia of the road wheels is usually very high, especially on a big-engined competition vehicle with large tyres. The rotational speed of the wheels, however, is only a small fraction of that of the engine. In first gear on the XK150S the overall ratio is 12.2 to 1. In this gear the torque absorbed in rotating the wheels is only about 3-4 per cent of the total engine torque. In overdrive a higher percentage of the 'lost' torque is used in rotating the wheels. Of the total lost torque of 5 per cent, 3½ per cent is absorbed in rotating the engine and 1½ per cent in rotating the wheels.

The Jaguar XK150S was no mean performer for its day, and could accelerate from 0 to 100 m.p.h. in 22.4 seconds. Several modern sports cars can halve this acceleration time. When this is achieved by using a highly tuned 3-litre engine instead of a more modestly tuned 5-litre engine less power is wasted in accelerating the rotating and reciprocating components. In this sense the smaller engine can be said to be more efficient.

It can be shown that the effective mass is highest when

(a) the ratio engine r.p.m./m.p.h. is high

(b) the ratio engine polar moment of inertia/total mass is high.

It can also be shown that every car has a limiting *effective* bottom-gear ratio. At this limiting ratio any change to a lower ratio (actually to a higher ratio when expressed as a numerical value) would increase the effective mass more than the gain in torque given by the ratio change. The overall effect would thus be a reduction in the rate of acceleration. For the SK150S the limiting effective gear ratio would be 17 to 1. The actual bottom-gear ratio of 12.2 to 1 is well inside this limiting value. For many modern racing/sports cars the limiting ratio will approach 10 to 1 and the designer of such projectiles should beware that he does not exceed this limiting effective ratio. Even though the bottom gear is a ratio only used once, from the starting line, the use of a ratio that is higher (numerically) than the limiting value will only result in a drop in acceleration.

While the Koffman method is the most accurate means available to the designer or project engineer for calculating the acceleration of a modified design over any desired speed range, the method is very laborious. Moreover many of us do not have access to the necessary data. A much simpler, but admittedly less accurate, method has been devised by the author.

Table 12.2 is based on the following formula:

$$t_{0\text{-}60} = (2W/T)^{0.6}$$

where W = the test weight in lb.
T = the max. engine torque, net in lb ft.

A comparison of the formula values and the Road Test values shows good agreement in the majority of cases.

MAXIMUM SPEED

There was a time when one could take out a high performance sports car on the public roads and find out its top speed in reasonably safety — but not so today. Today with maximum speeds often approaching 150 m.p.h. and in a few models even exceeding 200 m.p.h. to use the public roads for this purpose is asking for a brief notoriety in the daily papers, perhaps even a longer spell in one of Her Majesty's prisons! The testing staffs of the motoring journals are now finding it so difficult to make accurate measurements of this important yardstick of performance that they sometimes substitute an estimated value in their reports.

In Chapter Nine in the section on Drag coefficients we introduced the general formula for drag horsepower:

$$\text{HP}_{drag} = \frac{C_d \, A \, v^3}{146,600}$$

where C_d = drag coefficient
A = frontal area, sq ft
v = speed, m.p.h.

The horsepower absorbed in aerodynamic drag is about 70 per cent of the net b.h.p. at the flywheel. Thus if we know the net maximum power of an engine, the frontal area of the car and can make an inttelligent guess at the drag coefficient, this formula will give us a good approximation to the maximum speed. Since v varies as the cube root of these quantities no great accuracy is required in our estimate of C_d or A or even the net horsepower. For most modern shapes A can be estimated fairly accurately at:

$$0.9 \times \text{width} \times \text{height}$$

For older sports cars and particularly for cars with separate wings like the Lotus Seven and the Morgan the constant should be reduced to 0.8. To help the reader in his choice of a value for C_d when estimating the probable performance

Table 12.2 Acceleration time 0–60 mph (0–96 kph)

	Maximum torque net, T		Test weight W		Time in seconds for 0–60 mph (96 kph)	
	$lb\,ft$	Nm	lb	kg	by road tests	by formula $t = \dfrac{2W}{T}^{0.6}$
Aston Martin DBS V-8	400‡	542	4300	1950	5.7	6.3
Chevrolet Corvette Sting Ray	391†	530	3640	1650	6.1*	5.8
Datsun 280Z	163	221	2870	1300	8.3	8.5
Ferrari 308 GT4 2+2	210	285	2860	1297	6.4	7.2
Jaguar XJ-S	294	399	4150	1882	6.7	7.4
Lancia Beta HPE	127	172	2650	1200	10.0	9.4
Lamborghini Espada	290	394	4300	1950	7.8	7.7
Lotus Seven Series 4SE	96	130	1700	771	8.8	8.5
Lotus Eclat 523	140	190	2830	1284	8.5	9.2
Maserati Bora	339	460	3820	1733	6.5	6.5
MGB GT V-8	193	262	2790	1266	7.7	7.6
Morgan Plus Eight	210	285	2350	1066	6.7	6.5
Porsche 911 S	181	246	2675	1211	7.3	7.7
Reliant Scimitar GTE	172	234	2970	1347	8.7	8.4
de Tomaso Pantera	325	441	3460	1569	5.8	6.1
Triumph TR7	119	162	2580	1170	9.6	9.7
TVR 300 ML	172	234	2600	1179	7.5	7.7

*1968 *Motor* road test

†Estimated at 85% of SAE torque

‡Estimated by *Motor* staff (figures not available from manufacturer)

Table 12.3 Maximum speeds and drag coefficients

Make and type	Estimated frontal area		Maximum power net		Maximum speed from road test		Estimated drag coefficient C_d
	ft^2	m^2	bhp	kW	mph	kph	
Aston Martin DBS V-8	20.8	1.93	345‡	257	155	250	0.41
Chevrolet Corvette Sting Ray	18.2	1.69	340†	252	146*	235	0.50
Datsun 280Z	18.2	1.69	149	111	117	189	0.44
Ferrari 308 GT4 2+2	17.5	1.63	255	189	152	244	0.38
Jaguar XJ-S	19.5	1.81	285	212	155	250	0.36
Lancia Beta HPE	18.6	1.73	119	89	112	180	0.42
Lamborghini Espada	19.2	1.79	350	261	150	242	0.49
Lotus Seven Series 4SE	11.7	1.09	84	63	100	161	0.74
Lotus Esprit	20.0	1.86	160	120	138	200	0.31
Maserati Bora	17.7	1.65	310	232	160	258	0.39
MGB GT V-8	16.5	1.54	137	102	125	202	0.39
Morgan Plus Eight	15.7	1.46	168	125	125	202	0.56
Porsche 911 S	18.5	1.71	165	123	136	220	0.32
Reliant Scimitar GTE	19.4	1.81	135	101	118	190	0.39
de Tomaso Pantera	17.0	1.58	330	256	155	250	0.48
Triumph TR7	18.5	1.72	105	78	111	179	0.40
TVR 300 ML	16.7	1.56	142	106	125	202	0.40

*1968 *Motor* road test
†Estimated at 85% of SAE horsepower
‡Estimated by *Motor* staff (figures not available from manufacturer)

of a new design of car Table 12.3 has been compiled from published road test data. From this we see that a typical modern sports car has a drag coefficient of about 0.4. The best examples, invariably the result of painstaking testing in the wind-tunnel, give values approaching 0.3. A typical design of pre-war sports car, with flared wings, a slab fuel tank at the rear, a flat screen with only about 20 degrees rake, but with hood erect and side screens in place would have a value for C_d of 0.7 to 0.75. The Lotus Seven is in many respects a replica of this older design, but with modern materials and design techniques the weight is almost halved. Where the object is sheer acceleration good handling and a modest top speed the Lotus Seven formula still makes sense. If only we could persuade Colin Chapman there is still a market for an updated Lotus Seven perhaps he would design one, still at a kerb weight of about 1700 lb, but this time with a drag coefficient of 0.4 to 0.5.

13

The sports car in the future

'We are all working together to one end,
some with knowledge and design, and others
without knowing what they do.'

MARCUS AURELIUS

THE ENGINE

However much we may hate them we cannot escape the consequences of exhaust emission regulations on the future of the sports car engine. American car manufacturers have staggered from one crisis to another as the Federal emission standards have been tightened in successive stages to levels that have resulted in the addition of catalytic converters containing expensive and not very durable materials, air injection pumps, exhaust gas recirculation devices and very complex fuel injection systems. To add to the driver's misery some of these changes have resulted in poor drivability in traffic and an increase in fuel consumption.

Most governments in Europe have adopted the ECE specification known as ECE15. These standards are not as severe as the U.S. Federal or the Californian standards, since smog is not yet such a problem in our cooler climate. Even so several European sports car manufacturers have found the North American market quite profitable in the past and the larger manufacturers, such as Leyland and Mercedes-Benz and some enterprising small firms such as Lotus and Porsche are loth to abandon the market. If the Americans can do it — so can we!

It is difficult to make a direct comparison between the American standards and those specified in ECE15 since the driving cycles used in the acceptance tests of acceleration, cruise, deceleration, braking and idling are, following the inane decisions of most large committees, completely different. Sweden and Australia, however, have adopted the 1973 Federal test method and Table 13.1 serves to show the wide gulf that exists today between the Federal and Californian standards on the one hand and the rest of the world on the other. There is some consolation in the fact that the small-engined car is now favoured by a test method that measures emissions in grams per mile. The seven-litre gasoline guzzler carrying a single commuter into the city must eventually disappear from the scene.

Table 13.1

	Exhaust emission standards		
	CO (Carbon monoxide) gm/mile	HC (Hydrocarbons) sm/mile	NO$_x$ (Nitrogen oxides) gm/mile
Sweden/Australia	390	3.4	3.1
Present U.S. Federal	150	1.5	2.0
Present Californian	9.0	0.41	1.5
Proposed 1978 U.S. Federal	3.4	0.41	2.0

PROMISING ALTERNATIVES

We know that many of our brightest automobile engineers are not at all happy when they consider the problems of coaxing conventional petrol engines through the 1978 Federal test schedule. They are less happy when they think of the work involved maintaining these standards after the car has left the factory. Some even predict that the engine that has served us so well since the beginning of the century will be replaced by an entirely different engine within the next ten years. The automobile industry has not ignored these predictions. Large scale programmes have been undertaken to investigate all promising alternatives. At the same time they have not neglected to try out any feasible schemes to improve combustion and reduce the exhaust emissions from the conventional engine. The capital investment in the machinery to make the conventional internal combustion engine throughout the whole world is an astronomical figure. This will not be cast aside lightly. It will be of some value at this stage if we make an appraisal of all the promising alternatives.

The gas turbine

In 1951 Air Commodore F.R. Banks, in his James Clayton Lecture to the Institution of Mechanical Engineers, gave the following summary of the position of the automobile gas turbine at that time:

In the first place, the most suitable size of gas turbine to give reasonable efficiency is better fitted to the needs of the larger vehicle rather than the automobile — since it is more easy to build an efficient gas turbine of 250 shaft horsepower than one of 50 or 100 shaft horsepower. Scaling the engine down to these comparatively low powers demands lengthy and expensive development, to obtain the required efficiency of components such as the compressor, the combustion chamber, and the turbine.

Smoothness of operation and lack of vibration, inherent in the gas turbine, are now so good in the piston engine that a change to the former on these grounds alone could hardly be justified.

Working principle

For traction applications the gas turbine is fundamentally different from the aero gas turbine. Figure 13.1 serves to illustrate the 'two-turbine' principle as

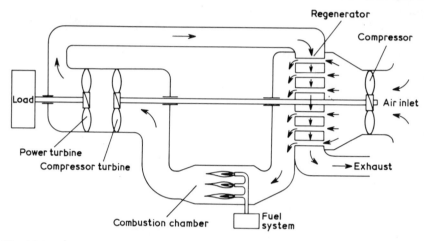

Fig. 13.1 Simplified gas turbine.

used in car and truck applications. The air/fuel mixture is burned in a combustion chamber and the resulting expanding gases are used to drive the first turbine, the compressor turbine. The compressor turbine provides the power to drive the compressor which compresses the air before it enters the combustion chamber. This compression of the intake air is as necessary in the gas turbine as in the piston engine; the greater the compression ratio, the more efficient the conversion of heat energy into useful work. The hot gases leaving the first turbine are expanded further through a second turbine, this being the power turbine which is connected through suitable gearing to the driven wheels of the vehicle. To improve the efficiency of the power unit the hot gases leaving the power turbine are passed through a heat exchanger or 'regenerator' as it is usually called by turbine engineers. This extracts heat from the gases before they are exhausted to the atmosphere and raises the temperature of the air entering the combustion chamber. The reader will have realised a fundamental difference between the gas turbine and the piston engine. In the former the processes of compression, combustion, expansion and exhaust are *continuous*, in the latter they are *cyclical*.

When we analyse the evidence reported during the 26 years since Air Commodore Banks made his authoritative statement we find that, despite considerable progress in this field, the goal of a commercially viable gas turbine to replace the automobile piston engine still eludes the thousands of engineers involved. General Motors, Ford and Chrysler in America and Leyland in Great Britain have spent millions of dollars on the development of the gas turbine. Only in the field of trucks and buses, where the size-factor, stressed by Banks, is in their favour, have they made any real progress. One of the current projects sponsored by the American Environmental Protection Agency is a seventh generation Chrysler automotive gas turbine. If all goes well full-scale production of this engine is planned for 1983.

The gas turbine gives very low hydrocarbon and carbon monoxide emissions and the problem of high concentrations of nitrogen oxides (NOx) that caused so much concern about five years ago has been solved by vaporising and pre-mixing the air/fuel mixture fed to the combustion chamber. Great advances have been made in the development of ceramic materials for the turbine blades thus permitting maximum operating temperatures to be raised from about 1000°C (1830°F) to about 1350°C (2450°F). This makes the gas turbine much more efficient and economical.

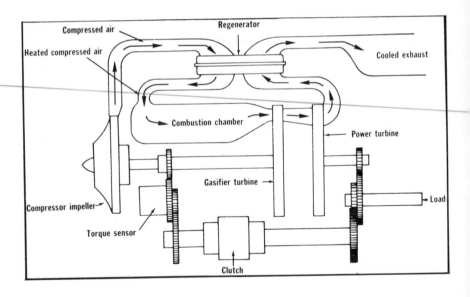

Fig. 13.2   GM Detroit turbine with power-transfer system giving economy and engine braking.

There remains one very challenging obstacle to the future of the gas turbine, the problem of cost. The mass production of investment castings for the aluminium alloy impellors, the development of inexpensive techniques to mould the turbine blades in sintered ceramix-metal mixtures, the development of cheap reliable regenerator cores; these and many other problems still occupy many fertile brains. It is very discouraging, but the small or medium-size gas turbine for automotive use seems very little nearer to-day than when we reviewed the position in 1969.

The application of the gas turbine to heavy road transport vehicles has made rapid strides in the last decade. A schematic layout of the 400 shaft horsepower turbine made by the Detroit Diesel Division of General Motors is shown in Figure 13.2. These engines have operated successfully in Greyhound long-distance buses. A power-transfer system is used to connect the power turbine shaft and the compressor (gasifier) turbine shaft under the automatic control of a 'torque sensor'. This system, not only gives the very desirable feature of overrun braking, but improves acceleration and economy.

Rotation combustion engines

It is 22 years since Felix Wankel invented his remarkable rotary engine. Today there are firms all over the world working under licence on the development of this engine. From Figure 13.3 we see that the 'rotating piston' is a three-sided rotor, eccentrically mounted on the output shaft and geared to it by an internal gear and pinion with a ratio of 3:1. Thus the output shaft makes three revolutions for every revolution made by the rotor. Both rotate in the same direction. Chambers are formed between the specially shaped outer casing (the geometric shape is called an 'epitrochoid') and the rotor, these chambers varying in volume as the rotor turns, thus giving alternate compressions and expansions as in the reciprocating engine. Intake and exhaust ports are provided in the periphery of the casing or in the end walls. Figure 13.3 will help the reader to understand how the 4-stroke cycle is obtained. Three expansion (working) strokes occur for every revolution of the rotor. Since the output shaft makes three revolutions in this time period only one working stroke occurs per revolution of the output shaft, which is the same number that occurs with a 2-cylinder 4-stroke reciprocating engine. The decision of the FIA racing committee to rate the Wankel engine at twice the swept volume of one of its chambers is therefore logical.

It will be seen that ignition is provided by the same sparking plug for successive firings. Conditions are obviously arduous for the single plug, since it receives no cooling from the induced charge as in a conventional engine. To prevent leakage across the rotor tips it is necessary to limit the size of the hole between the plug socket and the combustion chamber.

Gas sealing at the three tips of the rotor and at the end faces was a difficult problem in the early Wankel engines. Some designs suffered from excessive wear rates, others would flutter at a critical speed and this fluttering would soon gall the surface of the chamber and destroy the gas seal. Effective seals have now been developed by several of the companies working in this field, the sealing usually being least effective at low speeds. The intersection of the apex seals and the end-face seals on the NSU-Wankel engine is shown in Figure 13.4. The apex seal blade is free to slide in a radial direction, the inner portion being guided by a hardened steel bolt. The end-face seals extend from apex to apex and provide an interlock for the bolt. All parts are preloaded towards the faces

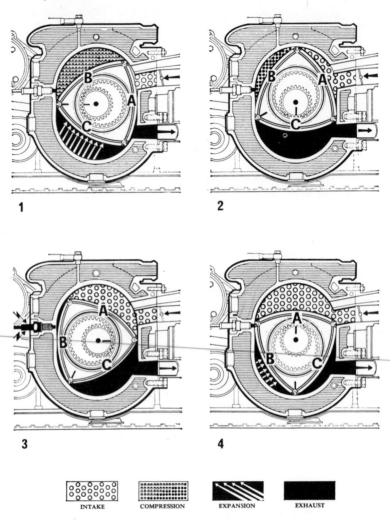

INTAKE   COMPRESSION   EXPANSION   EXHAUST

Fig. 13.3   Four-cycle operation of Wankel rotating combustion engine. An
eccentrically mounted three-lobe rotor, turning within an
epitrochoidal combustion casing, drives a centrally mounted
output shaft through an internal gear and pinion. The enclosed
volumes at A, B and C are successively expanded and compressed
in the manner of the four-cycle piston engine. The single
sparking plug carries a very high heat-load since it fires three
times per revolution of the rotor, or once per revolution of the
output shaft.

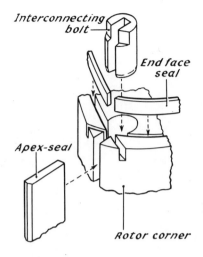

Interconnecting bolt

End face seal

Apex-seal

Rotor corner

Fig. 13.4 Components of the apex sealing system on the NSU-Wankel rotor.

to be sealed by corrugated springs. These springs do not provide sufficient pressure for sealing, this being provided by gas pressure acting behind the blades, as in the piston rings in a conventional engine.

Cooling of the outer casing is by water jackets, but the rotor is oil-cooled, being fed under pressure through the hollow shaft and by various passages in the hollow centre of the rotor. Circulation is maintained by means of a stationary extraction scoop.

Toyo Kogyo, the Japanese Company who make the Mazda car, have worked very hard on the many problems associated with the rotating combustion engine and have now produced a smog control system for their latest engine that operates on a *lean* mixture. This confounds many American experts who have been insisting on the need to operate on the rich side of a chemically-correct mixture in order to reduce the nitrogen oxides formed during combustion and to use a catalytic muffler or thermal reactor to burn away the excess hydrocarbons and carbon monoxide. The Mazda thermal reactor is maintained at a high temperature by means of an exhaust gas heated jacket and an efficient insulating cover. The former criticisms that the Wankel engine is uneconomical and unreliable could therefore be challenged by the New Mazda, but the weight of invested capital sunk into the manufacture of piston engines is still the greatest threat to this ingenious engine. Even so, if Toyo Kogyo can give a convincing demonstration that their engine is superior to the current piston engines, the changeover will eventually occur.

The diesel engine

The engine associated with the name Dr Diesel operates on the principle of 'compression ignition'. By this we mean that the compression ratio is so high that the temperature of the air towards the end of the compression stroke is high enough to ignite a spray of fuel injected a few degrees before TDC. No sparking

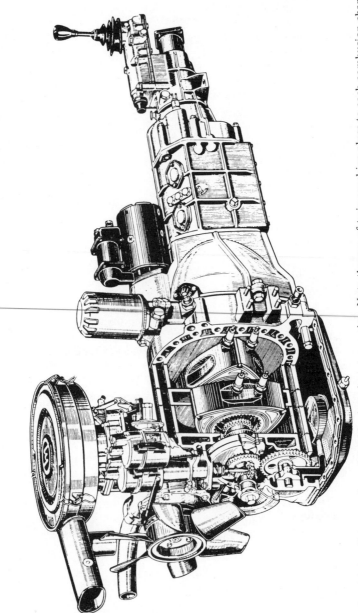

Fig. 13.5 Cutaway view of the Mazda twin-rotor engine. Note the use of twin sparking plugs to each combusion chamber.

plug is, of course necessary. A Diesel engine runs completely unthrottled, taking in a full charge of air at every induction stroke. Power is regulated entirely by the amount of fuel injected near TDC at the beginning of the working stroke. With no throttle to regulate the air flow only about 5 per cent of the oxygen is required for combustion at idle. At full power about 90 per cent of the oxygen is consumed. Any attempt to increase the metered quantity of fuel beyond this point results in incomplete combustion, exhibited by the emission of black smoke from the exhaust pipe. A petrol engine consumes 100 per cent of the oxygen supplied (neglecting the very small amounts of fuel only partially oxidised, i.e. the carbon monoxide). The petrol engine can also operate at much higher engine speeds. The speed of combustion in the Diesel engine is not as rapid.

In brief the Diesel engine, for the same overall bulk, produces about 70 per cent of the power of a petrol engine. Since the Diesel uses compression ratios as high as 20 to 1, heavier wall thicknesses are required in the combustion chamber walls and the cylinder walls, and a general increase in crankcase rigidity is necessary to withstand the higher loads transmitted to the crankshaft. For engines of the same weight we can therefore only anticipate the Diesel to produce about 60 per cent of the power of the petrol engine. On the credit side, the Diesel is very economical and a Diesel car will use only about two-thirds the fuel of the conventional car. This in itself is enough to explain the renewed interest shown by the automobile industry in the Diesel since the Middle East oil producers began to show their economic strength with such devastating results. Today 40 per cent of the cars made by Mercedes-Benz are Diesel-powered and many other well-known European car makers offer Diesel engines as an option on at least one model in their current range.

Turbocharging will be discussed later in the chapter but this could be the secret potion needed to achieve a successful mating of the overweight Diesel and the sports car of the future. Friedrich Van Winsen, the chief development engineer at Mercedes-Benz, recently expressed a conviction that a turbocharged Diesel could be produced in the near future that would be refined enough to meet the exacting requirements of his company's luxury cars *and at the same time conform with European pollution legislation*. In the author's opinion, such an engine could readily be adapted to power a future Mercedes sports car.

The Stirling engine

One of the problems that faced the Reverend Robert Stirling, his brother James and his son Patrick, when they tried to raise some interest in the Reverend Stirling's novel engine was to explain the working principle to businessmen with no knowledge of themodynamics. This was not surprising since little was known in 1843 about the laws that govern the conversion of heat energy into work. This was the year when the first Stirling engine was installed to drive the machinery at a Dundee foundry. Poor technology and unsuitable construction materials led to the comatose state of Stirling engine development for nearly a century. A few of the original engines survived as disused pumping engines to interest industrial archaeologists and a few were used in India to replace the *punka wallah*, the man servant who waved a fan from side to side to cool his master.

Modern materials and an understanding of the thermodynamics of the engine revived interest in this engine in 1937 when the N.V. Philips Company of Endhoven in Holland began a research programme to study its potential. This has grown into a world-wide interest, with General Motors and Ford in America and Mann and MWM in West Germany all participating in the search for a commercially viable engine.

The simple idea conceived by this Scottish Presbyterian minister in 1816 is illustrated in Figure 13.6. In this illustration no attempt is made to show the

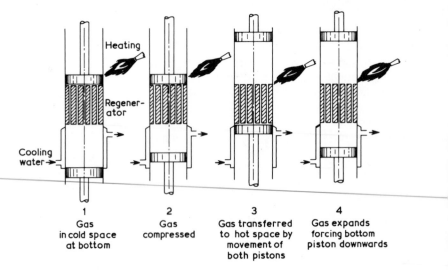

1	2	3	4
Gas in cold space at bottom	Gas compressed	Gas transferred to hot space by movement of both pistons	Gas expands forcing bottom piston downwards

Fig. 13.6   The Stirling cycle.

mechanism used to convert the reciprocating motion of the two pistons or to arrange the phasing of their relative movement. Many mechanisms have been devised and it is difficult today to predict which will prove to be the final solution. In the original engine a single cylinder is effectively divided into two working chambers by a heat exchanger or regenerator. The upper hot chamber and the lower cold chamber each contain pistons which are interconnected in some way to produce a pumping action (in many of the original engines) or to produce rotary motion. By suitable phasing of the cranks the gas in the lower chamber is first compressed, then transferred to the hot side through the passages in the regenerator which is designed to have a high heat storage capacity. The regenerator contains heat stored from the previous cycle. The heated gas enters the hot side which is maintained at a high temperature by *external* combustion of a suitable fuel and the gas expands and does useful work on the upper piston. The piston movements are reversed and the gas is transferred back through the regenerator. As the lower piston returns to its original lower position the hot gases, passing through the regenerator passages give up valuable heat to the regenerator. Heat is supplied continuously to the upper chamber; cooling by water or air is supplied continuously to the cold chamber. It will be realised that the Stirling engine like the steam engine is an external combustion engine.

The modern Philips engine uses hydrogen as the working fluid. Hydrogen has a high thermal capacity and because of its low viscosity the pumping losses through the minute regenerator passages are low. A compact 'rhombic drive' using contra-rotating cranks geared together gives the required phasing of the two pistons and a matrix of small diameter crimped wires acts as a regenerator.

There are no near-explosive pressure rises inside the Stirling engine; in fact no explosions inside or outside the cylinders. The Stirling engine is as quiet as the proverbial sewing machine, uses negligible amounts of oil and has shown few problems of wear or erosion. The working cycle is close to the ideal Carnot cycle. The Stirling engine therefore possesses the potential for a much higher thermal efficiency than the petrol engine. The extremely clean exhaust that can be given by a modern continuous combustion chamber operating on an excess of oxygen would be an added bonus. It is the ability to meet all reasonable future exhaust pollution demands that spurs on Stirling engine development. On the debit side the Stirling engine is still very heavy and bulky. It requires a radiator twice the size of the current petrol engines and is not yet able to cope with demands for quick changes in power output. The Stirling engine has much to offer as a stationary continuous speed engine, but its future in the automobile is still a distant prospect.

The steam engine

The steam engine is another power unit with the inherent advantages of a clean exhaust. Older Americans will remember the fine steam cars made by Abner Doble. His flash boiler used about 180 metres (600 ft) of small-bore seamless steel tubing as a boiler and an electrically-driven blower to control the excellent combustion of the kerosene/air mixture in the combustion chamber. The Doble steam car could be made ready to drive away 40 seconds after starting from cold; slow by modern standards but acceptable in the early twenties.

Two companies are active today in their unfailing belief in the steam engine. The Lear Motor Corporation, have an engine installed in a long-distance coach that is used for publicity purposes and the STP Corporation, have developed a completely sealed (no steam loss) system. The exhaust steam is condensed in a jet condenser and after cooling in a large radiator is returned to the boiler feed pump as shown in Figure 13.7. All the steam engines produced in recent years have been very bulky. When installed in a car they usually require the whole of the engine compartment and the boot (trunk) to house the engine, condenser, boiler and other auxiliaries. It would be pleasant to see a lightweight steam engine in a sports car some day. The excellent low-speed torque would be very welcome. Somehow it seems to be many many years away.

JET CONDENSER

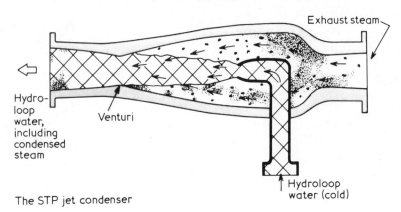

The STP jet condenser

CLOSED HYDROLOOP CYCLE−
AUTOMOTIVE STEAM ENGINE

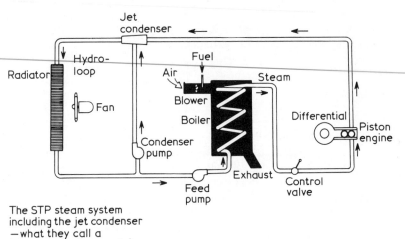

The STP steam system
including the jet condenser
—what they call a
'closed hydroloop cycle'

STEAM POWERED FAMILY CAR

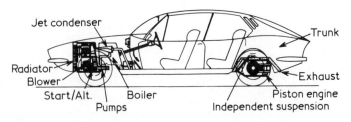

Fig. 13.7   The STP steam car project.

PETROL ENGINE DEVELOPMENTS

Stratified charge

Otto patented a system in which combustion starts in a rich mixture and progresses into a lean one. His aim was to reduce the shock-loading on the piston. This is the first known reference to what we now call 'stratified charge' where a small quantity of mixture on the rich side of chemically correct is situated near the sparking plug, and a very lean mixture occupies the rest of the combustion chamber. The concept is that the rich mixture, once ignited, will carry combustion like a flaming torch through the lean mixture. By designing the combustion chamber to effect this action it is hoped to burn a much leaner, overall mixture than would be possible using a homogeneous mixture. Harry Ricardo was one of the first to see the possibilities of the stratified charge engine and he experimented on such an engine as early as 1915. Since then hundreds of patents have been taken out on special cylinder head designs to achieve efficient stratification followed by good combustion. Some of these patents have resulted in experimental engines and a few of these engines have shown a measure of success.

The weakest homogeneous mixture that a conventional spark-ignition engine will run on without an occasional misfire is about 16 to 17 lb of air to 1 lb of fuel. Overall air/fuel ratios as lean as 60 to 1 have been burned successfully in stratified charge engines, but such an engine can only operate at a constant speed and may be regarded as a very clever laboratory experiment. On a more realistic level several practical engines have been produced in recent years that will operate in the range 20 to 25 to 1.

Stratified charge engines fall into two generic classes, single chamber designs and dual chamber designs. Fuel injection is a *sine qua non* for the success of the single chamber system. A very high rate of air swirl is required into which the fuel is injected tangentially. The mixture resulting from this spray becomes stratified by the centrifugal action of the intense swirl, the richer mixture being

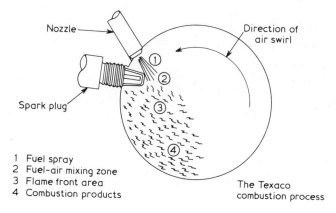

1 Fuel spray
2 Fuel-air mixing zone
3 Flame front area
4 Combustion products

The Texaco combustion process

Fig. 13.8 Diagram of the Texaco combustion process.

centrifuged to the outside. This principle was used in the Texaco TCCS engine and appears in a modified form in the German MAN bowl-in-piston engine where the fuel is sprayed on the hot surface of the bowl. Combustion proceeds radially inwards as the fuel evaporates from the hot surface.

The majority of workers in this field show a preference for the dual chamber system. The author worked on an experimental engine of this type fifteen years ago. This was the 'Spitfire' system, patented by Claude May and developed in the laboratory of the Walker Manufacturing Company in Racine, Wisconsin. A close approach to the Spitfire system was described in a recent paper by Professor Lev A. Gussak on the Russian LAG process. This engine carries a small primary combustion chamber connected to the main chamber by a very small diameter throat. A rich mixture is fed to the prechamber and a very lean mixture to the main chamber. A secondary, small inlet valve is used in the prechamber. By using such a valve the admission of the carburetted rich mixture can be controlled to begin at the optimum time before TDC. According to Professor Gussak, the burning gases violently ejected through the tiny throat carry micro-eddies of gas pre-conditioned for combustion as well as other small centres of ignited mixture that spread combustion throughout the main chamber. The pre-conditioning of the combustible mixture before true ignition is a complex physical and chemical phenomenon involving ionisation of the molecules followed by pre-flame oxidation. It is argued by Professor Gussak that the ignition points and the pre-conditioned gas pockets act like an avalanche as combustion spreads throughout the lean mixture.

In conventional engines a mixture leaner than about 17 to 1 is not only difficult to ignite but the spread of combustion is so slow that it is not completed before the exhaust valve opens.

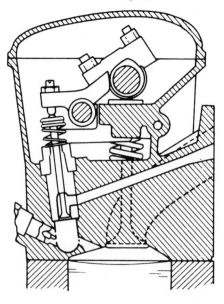

Fig. 13.9
The Leyland stratified charge
engine using carburetted
mixture to both chambers.

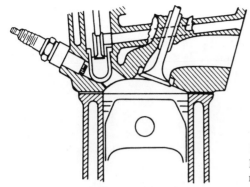

Fig. 13.10
Honda's CVCC engine, the first in
regular production.

The Leyland dual chamber engine shown in Figure 13.9, designed for use in the Triumph Dolomite, bears a strong resemblance to the Russian design. The sparking plug is on the left of the prechamber, this chamber being fed by a carburetted rich mixture as in the LAG engine. The Honda CVCC engine (Figure 13.10) is used in the production Honda Civic. In this case again separate carburetted mixtures are used to feed the two chambers. Mercedes-Benz, however, prefer to use a fuel injector in the prechamber and a carburettor to supply the lean main mixture.

The Honda engine has not yet achieved any great economy but their Civic saloon complies with the current Californian emission standards and gives nitrogen oxide levels that are low enough to meet the current Japanese standards which are even lower than those in California. Nitrogen oxides are formed at

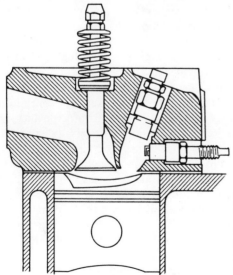

Fig. 13.11
The Mercedes-Benz pre-chamber
design. A carburetted mixture is
supplied to the main chamber,
with fuel injection in the
pre-chamber.

high temperatures and the major part of the mixture in this type of engine is burned at a lower pressure and temperature than in the conventional engine.

It is of interest to sports car owners that Porsche have an experimental dual-chamber engine. This may not be the first to appear in a production sports car, but the author will be very surprised if we do not see a stratified charge engine in a sports car in the early eighties.

Turbocharging

It is now commonplace for medium and heavy truck Diesel engines to be turbocharged. As a consequence compact, low-cost reliable turbochargers are available as off-the-shelf components for any specialist sports car manufacturer who wishes to boost the power of his engine. Turbocharging for passenger cars was used for a period in the sixties when the firm of AiResearch, in conjunction with General Motors, designed turbocharger installations for the Corvair, Oldsmobile and various Pontiac models. Using 100 octane fuel it was possible to increase power output by about 100 per cent with complete reliability.

A turbocharger uses the pressure and temperature energy in the exhaust gases to drive a compressor to increase the induction pressure substantially above atmospheric pressure. Supercharging as we knew it on pre-war racing cars used mechanically driven compressors and these absorbed a considerable amount of the gross power that came from the increase in induction pressure. Apart from a certain increase in exhaust back pressure the additional power produced by turbocharging is all in the American vernacular 'for free'.

A typical turbocharger, an AiResearch Type T-04B, is shown in cross-section in Figure 13.12. The compressor is on the left and is an investment casting in aluminium alloy. The air flow is in the normal centrifugal supercharger direction, i.e. inwards from the left and outwards from a tangential passage from the scroll chamber. The impellor carries 16 radial blades. The flow through the gas turbine is in the reverse direction, the gas passing from the manifold into dual scroll chambers that form vortices converging on the curved blades of the turbine rotor. Expansion of the exhaust gas through the turbine, with the exhaust manifold pressure maintained at a much higher pressure than is normal in unsupercharged engines, provides the power to drive the compressor. The unit is quite compact since rotor diameters seldom exceed 80 mm (3.2 in) but they rotate at speeds as high as 120,000 r.p.m., about 10 times the maximum speed of a Grand Prix engine. The double rotor unit is dynamically balanced at assembly and by careful design very little end-thrust need be taken up by the fully floating bushes. Oil is supplied to these bearings at engine oil pressure and is drained back to the sump. The bearing housing has seals at each end. Oil consumption with good maintenance should therefore be nil.

One difficulty in matching the turbocharger installation to the demands of a petrol engine lies in the rising delivery characteristics of a centrifugal blower with increase in speed. A turbocharger designed to give the desired pressure in the middle range of the engine speed will produce a boost pressure that is much too high at maximum engine speed, leading to heavy detonation and almost

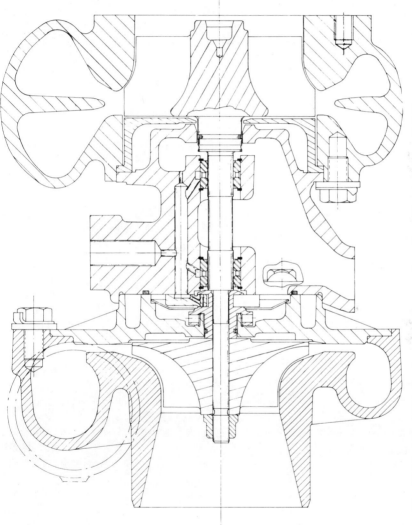

Fig. 13.12 Typical turbocharger in cross-section, the AiResearch Type T-04B.

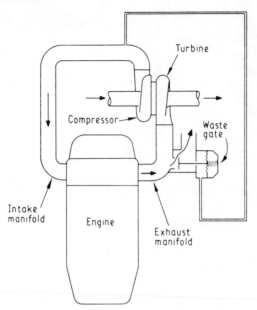

Fig. 13.13   Waste gate control system for turbocharging (shown diagrammatically).

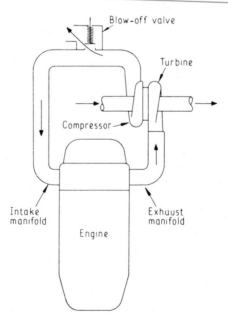

Fig. 13.14   Compressor blow-off control system.

certain engine failure. Three control methods to overcome this problem are in use today.

Waste-gate. The control scheme illustrated in Figure 13.13 spills exhaust gas through a waste-gate, thus by-passing the turbine. The simple control device shown here is a diaphragm valve that opens the waste-gate as the intake manifold pressure rises to the control point and closes it again as the engine speed falls. More sophisticated control valves that would give a boost curve that rises or falls at a chosen rate are of course possible.

Compressor blow-off valve. Excess air delivery can be blown off by a suitable valve as shown schematically in Figure 13.14. This simple system cannot be used of course with the carburettor fitted on the atmospheric side of the compressor, but is well suited to fuel-injected engines. The thermal efficiency suffers since work is performed in compressing air which is then discharged to atmosphere.

Turbine outlet restriction. A fixed orifice is sometimes placed downstream of the turbine to reduce the available turbine energy at high speeds. This tends to give higher maximum exhaust back-pressures than the other two methods.

The Turbo Porsche is a fully developed system using the waste-gate control system. The caption under Figure 13.15 explains the workings of the system. The Bosch K Jetronic fuel injection has already been described in Chapter five. Many firms with emission problems are now adopting fuel injection since it gives such a close control of air/fuel ratios. The compressor recirculation circuit controlled by valve 3 is the Porsche answer to the old problem that plagued General Motors in the sixties. The Corvair Monza Spyder exhibited an agonising flat-spot when full power was again required after coasting. It could take up to three seconds after flooring the accelerator again before the gases in the exhaust system built up a high enough pressure ratio across the turbine to give any useful power from the compressor.

Air/fuel ratio control

Cars like the Turbo Porsche have been developed expressly with the North American market in mind and with the turbocharger controls described above and the latest K Jetronic fuel injection it is well able to meet the current Federal emission standards. Many development engineers however have recently expressed grave doubts of their ability to meet the proposed 1978 Federal standards. The Swedish Saab company is one firm that has not yet given up hope. In fact, as we write this chapter it is reported that the Saab Turbo has passed these very severe 1978 emission tests and has achieved this with a turbine control system largely similar to the Porsche system. They have the assistance of two additional devices the *three-way catalyst* and an *automatic air/fuel ratio control*.

The three-way catalyst was found in the late sixties by the Ford specialists working in this field. In theory, to oxidise CO and HC in a catalyst bed one needs a lean mixture. To reduce NOx the mixture should be rich. Despite these simple theoretical considerations it was found that certain catalysts, largely platinum with about 10 per cent of rhodium, could do a 'three-way clean-up' of

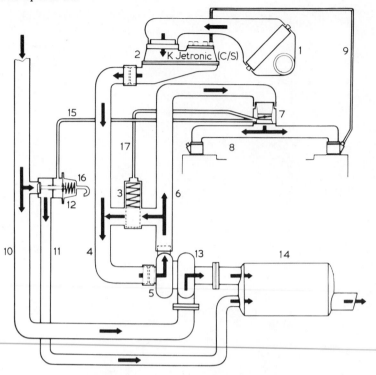

The engine draws in atmospheric air through air filter (1), mixture control (2), and induction pipe (4) which then flows through compressor (5) of the supercharger, pressure line (6), throttle housing (7), air manifold (8) and enters the engine.

The engine exhaust gases pass through exhaust manifold (10), supercharger turbine (13), muffler (14) and then discharged to atmosphere. The exhaust gas flow drives turbine (13) which again drives compressor (5), supplying compressed air to the engine. The supply pressure of compressor (5) is limited by bypass valve (12) in exhaust manifold (10); when the supply pressure of compressor (5) exceeds a predetermined value, bypass valve (12) is opened by the excess pressure in control pipe (15) so that the exhaust gas flow passed through bypass line (11) around turbine (13) directly to muffler (14). For maintaining the supercharger speed, e.g. under coasting conditions or to ensure quick engine response when accelerating, a connection pipe with blowoff valve (3) is provided between induction pipe (4) and pressure line (6). With the throttle in closed position, blowoff valve (3) in control line (17) is opened due to the differential pressure so that the inlet air passing around compressor (5) ensures the required supercharger speed.

Fig. 13.15   Diagram of Porsche turbocharging control system as used on Turbo model.

all the pollutants. The problem with the three-way catalyst, insoluble in the sixties, was the extremely narrow band of air/fuel ratios required before all three reactions could occur. If for example the fuel in use had a stoichometric (chemically correct) air/fuel ratio of 14.6 the mid-point of the control band had to be very slightly on the rich side of this value, i.e., 14.5. Moreover, and this was the real challenge, all three reactions would only be achieved if the control band was held to limits of plus or minus 2 per cent of the mid-point under all operating conditions. When we remember that many induction manifolds in pre-emission days gave variations of plus or minus 10 per cent from cylinder to cylinder we see why the three-way catalyst was put on the shelf.

A few years ago the breakthrough came with the invention of Lambda-Sonde. *Lambda* is the Greek letter used by German engineers to represent air/fuel ratio and *Sonde* is the German word for sensor. The Lambda Sonde is more correctly described as an oxygen sensor. The German Bosch Company is one of the firms active in this field and their sensor has now an assured life of 15,000 miles and can control air/fuel ratio to the tight band demanded by the three-way catalyst. The complete metering system developed by Bosch uses K Jetronic injection in conjunction with a 'feed-back system' using a signal from the Lambda-Sonde, situated in the exhaust manifold, to indicate to the electronic control module when the exhaust gas oxygen content has moved away from the control value by a small amount. The signals from the sensor are interpreted by the control module which then proceeds to regulate the quantity of fuel injected. The Volvo application is shown in Figure 13.16. When this engine was tested in California the chairman of the California Air Resources Board called it 'the most significant breakthrough ever achieved.'

One thing is certain. Engines will become much more complex. Apart from

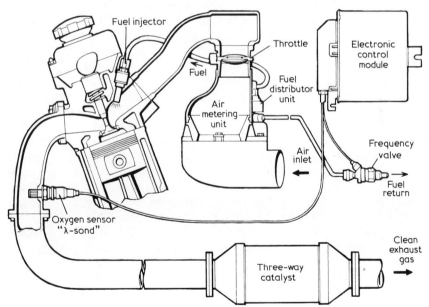

Fig. 13.16 Volvo's thinking engine. Schematic view of Volvo's Lambda-Sonde equipped engine where the oxygen content of the exhaust gas is measured and the air/fuel ratio automatically corrected to maintain a clean exhaust.

the increased cost, which we all regret, it is now apparent that the days of the do-it-yourself mechanic are numbered. Those familiar with any of the earlier editions will now realise why the chapter on Tuning has now been omitted. Under American law, carburettors are now sealed against unauthorised mixture adjustments. The practice will probably be adopted by other countries in the future.

THE TRANSMISSION

In our companion book, *Design of Racing Sports Cars*, a strong case was advanced for the use of automatic transmission in racing sports cars. So many long-distance races have been lost through a clumsy gear change on a manual gearbox by a tired driver. The shock loads created by one careless gear change can strip teeth from a gearwheel or break some other component in the drive train. The use of sticky tread compounds and the uncanny grip of wide tyres has increased this danger.

When we consider the less arduous conditions of a production sports car used by a reasonably experienced driver, the danger of complete transmission failure recedes but the provision of an automatic transmission will remove one chore from the driver in a traffic-packed situation and leave him more time to concentrate on weaving his way through the traffic stream. With a modern well-designed 3-element torque converter coupled to a 3-speed automatic gearbox a sports car loses very little in terms of acceleration, fuel economy and maximum speed. Current automatic gearboxes use hydraulic control systems to operate the friction bands that engage the planetary gear trains. With the proven reliability of solid-state electronic equipment it is probable that future automatic gearboxes will be controlled electronically.

TYRES AND SUSPENSION

One cannot predict the tyre profile ratio that will eventually become the norm on production sports cars but a fair guess would be that the 50 Series will seldom be exceeded in the downward trend since lower profiles become unacceptable on practical grounds. This limitation is very apparent in the case of the front-engined car where ultra wide tyres intrude on the space occupied by the engine and its increasing number of auxiliary components.

Suspension geometry is now largely dictated by the tyres since the low profile tyre must be maintained very close to the vertical plane if it is to perform well.

No-roll suspensions

It is always possible to adopt one of the no-roll suspensions developed over the last twenty years, since with a body that never rolls one can design a suspension geometry that maintains all four wheels perfectly upright in a tight turn. The gain in cornering power is quite substantial. When tested by *Motor* a Rover 3500 saloon fitted with the AP 'stabilised suspension' could negotiate a test chicane at

54.5 m.p.h., an increase of 6 m.p.h. over the standard car. Since centrifugal force varies as the square of velocity this represents a gain of about 25 per cent in cornering power.

Several engineers have designed workable no-roll suspension systems. As early as 1961 the writer tested a Chevrolet fitted with the Kolbe *Curve-Bank* suspension which was designed to lean inwards on corners. This would be a mistake with modern low-profile tyres but the system could easily be set up to give a flat ride. About six years later came Norbert Hamy's *Trebron* system in which a sideways displacement of the body under centrifugal force is used to generate forces to hold the wheels upright in a corner. There have been others but none we know that have reached production or have been used successfully in racing. The latest sophisticated design, as tested on the Rover by *Motor*, comes from that enterprising component manufacturer Automotive Products of Leamington Spa. It uses the self-levelling principle developed by Citroen, but with an important difference, the hydro-gas strut has a split-second reaction time. If you stand on the front bumper of a CX Series Citroen (with the engine running) the front end dips and then slowly rises back to the controlled height. The delay time is about ten seconds. If you stand on the front of a car fitted with the AP system no apparent movement occurs.

The secret of the AP control system is a small pendulum mass, mounted on a spring and provided with a damper. The power to correct the ride height of each suspension leg is provided by a large hydraulic pump capable of a high flow of oil at a pressure of 290-360 kN/m² (2000-2500 lbf/in²). Full pump output, only required when taking a corner or chicane at speed, is 11 kW (15 b.h.p.), although the system is not designed simply to prevent roll. It also prevents pitch,

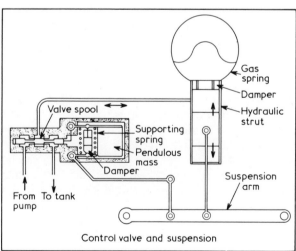

Fig. 13.17   One suspension leg of the Ap stabilised suspension, showing schematically the hydraulic control system.

dive and squat. In other words it is in the words of the makers a 'stabilised suspension'.

Figure 13.17 is a schematic representation of a single suspension unit. The inert gas contained in the ball and separated from the hydraulic fluid by a flexible diaphragm is the suspension spring. By adding or subtracting flud from the space between the diaphragm and the piston in the suspension strut the level of the car body at that particular corner of the car can be adjusted upwards or downwards. The signal to add or extract hydraulic fluid comes from the balanced three-way valve. Change in level is sensed by the 'pendulous mass', which is supported on a coil spring and supplied with its own hydraulic damper. This mass-spring-damper unit is tailored to match the particular suspension system precisely, in frequency and damping characteristics. The behaviour under single wheel bumps is as follows: As the suspension arm moves upwards to compress the suspension spring (the gas contained in the ball) an upward force is created which lifts the body upwards. The pivot of the offset pendulum moves upwards with the body and, with no movement of the pendulum, the spool of the three-way valve would move to the left to extract fluid from the suspension leg. As already stated the pendulum, spring and damper unit have been designed to behave as a perfect model of the car suspension. Consequently, the pendulum rises at the same speed as the body. The net effect on the valve spool is to create no signal, both on bump and rebound of a single wheel. A change due to roll, however, is not as transient as a single wheel bump or rebound, which is completed in about a hundredth of a second. Roll, pitch, brake dive and acceleration squat are all suspension movements of relatively long duration and the system responds to these to maintain a level ride at all times. In the experimental Rover system two hydraulic valves are used at the front with a single central valve at the rear. The two front valves control roll, pitch and body height. The single rear valve only controls pitch and height. Additional hydraulic cylinders are incorporated in the rear suspension struts. These are diagonally connected to the front control valves. In this way a roll couple can also be applied to the rear when cornering. Moreover, by varying the size of these additional rear units the front and rear roll couples can be matched to give well-balanced behaviour when cornering.

All this, as it stands today, represents an expensive and complicated piece of equipment. Even with the help of a large order for a popular car it is difficult to see the additional retail cost being held below £100. On a specialist sports car costing £10,000 a specially tailored system might add £300 to the retail price — an extra 3 per cent — not a great price to pay for improved cornering power and comfort. From the designer's viewpoint a fully stabilised suspension system means that he can forget all about roll-centre heights, roll steer effects, anti-roll bars and the influence of wheel camber change on cornering behaviour. For the designers of luxury cars it means that a very soft suspension can be used. Perhaps Rolls Royce or Mercedes-Benz will be the first customers.

BRAKING

Despite all the work, particularly in the U.S.A., to cocoon the occupants of a car against the results of an accident the author still believes that more thought should be given to improving handling and braking under adverse conditions so that accidents are less likely to happen. Anti-lock braking could give a worthwhile contribution to this safety philosophy.

Those drivers who feel confident they can handle a car safely on slippery roads should consider the results of an exhaustive survey recently carried out by Calspan Corporation under the auspices of General Motors. Sixty men and forty women, all carefully selected as representative of typical road users, with an average age of 38 and an average driving experience of 19 years, were subjected to a series of driving tests. The report stated 'The typical driver did not use the full potential of the car in terms of its cornering capabilities and handling qualities. In most instances, the driver resorted to hard or panic braking in simulated emergency situations, often locking up all four wheels and thus losing steering control.'

An interesting sidelight was that the men were shown to be more aggressive in their driving. They drove at higher speeds, but were not shown to be any more capable of handling a car in an emergency than the women. When asked to rate their driving ability *before taking the tests* 54 of the 60 men said they were above average; only 20 of the 40 women made this claim. There is no need for comment on this aspect of the tests, but the case for the provision of a braking system that is less dependent on driver ability is well demonstrated.

Many accidents occur through panic braking. With locked rear wheels the car either spins or yaws into the approaching traffic. With locked front wheels the car slides in a straight line, despite the efforts of the driver to steer the car. An experienced driver with a cool head can use the quick on-off-on-off brake application technique on slippery surfaces to take advantage of the relatively efficient braking given just before the wheels lock-up completely. A system that senses the onset of wheel lock-up and uses the on-off-on-off technique automatically would turn us all into top rally drivers — in one aspect at least. It has been shown that on most flooded, greasy or icy surfaces maximum braking force is given with a slip of 10 to 15 per cent relative to the road surface. At 100 per cent slip, i.e. a locked wheel, the braking force is negligible. On a dry surface in good condition, however, the degree of slip is not important and good braking is given with locked wheels.

Dunlop was the first firm to make a serious attempt to introduce anti-lock braking with their Maxaret system in the late fifties. Pioneer work on this system led to the introduction of small-scale production on the Jenson FF (Formula Ferguson) four wheel drive sports saloon. The Maxaret system had a wheel-locking sensor with an on-off frequency of about six cycles per second. Later systems, such as the WSP (Wheel Slide Protection) system developed by Girling and Lucas in Great Britain and the Bosch system in Germany have a re-cycle time of 10 to 12 per second. A very high speed of response is essential since a wheel may pass from a dry surface, across a patch of ice, then back to a dry surface again in even less time than a sixth of a second.

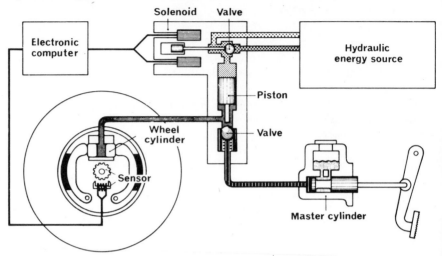

Fig. 13.18   Diagram of the Bosch anti-lock braking system.

Figure 13.18 is a diagram of the Bosch system. The pressure-relieving piston is normally held in the lower position during braking by the anti-lock pressure system. Release of pressure on the wheel cylinder is triggered by a signal from the wheel-lock sensor to the electronic control box. An electronic pulse from this opens a solenoid-operated ball valve, thus releasing the pressure above the piston. The piston rises, thus relieving the pressure on the wheel cylinder and, by means of a stalk on the base of this piston, isolating the normal brake pressure by closing another ball valve. In this Bosch system the pressure relieving piston is held in the lower position by the superior pressure of the anti-lock system. This hydraulic pressure is supplied from a reservoir and an electrically-driven pump that continues to operate from battery voltage if the engine stops.

With the Girling-Lucas WSP system the pressure relieving piston is held in the minimum volume position by a strong spring. Failure of the electrically-driven pump in this system therefore leaves the normal braking fully operative. Most of the difficulties associated with anti-lock braking have now been solved. Some development engineers are approaching the concept of full-scale production with great caution, perhaps a commendable failing when lives are at stake if unexpected defects are revealed by the hard school of public abuse.

THE LONG-LIFE CAR

Since we pay so much for a well-engineered sports car today, it is a logical step to design the car for long life. This is a very complex subject and is certainly contrary to the policy of planned obsolescence that has kept Detroit in business for so long. However, we are the customers and the idea of a car that will last about twenty years appeals to many of us. Today we work hard to earn money so that we can buy a new car every two or three years so that other men in the motor industry can also keep on working hard, etc, etc. Meanwhile the raw materials we need for new cars are becoming more and more scarce and the mountains of rusty old cars are such an embarrassment that some authorities are dumping them in the sea. A few companies are beginning to look at the concept of the Long-Life Car, notably Volvo and Porsche whose cars are already well respected for their durability. We should give them every encouragement.

14

Design studies

THE JAGUAR

William Lyons began as a body builder fifty-five years ago. It was therefore fitting that his final act before retiring was to assist the late Malcolm Sayer to design the body for the XJ-S sports car. Malcolm Sayer was a brilliant aerodynamicist and over the years Sir William had developed an uncanny flair for designing bodies that appealed to the public.

The early bodies that were made by the Swallow Side Car and Coach Building Company in Blackpool were rather flamboyant and many connoisseurs of the period suggested they were even vulgar. Perhaps the bonnet and scuttle of the SS1 was too long for a car with such a small engine and a top speed of only about 65 m.p.h., but William Lyons was selling his cars to the public, not to connoisseurs and the public associated long bonnets with dashing exotic sports cars. After the long years of the Depression they yearned for exciting sports cars. Unfortunately, they were not able to afford them. The SS1 was in truth a 'dream car'.

The years 1933 to 1935 marked a turning point in the William Lyons story. The motor-cycle sidecar business was sold to a sub-contractor and a public company was formed to make nothing but cars. This new company, SS Cars Ltd, would no longer build bodies to fit chassis made by other companies. They began to design and build their own cars. Bill Heynes left the Humber Company in 1935 to start work on a new chassis, a conventional design, but one with an exceptionally stiff frame and excellent Girling brakes. Harry Weslake designed two new six-cylinder overhead valve engines and it was in September 1935 that the new SS Jaguars were announced. At a price of £285 for the 1½ litre model and £365 for the 2½ litre they were remarkable value for money. Many wondered how long they would hold together and must have been rather disappointed when they eventually saw them survive to become valuable classic cars. The Jaguars were handsome, comfortable and well constructed and the 2½ and 3½ litre 2-seater SS 100s that followed in 1936 and 1937 were not only fine cars, they were real sports cars. That, after all is the subject of this book. The 3½ litre model gave a genuine 100 m.p.h., very rare in pre-war sports cars and would accelerate from 0 to 60 m.p.h. in 12 seconds.

After the war the company name was changed again, this time to Jaguar Cars Ltd, and their first sports car, shown for the first time at the 1948 Motor Show in London, was the memorable XK120, a car that is now cherished as a major classic. Few cars have been welcomed with such enthusiasm as the XK120. In those early post-war years the British public was still rationed for food, excitement and personal transport. The news of this truly beautiful magnificent sports car spread so fast there was no need for high-pressure publicity. Jaguar had certainly built 'a better mousetrap' and the public beat a path to their door.

Many of the small companies that existed by assembling fairly effective and rugged sports cars from bits and pieces supplied from various component manufacturers found they could no longer compete with this fine new sports car. During the fifties the XK120, the XK140 and XK150 continued to challenge the best in Europe. Later variants were more close to racing cars, being developed to meet the increasing opposition from Ferrari, Maserati and Mercedes-Benz on the racing circuits of the world. This was the heyday of sports car racing for Jaguar and the C-Type and D-Type scored an impressive list of successes including five outright wins at Le Mans. The production Jaguars had many successes. The XK120 shown in Figure 14.1 was a replacement for NUB120, now in the Jaguar museum. NUB120 driven by Ian Appleyard with his wife Pat (née Lyons) as navigator, won a Coupe des Alpes three times in succession.

After a serious fire at the Browns Lane Works in 1957 production plans for a modified version of the D-Type, to be sold on the American market as the XK-SS, were abandoned. The design and development departments concentrated their efforts on a completely new sports car, one using independent rear suspension on a Jaguar for the first time. This was the XK-E usually called the 'E-Type.'

The E Type, introduced in 1961, maintained the tradition that had started with the XK120, that a production sports car should be docile in traffic, well-mannered at all times and comfortable on a long journey. Many American housewives, taught to drive at High School on an American sedan with automatic transmission, are not daunted by this piece of exotic machinery and love to use it to bring home the groceries. The engine in the E Type was still the long stroke 6-cylinder engine shown in Figure 3.8. This engine first appeared in 1948 with a bore of 83 mm and a stroke of 106 mm to give a swept volume of 3.44 litres. The bore of the E Type was increased to give a capacity of 3.8 litres and later, with a bore of 92.07 mm the capacity rose to 4.235 litres. Since the stroke remained at 106 mm the engine lost some of its extreme stroke/bore ratio. Even so, Ferrari, Lotus, Maserati, Mercedes and Porsche had all gone over-square by this time.

Fig. 14.1 The William Lyons touch. The aesthetic aerodynamic appeal of the XK120 Jaguar, introduced in 1948. Ian and Pat Appleyard in the Alpine Rally. (*Motor* photograph).

The E Type body was as advanced in style as its engine was old-fashioned. In some respects the oval cross-section was reminiscent of the earlier D Type and the appearance of the car was welcomed by the aficionada who write in such magazines as 'Car and Driver' and 'Road and Track'. The latter magazine described it as 'The greatest crumpet collector known to man.' This could be true, but we are concerned here with technical matters and their criticism of the archaic gearbox with its slow synchromesh and very long travel between gears was well merited. A car with such potential can be ruined if so much time is wasted changing gears. Jaguar became aware of this criticism and an excellent 4-speed gearbox appeared in 1964 to make the car a delight to drive.

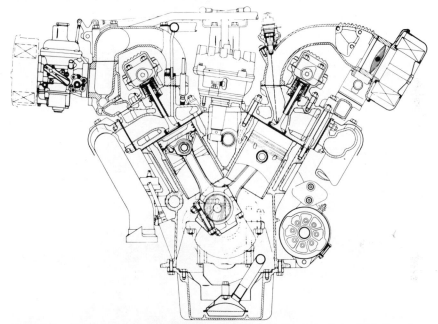

Fig. 14.2   V-12 engine cross-section showing carburettor layout on the left and fuel injection on the right.

In 1971 the E Type appeared with a new engine, a 12-cylinder of 5.342 litres with the cylinders arranged in a 60 degree V. The bore was 90 mm and the stroke 70 mm, in striking contrast to the stroke/bore ratio of the older 6-cylinder engine. In the development programme leading up to this engine there were two parallel projects, the first engine having a double overhead camshaft head on each bank of cylinders, the second having only a single OHC head per bank. The first engine, as one would expect developed more power — about 30 per cent in competition tune and about 10 per cent more in its planned production form. For several reasons the DOHC design was dropped, the major reason being the width between the outer camboxes and the additional height. The width conflicted with the space needed to give sufficient steering lock and the height of this engine could not be accommodated under the falling bonnet-line planned for the new generation of Jaguars.

THE XJ-S

The new series of Jaguar saloons offer a choice of three engine sizes, two 6-cylinder of 3.4 and 4.2 litres and the new 12-cylinder of 5.3 litres. For the new sports car, the XJ-S, introduced in September 1975 only the V-12 is fitted. The finalised production engine is fitted with Lucas electronic fuel injection as described in Chapter five and Lucas electronic ignition as described in Chapter six. It will be seen from Figures 14.3 and 14.4 that the XJ-S bears little resemblance to the E Type. It is also substantially larger, being 11 cm (4.5 in) wider and 43 cm (17 in) longer.

Fig. 14.3   Front view of Jaguar XJ-S.

The new XJ-S has been classified by some motoring journalists as a 'sports saloon', not a sports car. This could be true. In the words of *Motor* it is 'one of the world's most desirable cars.' They also say it is 'no replacement for Jaguar's classic two-seater.' The two-seater sports car has always been a young man's car and it would appear that the Leyland marketing organisation has decided the supply of young men who can afford a two-seater with a top speed of 150 m.p.h., a fuel consumption of about 14 m.p.g. and an insurance premium well into three figures is fast running out. For these young men they offer the Triumph Spitfire and TR7 and the MG Midget and MGB. The market they

Fig. 14.4 Ghosted view of XJ-S.

Fig. 14.5   The V-12 engine installed. A very full engine compartment.

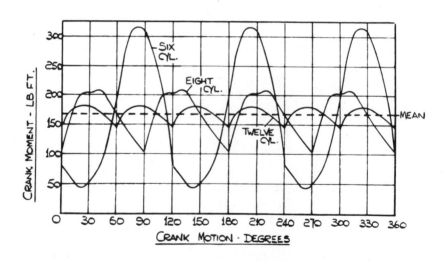

Fig. 14.6   Torque characteristics of 6, 8 and 12-cylinder engines.

envisage for the XJ-S is the more mature and certainly the more financially successful businessman. In this class the new Jaguar 'sports saloon' is highly competitive. The Aston Martin DBS which could be bought for under £8000 in 1972 now costs £16,999. In these hard times even a well-paid top executive will be tempted when replacing his older Aston Martin by the new Jaguar at £12,500. Even today there are still a few customers left for Aston Martin. There is already a long waiting list for the new Lagonda recently announced at an estimated selling price of £30,000.

The engine

Many aspects of the engine have already been covered in the rest of the book. An external view of the engine is given in Figure 14.5. It lacks the finely sculptured beauty that we once saw under the bonnet of a Bugatti or the early

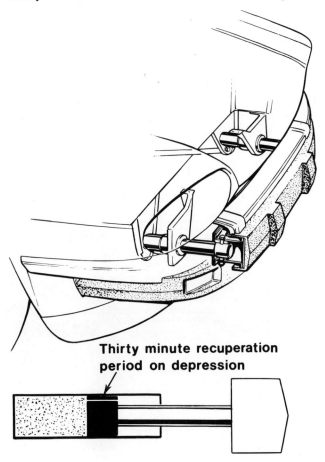

Thirty minute recuperation period on depression

Fig. 14.7 The XJ-S 'hydraulic' bumper. The working fluid is a silicone wax.

Ferraris. The impression is of a plumber's nightmare. Fortunately the rest of the XJ-S has more aesthetic appeal and the inside of the engine compartment should only be seen today by garage mechanics — at fairly infrequent intervals.

The smooth torque given by the V-12 is well illustrated in Figure 14.6. Torque variations are not great on a V-8; a V-12 is almost as smooth as a turbine. The power of the new engine is 285 b.h.p. DIN. The 4.2 litre E Type engine had an advertised power of 265 b.h.p., but these were SAE *gross* figures, a gross exaggeration as explained in Chapter twelve. Aluminium alloy is used for the major structural components of the new engine, an open deck sand casting in LM 25 for the block/crankcase and LM 25WP for the cylinder head. The tappet block, oil cooler, induction system, and all external covers are in aluminium alloy. The sump, however, is a steel pressing, a sensible precaution against the more venturesome drivers who occasionally knock holes in cast sumps on rocky terrains.

Special features of the XJ-S

The body
The steel monocoque body shell is designed to meet all current Federal safety regulations. It incorporates '5 m.p.h. — no damage' bumpers which act like the hydraulic buffers at railway terminals. The hydraulic medium is a silicone wax which absorbs the kinetic energy of the impact and slowly restores the bumper

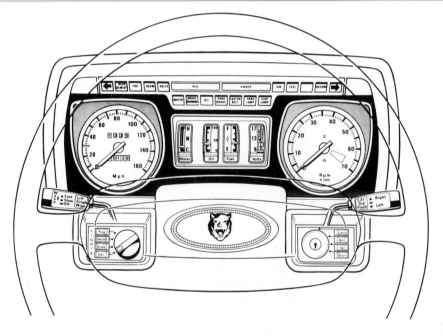

Fig. 14.8   The XJ-S instrument binnacle and fingertip controls. A study in ergonomics.

Fig. 14.9 The XJ-S front seats.

Fig. 14.10 The XJ-S rear seats.

to its original position. Anyone with a pre-disposition to 'parking by ear' should remember that the two struts take about thirty seconds to regain their normal position.

The new Jaguar body is well sound-proofed by means of damping pads and deep-pile felt-backed carpeting. In this respect the car is a serious challenge to the most expensive luxury cars. Anyone equating sports cars with noise and fury should look elsewhere for his next car. The XJ-S is designed to give high performance with the minimum of fuss.

The instruments

The XJ-S instruments are contained in a single nacelle as shown in Figure 14.8. Between the speedometer and the tachometer the four critical indicators of water temperature, oil pressure, fuel contents and battery conditions are grouped together for easy reading. Along the top of the nacelle are 18 warning lights to monitor 18 major mechanical and safety functions. The instrument nacelle is wired by printed circuits and connected into the main wiring loom by two multi-pin plugs.

General specification

Engine

Type	Four-stroke — petrol engine — water cooled	
No. of cylinders	12 in 60° Vee	
Bore	90mm	3.54 ins
Stroke	70mm	2.76 ins
Capacity	5343 cc	326 cu ins
Piston area	763.2 cm²	118 sq ins
Compression ratio	9.0:1	

Performance

Power	285 DIN HP at 5800 rpm	
Torque	40.7 mkg	294 lbs/ft at 3500 rpm

Cylinder block

Type	Open deck
Material	Aluminium alloy LM25
Pistons	Aluminium alloy solid skirt with combustion chamber in top.
Piston rings	Three — two compression and one multi-rail oil control.
Crankshaft	Three plane, seven main bearings. Tufftrided manganese molybdenum steel.

Cylinder heads

Material	Aluminium alloy LM25 WP
Camshafts	Two — one per bank
Valve layout	Single overhead camshafts operating bucket type tappets.
Valve lift	9.525 mm 0.375 ins

Engine *continued*

Tappets type	Inverted bucket	
Tappet clearance inlet	0.30—0.35 mm	0.012—0.014 ins
exhaust	0.30—0.35 mm	0.012—0.014 ins
Valve timing inlet	17° BTDC	59° ABDC
exhaust	59° BBDC	17° ATDC

Sump

Type	Steel pressing with internal baffles.

Lubrication

Type	Pressure	
Pump type	Internal and external gear with crescent type cut-off.	
Normal running pressure	4.9 kg/sq cm	70 psi
Filter	Full flow paper element.	

Ignition

Type	Lucas Opus Mk II electronic.
Firing order	1a, 6b, 5a, 2b, 3a, 4b, 6a, 1b, 2a, 5b, 4a, 3b.
Distributor	Lucas magnetic impulse type.
Ignition timing	Stroboscopic 10 BTDC at 750 rpm
Spark plugs	Champion N10Y
Gap	0.625 mm 0.025 ins

Injection
Type	Lucas electronic manifold injection.
Enrichment	Automatic cold start injector.
Induction manifolds	Two 6-branch aluminium alloy.

Fuel system
Type	Recirculating.
Pump	Lucas electric permanent magnet motor.
Fuel specification	97 octane — four star.

Electrical equipment
Polarity	Negative.
Battery	Lucas CP 13
Battery capacity	68 amps at 20 hour rate.
Starter	Pre-engaged
Alternator	Lucas 20 ACR
Alternator capacity	60 amps at 3500 engine rpm.
Horns	Twin Lucas self earthing.

Cooling system
Type	Water pressurised. Impeller pump belt driven off crankshaft.
Pressure	1.056 kg/cm^2 15 psi
Radiator	Marston Superpak crossflow.
Thermostat	Two wax type opening at 82° C
Fans	12 bladed steel fan with viscous coupling and thermostatically controlled electric 4 bladed fan.

Exhaust
Layout	Four downpipes merge into two double skinned pipes. Two main and two rear silencers.
Exhaust emissions (North America)	Exhaust emission controls incorporate exhaust port air injection, exhaust gas recirculation and a catalytic reactor for each bank.
Evaporative loss	Engine anti-run-on valve. Vapour from the fuel tank is piped via a separator cannister to a charcoal cannister which is purged by manifold depression.

Transmission
Manual
Gearbox	4-speed all synchromesh.	
Clutch	Single dry plate.	
Plate diameter	267 mm	10.5 ins

Automatic
Gearbox	Borg Warner Model 12 3-speed.
Torque Convertor	2.0:1 ratio

Transmission *continued*

Ratios	Manual	Automatic
	1st 3.238:1	2.39:1
	2nd 1.905:1	1.45:1
	3rd 1.389:1	1.0:1
	4th 1.0:1	
	Rev 3.428:1	2.09:1
Axle ratios	3.07:1	3.07:1
Overall ratios	Manual	Automatic
	1st 9.94:1	7.34/14.68
	2nd 5.85:1	4.46/8.92
	3rd 4.26:1	3.07/6.14
	4th 3.07:1	
	Rev 10.51	6.41/12.82

Brakes
Type	Disc brakes all round.	
Layout	Dual circuit split front to rear with pressure differential warning actuator.	
Servo	In line tandem vacuum servo.	
Discs – front	Type	Ventilated cast iron.
	Diameter	284 mm 11.18 ins.
Discs – rear	Type	Cast iron with damper ring in periphery.
	Diameter	263 mm 10.38 ins
Calipers – front	4 piston caliper	
Calipers – rear	2 piston caliper	
Friction materials	Discs – Ferodo 2430	
Rubbed area		
– front	1624 cms^2	252 sq ins
– rear	956 cms^2	148 sq ins
–total	2580 cms^2	400 sq ins

Suspension
Front layout	Fully independent semi-trailing wishbones and coil springs. Anti-dive geometry. Girling Monitube dampers. Anti-roll bar.
King pin inclination	$1\frac{1}{2}^\circ \pm \frac{1}{4}^\circ$
Castor angle	$3\frac{1}{2}^\circ \pm \frac{1}{4}^\circ$
Camber angle	Positive $\frac{1}{2}^\circ \pm \frac{1}{4}^\circ$
Alignment	1.39–3.12 mm $^1/_{16}$–0.125 ins
Springs – free length	12–14 ins
– rate	423 lb/ins
Anti-roll bar diameter	22.2 mm 0.875 ins
Rear layout	Lower transverse wishbones with drive shafts acting as upper links. Radius arms. Twin coil spring and damper units. Girling Monitube dampers. Anti-roll bar.

Suspension *continued*

Camber angle	¾° negative ± ¼°	
Anti-roll bar diameter	14 mm	0.562 ins

Wheels and tyres

Wheels – type	GKN Kent Alloy. Light alloy wheels to Jaguar design.
Size	6JK rim. 38.1 cms (15 ins) diameter.
Tyres	Dunlop SP Super steel braced with block tread pattern.
Size	205/70 VR 15

Steering

Type	Adwest power assisted rack and pinion with energy absorbing column.
Wheel diameter	393.7 mm 15.5 ins.
Turns lock to lock	3 turns
Overall ratio	16:1 with an 8 tooth pinion.
Pump	Saginaw rotary vane.

Body

Type	All steel monocoque construction. Two door four seater with forward opening bonnet and large boot.
Exterior features	Complete underbody protection. Driver's door mirror. Front air dam and undershield. Radio aerial. Flush fitting filler cap cover. Recessed door handles.
Bumpers	Wrap-around front and rear bumpers consisting of a steel armature mounted to Menasco struts and with a synthetic rubber cover. Designed to meet 5 mph impact tests.
Glass	Laminated windscreen with toughened side and rear windows. Tinted glass is standard. Electrically heated rear window.
Locks and keys	Doors are fitted with high anti-burst load locks with flush fitting interior and exterior handles. Electrically operated central door

Body *continued*

locks. Separate keys for ignition, doors and boot and glove locker. Bonnet release and locking lever below facia.

Dimensions

Overall –		
length	4.87 m	191.72 ins
height	1.26 m	49.65 ins
width	1.79 m	70.60 ins
Wheelbase	2.59 m	102.00 ins
Front track	1.47 m	58.00 ins
Rear track	2.49 m	58.60 ins
Ground clearance	140 mm	5.50 ins

Interior dimensions

Headroom –		
front	914 mm	36.0 ins
rear	826 mm	32.5 ins
Maximum width–front	1422mm	56.0 ins
width–rear	1346 mm	53.0 ins
Seat squab to brake pedal	521–362 mm	20.5–14.25 ins

Luggage compartment

Maximum –		
height	565 mm	22.25 ins
depth	572 mm	22.5 ins
width	991 mm	39.0 ins
Capacity	0.43m³	15 cu ft
Weight	1687 kg	3710 lb

(Weight includes automatic transmission, automatic air conditioning, energy absorbing bumpers, door side intrusion members, electric windows, central door locking, radio with electric aerial but less fuel).

THE LOTUS

Automobiles, like people, suffer the ignominy or enjoy the privileges of Class. Class is decided to some extent by money, but not entirely. The position in the Class structure depends upon public recognition, as many a Texas cattle-baron has learned. Rolls Royce, Cadillac, Ferrari and Mercedes-Benz have never known any other class but that of aristocracy, while Chevrolet, Volkswagen and Morris are unashamedly working class. In one generation Colin Chapman has pulled Lotus out of its lowly origins of the fifties when he made kit-cars to be assembled by young drivers with very little money but lots of enthusiasm, through the middle class status of the first Elite, the Elan and the Europa into what is now accepted by the motoring press as the top echelon of the Middle Classes, if not yet the Aristocracy. In January 1977 *Motor* compared the Esprit, the new Lotus mid-engined sports car costing £8000 very favourably with the Porsche 911 Lux at £11,500 and the Ferrari Dino 308 GT4 at £11,700. The front-engined Elite (the second model to carry this name) is now available with automatic transmission, air conditioning and electric windows. The Elite has four comfortable seats and is sometimes seen as a chauffeur-driven company car. Company cars with a touring fuel consumption of 25-30 miles per Imperial gallon are beginning to appeal today even to company accountants.

A coloured spread of the Lotus Elite with thoroughbred horses in the background is evocative (to those of us old enough to remember) of the Bugatti, *le pur sang* of the automobile world. One can look for points of similarity in the style and thoughts of these two creative engineers, but one essential difference is that 'value analysis' was not invented in Ettore Bugatti's day and would have been scorned by him if it had. Colin Chapman would be the first to point out that the Bugatti company did not survive. To survive as a sports car manufacturer one must strive, not only for near-perfection, but for near-perfection at an acceptable price.

Lotus Cars Ltd of Hethel, near Norwich, make about 3,000 cars a year, fewer than General Motors make before lunch. Colin Chapman has no desire to emulate General Motors in output, only in their ability to stay in business. They admit at Hethel that their slant-4 engine is in effect one half of a V-8, but they will study the market very carefully before they are tempted to put a 4-litre engine in one of their cars. In a world starved for fuel a 2-litre engine is very close to the optimum for a sports car.

Self-sufficiency is now the watchword at Hethel. For the first time since Colin Chapman began to build his own cars in a small lock-up garage in North London in 1948 he is no longer dependent on outside suppliers for engines. The Lotus 4-cylinder 16-valve DOHC engine has been developed into a remarkably smooth reliable power unit. The cylinder head and cylinder block are die-cast in aluminium alloy and all components are now manufactured in the new Lotus machine shop on tape-controlled machines. Bodies and chassis components are made at Hethel. Even the air conditioning units are made on site. The only bought-out major components are the gearboxes and final drive units, a practice not unknown among much larger companies.

In Chapter seven we advanced reasons for rejecting front-wheel drive for a

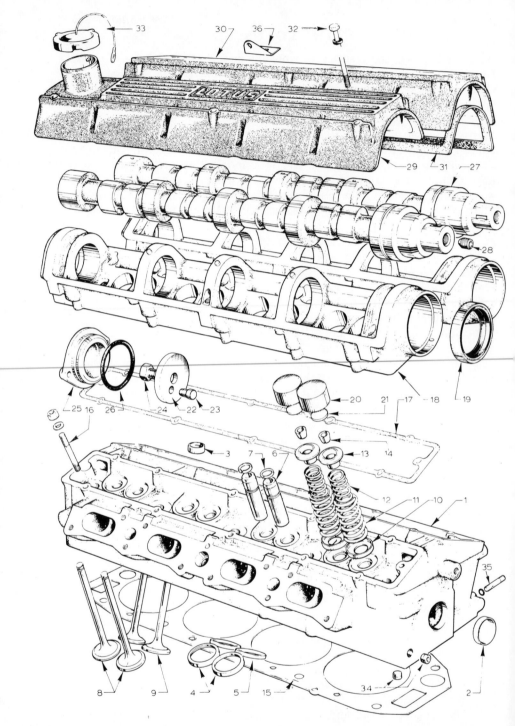

Fig. 14.11 Cylinder head and camshaft components on the Type 907 4-valve engine.

high performance vehicle. One can design a front wheel drive car to outperform all others in a fast bend, but it is possible to reach a *point of no return*. It is flattering to think that Colin Chapman is motivated by similar thoughts. Only two layouts are considered at Lotus. For a four-seater or 2 + 2 (what we once called an 'occasional 4-seater') Lotus prefer a front engine driving the rear wheels. For a more sporting 2-seater the engine is placed immediately behind the seats, a mid-engine layout with rear drive. The Elite and Eclat are variants on the first theme. The Esprit, designed for those with 'spirit' is a challenge to all those expensive continental mid-engined sports cars from the Ferrari Dino to the Lamborghini Urraco and, of course, to the Porsche 911 with its overhung rear engine.

THE ELITE

The 500 Series begins with the basic 501, no spartan specification this, since it is equipped with heater and radio, electric windows, heated rear window and rear window wiper and washer and inertia-reel front seat belts. The 502 specification carries the additions of air conditioning, stereo radio tape deck, quartz-halogen headlights, tinted glass and a more expensive trim. The 503 specification extends to power steering and the 504 carries an automatic transmission. Since lovers of automatics are assumed to be lazy the 504 specification also includes electric aerial extension.

The engine

This is a slant-4 with a cylinder bore size of 95.2 mm (3.75 in) and a stroke of 69.2 mm (2.72 in). The head, block, crankcase oilpan, camshaft carriers and cam covers are all die-cast in aluminium alloy. The engine is canted at an angle of 45 degrees to give the low bonnet-line necessary in the Elite to achieve the wedge profile. The provision of a timing-belt drive for the two overhead camshafts has been described in Chapter Four and an external view of the engine as used in the Team Lotus racing cars can be seen in Figure 4.7. An exploded view of the camshaft and cylinder head components is given in Figure 14.11. The inherent stiffness that an oversquare bore/stroke design gives to the short block and crankcase is well illustrated in Figure 14.2. The Lotus head shows a strong Cosworth influence, having a narrow valve angle and siamesed inlet porting to feed the 8 inlet valves. The 4 siamesed ports are fed by two Dellorto twin-choke DHLA 45E carburettors.

With a specific power of 80 b.h.p. per litre from a 4-cylinder engine one would have accepted a few years ago that a certain amount of roughness was inevitable. The continuous development of this Type 907 engine over a period of about five years has reduced mechanical noise and vibration to a low level. Oil consumption was a little high on early engines but this is now reduced to an acceptable negligible amount. Since the Elite was introduced in 1974 an intensive development programme has been carried out to refine the engine. Revised inlet ports have given improved torque at low speeds and a lighter flywheel has improved acceleration. The new standard of smoothness and freedom from vibration is given by careful matching of combustion chamber volumes and a higher standard of balancing of rotating and reciprocating components.

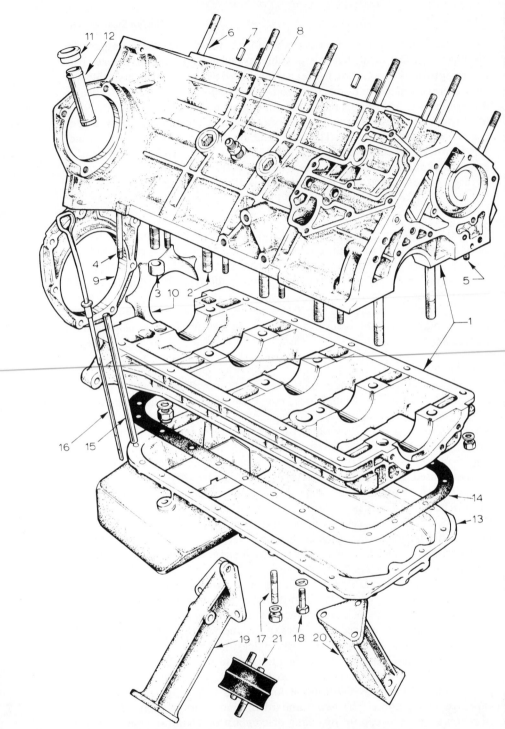

Fig. 14.12 Cylinder block, lower bearing housing and sump on the Lotus engine. Note the increased stiffness given by integrating the lower main bearing halves into a single ladder-like component.

Fig. 14.13 The Lotus Elite.

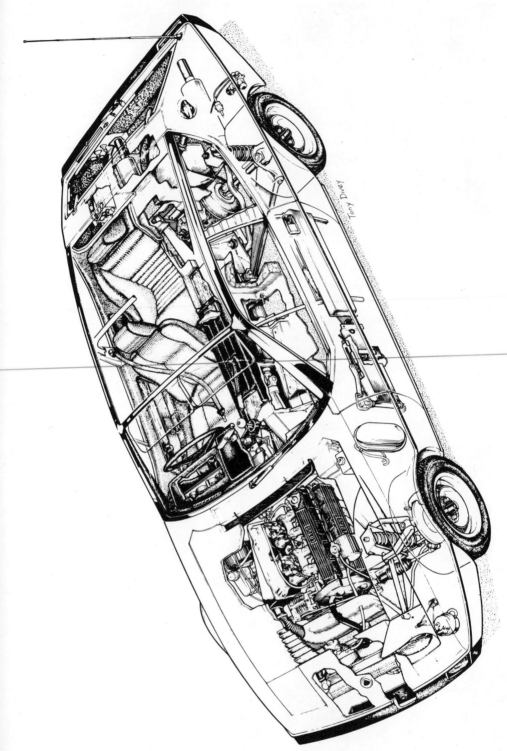

Fig. 14.14 The Lotus Elite; a ghosted view.

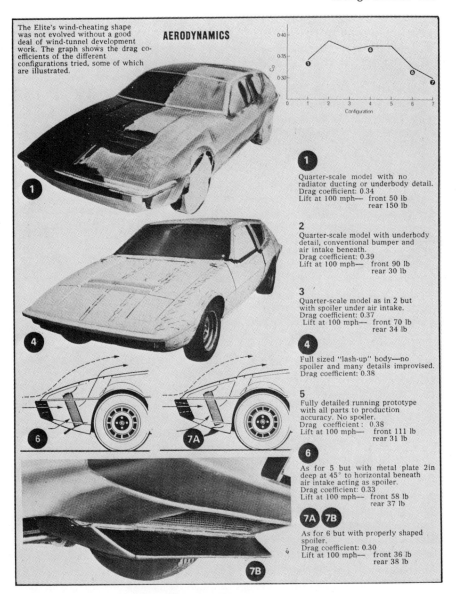

The Elite's wind-cheating shape was not evolved without a good deal of wind-tunnel development work. The graph shows the drag co-efficients of the different configurations tried, some of which are illustrated.

AERODYNAMICS

1
Quarter-scale model with no radiator ducting or underbody detail.
Drag coefficient: 0.34
Lift at 100 mph— front 50 lb
rear 150 lb

2
Quarter-scale model with underbody detail, conventional bumper and air intake beneath.
Drag coefficient: 0.39
Lift at 100 mph— front 90 lb
rear 30 lb

3
Quarter-scale model as in 2 but with spoiler under air intake.
Drag coefficient: 0.37
Lift at 100 mph— front 70 lb
rear 34 lb

4
Full sized "lash-up" body—no spoiler and many details improvised.
Drag coefficient: 0.38

5
Fully detailed running prototype with all parts to production accuracy. No spoiler.
Drag coefficient: 0.38
Lift at 100 mph— front 111 lb
rear 31 lb

6
As for 5 but with metal plate 2in deep at 45° to horizontal beneath air intake acting as spoiler.
Drag coefficient: 0.33
Lift at 100 mph— front 58 lb
rear 37 lb

7A 7B
As for 6 but with properly shaped spoiler.
Drag coefficient: 0.30
Lift at 100 mph— front 36 lb
rear 38 lb

Fig. 14.15 Wind tunnel testing of the Elite. Step by step improvements.

The gearbox

Originally introduced with a 4-speed box the Elite now uses a Lotus designed box with five speeds. Fourth drive is a direct drive with an effective ratio of 0.8 to 1 on fifth. 116 m.p.h. is given at 7,000 r.p.m. on fourth gear. The Elite can potter down to 30 m.p.h. in top gear, but for real acceleration the driver must

Fig. 14.16   The interior of the Elite

make full use of the gearbox. Since this has such an excellent slick gear change this is more of a pleasure than a chore.

For those who prefer it a ZF automatic transmission is available.

The body

The clean wedge profile of the Elite body can be seen in Figure 14.13. The ghosted drawing in Figure 14.14 also shows body construction details and other features such as the suspension layout. The GFRP body and its incredibly smooth surface finish has been fully described in Chapter nine. Figure 14.15 is a resumé of the wind tunnel development work that led to the final drag coefficient of 0.30, a reduction of 15 per cent on that given by the Europa. It is to be noted that the total *drag* of the Elite body will be higher than that of the Europa since the frontal area of the Elite is so much greater. The Elite is actually half an inch wider than the Rolls Royce Silver Shadow! It is of course much shorter and lower. By European standards this is wide for a 2-litre car and it tends to take up more than its share of the road in its native Norfolk lanes. In North American and Australia the Elite is still a small car. The Chevrolet Caprice and the Australian-built Ford Fairmont are both about three inches wider. In its own country the American sedan is given wide roads, wide parking slots and big garages. In such surrounding the Elite makes the typical 'compact' look very big.

With a front track of 4 ft 10½ in and a rear track of 4 ft 11 in, even wider than the Jaguar XJ-S, it would have been difficult to pare down the overall body width since the doors must be deep enough in section to accommodate the box-section girders needed to withstand the side impact test specification of the U.S. Federal laws. The interior of the Elite is carefully planned, giving space for the driver and front passenger of fairly ample proportions. By seating the rear passengers in a knees-up reclining position, that is much more comfortable than it sounds, it is possible to give quite acceptable rear seating for two 6 foot passengers in a car with a height below 4 feet. The interior of the Elite is shown in Figure 14.16.

General specification

Engine

Cylinders	4 in line
Capacity	1973 cc (120.4 cu in)
Bore/stroke	95.2/69.2 mm
	(3.75/2.72 in)
Cooling	Water
Block	Aluminium
Head	Aluminium
Valves	Dohc, 4 per cylinder
Valve timing	
inlet opens	25° btdc
inlet closes	65° abdc
ex opens	65° bbdc
ex closes	25° atdc
Compression	9.5:1
Carburetter	Two Dellorto DHLA 45E
Bearings	5 main
Fuel pump	SU electrical
Max power	155 bhp (DIN) at 6500 rpm
Max torque	135 lb ft (DIN) at 5000 rpm

Transmission

Type: 5 speed manual or automatic
Clutch: 8.5 ins (21.59 cms) diaphragm spring cable operated.

Manual Internal Ratios and mph/1000 rpm

5th (O/D)	0.800:1	20.8
4th	1.000:1	16.6
3rd	1.370:1	12.1
2nd	2.010:1	8.3
1st	3.200:1	5.2
Reverse	3.467:1	
Final drive	44.11:1 (optional 3.72:1)	

Automatic Internal Ratios and mph/1000 rpm

Drive	1.00:1	16.6
2nd	1.45:1	11.5
1st	2.39:1	6.96
Reverse	2.09:1	

Transmission *continued*

| Final drive | 4.11:1 |

Body/chassis

| Construction | GRP body, steel backbone chassis |
| Protection | Underseal on chassis with flame retarding resin and intumescent paints |

Suspension

| Front | Independent by wishbone, transverse link, coils, telescopic dampers, anti-roll bar bar |
| Rear | Independent by transverse link semi-trailing arm, coils, telescopic dampers |

Steering

Type	Rack and pinion
Assistance	Yes
Toe-in	0.125 ± 0.06 in
Camber	0° ± ½°
Castor	3° + 1° = ½°
King pin	9°
Rear toe-in	0.25 ± 0.06 in.

Brakes

Type	Disc front, inboard drum rear
Servo	Yes
Circuit	Dual

Wheels

Type	Alloy 7J x 14
Tyres	Dunlop SP Sports Super 205−14/60
Pressure	22 psi f/r (high speed)

Electrical

Battery	12 v 50 Ah
Polarity	Negative
Generator	Alternator, 60 A
Fuses	9
Headlights	2 x 75/70 W

The suspension

The shape of the backbone frame described in Chapter nine begins to make sense when the rear suspension is studied. A transverse beam at the rear of this frame provides a rigid structure to transmit the vertical loads from the coil spring mountings to the backbone. The narrowness of the backbone itself gives full scope to the designer to use long semi-trailing arms to locate the wheel hubs and to provide the desired amount of swing-axle effect. A perimeter frame as used by some earlier designers to support GFRP bodies would encroach on the space needed for long semi-trailing arms. The mid-engine position used on the Esprit does in fact encroach to a certain extent on this space as will be discussed later. Lateral location of the wheel hub on the Elite is provided by the fixed length drive shaft and a secondary lateral link.

The forked front section of the backbone frame carries vertical pillars on each side which act as upper spring locations for the front suspensions (See Figure 9.5). An upper wishbone link is used on the front suspension with a single lower transverse link and an anti-roll bar. Telescopic dampers are used front and rear.

Performance

The Elite cannot quite match the top speed or the vivid acceleration of the more powerful competition. On the credit side most of the competition needs at least 50 per cent more fuel to travel between two points. Maximum speed of the Elite is 20-25 m.p.h. lower than that of the 3-litre Ferrari Dino 308 GT and the 3-litre Maserati Merak, but a top speed of about 120 m.p.h. is high enough for most drivers. With a zero to 60 m.p.h. acceleration time of just under 8 seconds the Elite yields about 1.5 seconds to the Ferrari and the Maserati. On the credit side again it is difficult to find another 4-seater to match the cornering power of the Elite. The combination of Lotus suspension finesse and the new Dunlop 60 profile steel mesh radial tyres seems unbeatable. When tested by *Motor* they concluded their report as follows:-

'So highly do we regard this superb car in its latest form that all members of the test team were duty bound to sample it in order to renew the standards by which they must now judge rivals, some of them much more expensive than the Lotus.'

THE ECLAT

The Eclat is not a full 4-seater like the Elite. It is a more sporty 2 + 2 for those who prefer the engine at the front and will sacrifice a little space and headroom at the rear to reduce the frontal area slightly and reduce the weight by about 40 kg (90 lb). The Eclat does not have an opening rear window as on the Elite. The roof line is lower at the rear and the rear view afforded to the driver is also reduced. The luggage space, oddly enough, is slightly larger.

There is a basic Eclat, priced £1100 below that of the cheapest Elite. This Type 520 Eclat is the only option with a 4-speed manual gearbox, 5½ J × 13 steel wheels and 70 profile Goodyear G800 Grand Prix tyres. The 521, 522 and

Fig. 14.17 The Eclat

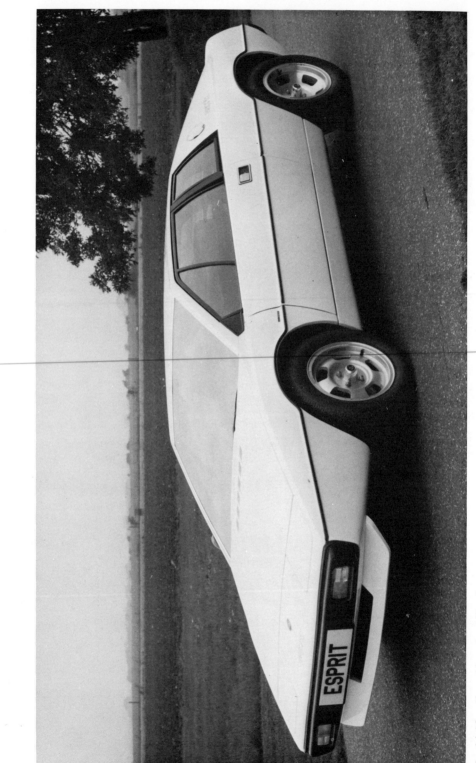

Fig. 14.18   the mid-engined Esprit.

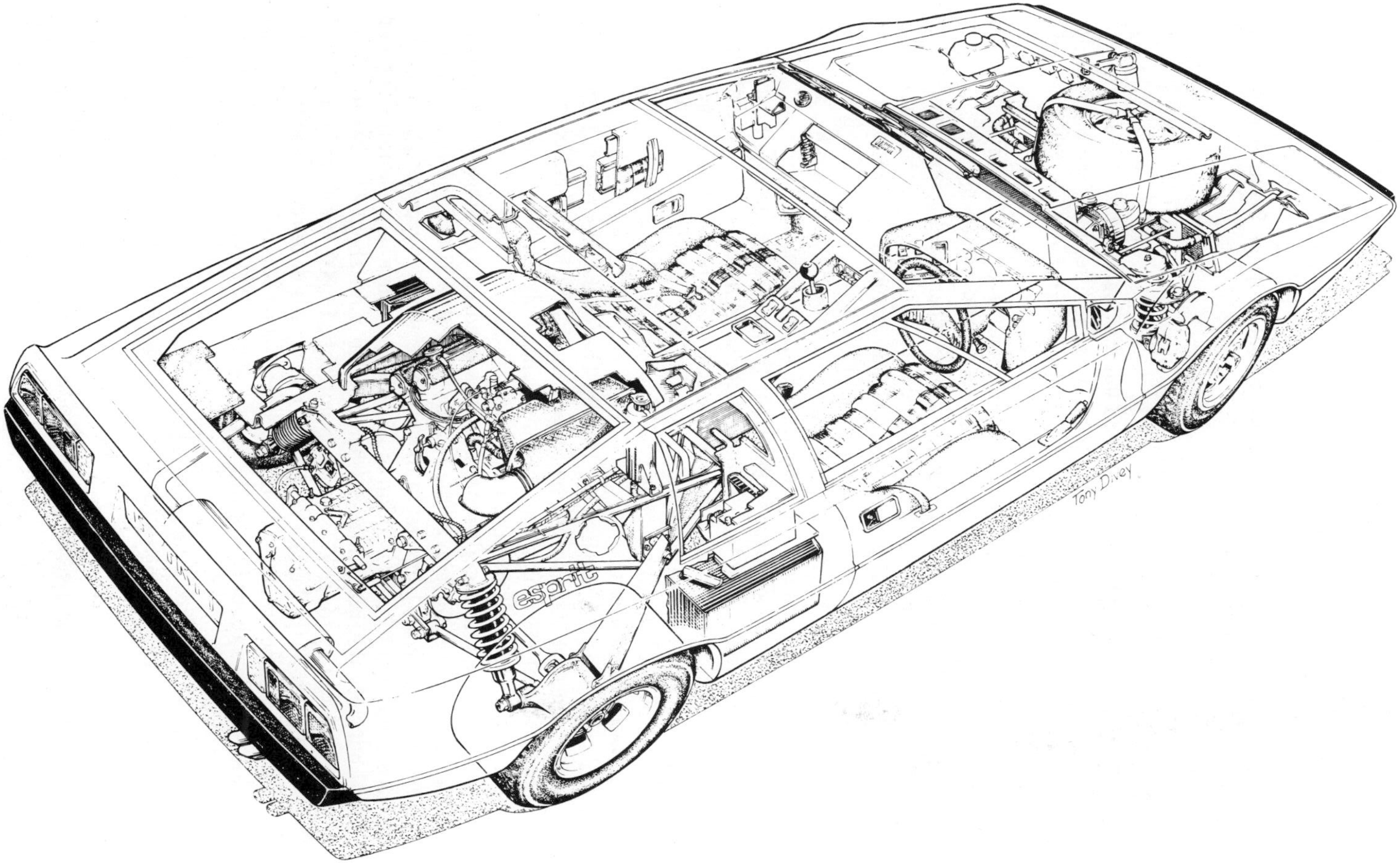

Fig. 14.19 The Esprit, a ghosted view.

523 are equipped with 7J × 14 alloy wheels and the more expensive Dunlop SP Sports Super 205/60 VR tyres. They also have a five-speed manual gearbox as in the Elite. The 522 carries the air conditioning option and the 523 has power steering. Automatic transmission is not available on the Eclat. A rear view of the Eclat is shown in Figure 14.17.

THE ESPRIT

If the Elite is the replacement for the Elan it is logical to see the Esprit as the replacement for the Europa. This is an oversimplification. There was little in common in the external appearance of these earlier models. The three new Lotuses, however all bear a strong family likeness.

The Europa came in for much criticism for its poor visibility, particularly over the rear-quarters. Not all the criticism was fair. One editor of a New York car magazine made fun of the difficulties he experienced getting in and out of the car. In truth he was really too old and too fat for a Europa! Very few active young men complained on this score, but the Renault power unit only produced 67 b.h.p. in the original form and 78 b.h.p. in the S2 version. The car was aerodynamically efficient and this gave it a top speed of 115 m.p.h., but the car sadly lacked acceleration for a car with such potential.

The body on the new Esprit follows the general wedge outline of the Elite. In fact the lower half of the body is made in the same mould as the Elite. Body and interior were styled by the European designer Gingiaro. He gave the body an even lower profile than the Elite and Eclat. With a height of 3 ft 7¾ in, the Esprit is 3¾ in lower than the ferrari Dino and the Porsche 911 at 4 ft 4 ins in almost towers above it.

The kerb weight of the Esprit is 1980 lb. That of the Europa was 1465 lb. With an allowance of 300 lb for 2 passengers the Esprit has an effective power to weight ratio of 157 b.h.p./ton; the Europa had only 99. Where the Europa took 10.7 seconds to reach 60 m.p.h. from rest, the Esprit takes 6.8 seconds and will reach 100 m.p.h. in slightly more than 20 seconds. To complete the comparison the power to weight ratio of the Ferrari Dino 308 GT4 is 182 b.h.p./ton. The Dino will accelerate from rest to 100 m.p.h. in about 16 seconds. The Esprit will give a touring fuel consumption of 25 miles per Imperial gallon, the Dino only 18, but does this really matter when one has paid about £12,000 for the car delivered to the door? The Esprit is not only £3,000 less expensive than this lowest prices of the Ferrari range, but a comparison of replacement part costs must carry some weight, even to pop stars. To replace a broken windscreen on the Lotus costs about £80, on the Ferrari about £220, on a Lamborghini about £450.

An external view of the Esprit is given in Figure 14.18, a ghosted line drawing in Figure 14.19. The interior is shown in Figure 14.20.

The engine

The same engine is used in all three models. In the Esprit, however, it occupies

Fig. 14.20 The interior of the Esprit.

the space allocated to the rear passengers in the Elite, driving the rear wheels through a transaxle, the gearbox being overhung as in modern racing cars.

The gearbox

Maserati, now under the financial control of the Citroen company, make the 5-speed transaxle for this Lotus model. The gear linkage was originally designed for the Maserati-powered Citroen SM and is found to give the proverbial butter-slicing changes, no mean achievement with such a remote gearbox location. As in the front-engined models fifth gear is used as an overdrive, although in this gearbox none of the gears give a direct drive.

The body

The chisel-nose of the Esprit is even lower than that of the Elite and Eclat, since the only major bulk housed at the front is the spare wheel. This, in practice can be a disadvantage since the front extremities of the car cannot be seen when parking. A similar objection can be raised to the rear visibility. On the open road this is no great handicap since there is a rearview mirror and very few cars attempt to pass. There has been a marked improvement on the letter-box slot rear window with built-in side blinkers that damned the Europa in the motoring press. The Esprit demands a change in driving technique when entering angled road junctions. The drivers of vans (panel trucks) have a good survival rate in modern traffic conditions and they have an inferior rear quarter vision. If we may throw out a wild suggestion, is it not possible to use fibre-optics or some other periscopic system to transfer a view of what lies behind the car on a display panel in front of the driver?

The suspension

Front and rear suspension are identical in principle to that used so successfully in the Elite. One noticeable difference is the shortening of the semi-trailing links in the Esprit. This is necessitated by the mid-engine location. The Esprit has 205/60 HR 14 tyres at the front and 205/70 HR 14 at the rear. The tyre pressures of 18 p.s.i. front and 28 p.s.i. rear reflect this imbalance, accentuated further by the rear-end weight bias resulting from the engine location.

Despite these fundamental differences from the front-engined Lotuses the Esprit corners and handles so well that the majority of professional testers are tempted to 'chicken-out' from testing to the ultimate. The low polar moment of inertia makes the Esprit more responsive to rapid changes in direction than the Elite and the Elite is no sluggard by contemporary standards. If the driver ever becomes so carried away as to exceed the limits of adhesion on a tight bend the car spins off, which is usually much safer than ploughing straight ahead.

Performance

When tested by *Motor* the Esprit carried a total weight, included 100 lb of test equipment, of 2630 lb. This was 370 lb lighter than the fully equipped Elite tested 18 months earlier by the same magazine. The Esprit is higher geared; 5.69 m.p.h. per 1000 r.p.m. in bottom gear and 8.56 m.p.h. per 1000 r.p.m. in second versus values of 5.2 and 8.3 on the Elite. This higher gearing tends to offset the weight advantage and the acceleration figures for 0-60 m.p.h. and 0-100 m.p.h. were only marginally reduced. The top speed was not measured but was adjudged to be in excess of 130 m.p.h. or about 10 m.p.h. faster than the Elite. Such figures do not express the appeal of the Esprit. It is not sufficient to say 'the Esprit is an enthusiasts car' since Lotus have been making nothing else since they went into business. The Esprit is much closer to the modern racing car which is controlled in a corner as much by the accelerator as by the steering wheel.

General specification

Engine

Cylinders	4 in line
Capacity	1973 cc (120.4 cu in)
Bore/stroke	95.2/62.9 mm
	(3.75/2.72 in)
Cooling	Water
Block	Aluminium
Head	Aluminium
Valves	Dohc
Valve timing	
inlet opens	27.5° btdc
inlet closes	52.5° abdc
ex opens	52.5° bbdc
ex closes	27.5° atdc
Compression	9.5:1
Carburettor	2 Dellorto DH LA 45E

Engine *continued*

Bearings	5
Fuel pump	SU electrical
Max power	160 bhp (DIN) at 6200 rpm
Max torque	140 lb ft (DIN) at 4900 rpm

Transmission

| Type | 5 speed manual |
| Clutch | 8.5 in dia diaphragm spring |

Internal ratios and mph/100 rpm

Top	0.760:1/22.1
4th	0.970:1/17.3
3rd	1.320:1/12.7
2nd	1.940:1/8.7
1st	2.920:1/5.8
Rev	3.460:1
Final drive	4.375:1

Body/chassis

Construction	GRP body, steel backbone chassis
Protection	Undersealant on chassis

Suspension

Front	Ind. by unequal length wishbones, coil springs and anti-roll bar
Rear	Ind. by lower transverse links, fixed length drive-shafts, semi-trailing arms and coil springs

Steering

Type	Rack and pinion
Assistance	None
Toe-in	3–5 mm (0.12 – 0.20 in)
Camber	0–½°
Castor	3° ± ½°
King pin	9°
Rear toe-in	8-10mm (0.32 – 0.39 in)

Brakes

Type	Discs all round (inboard at rear)
Servo	Yes
Circuit	Split, front/rear
Rear valve	No
Adjustment	Self-adjusting

Wheels

Type	Alloy sports pattern; 7J rear; 6J front
Tyres	205/70 HR 14 rear; 205/60 HR 14 Dunlop SP Sport front
Pressures	18 psi front; 27 psi rear

Electrical

Battery	12V, 44Ah
Polarity	Negative earth
Generator	Alternator
Fuses	4
Headlights	4x5″ Sealed beam 75/60 watt

THE MERCEDES

The history of the Daimler-Benz Company is the history of the automobile itself. If we dismiss the vague claims of Lenoir in 1862 and Markus in 1875 as the inventors of the first petrol driven automobile we are left with the well-authenticated claims of Gottlieb Daimler and Karl Benz between 1885 and 1886. After working on the test bed in 1885, Daimler's four-stroke petrol engine was installed in what became his first limited production road vehicles at the end of that year. Karl Benz was working on a two-stroke engine as early in 1880, but his motor vehicle patent only appeared in 1886. The merits of the four-stroke engine were known to Benz but Otto had already patented the system in 1877. Benz worked for five years on a three cylinder engine in which one cylinder pre-compressed the air, one pre-compressed the combustible gas and the third was the working cylinder. By the time Benz was able to finance the construction of his first motor vehicle in 1885 Otto's patent had been challenged in the courts and invalidated. It was July 1886 before the first Benz three-wheeler petrol-driven carriage appeared on the public roads, fitted with a single cylinder four-stroke engine having cam-operated valves and electric ignition. On this evidence it would appear that Daimler had the prior claim to the first practical automobile. Professor Kurt Schnauffer of the Technische Hochschule at Munich, who has made a study of the subject, insists that 'Carl' Benz made the first successful automobile. He also spells his Christian name with a 'C', while the Daimler-Benz literature use a 'K'. It is purely a question for historians. Since the two companies started by these great pioneers amalgamated in 1926 all rivalry on this issue must surely have died.

Gottlieb Daimler must have guessed that sales would soon take off like a rocket but he died at the turn of the century and it was left to his old friend Wilhelm Maybach to take over the technical and commercial control of the company. Karl Benz died in 1929, three years after the amalgamation. Like Henry Ford he had always hated motor racing, but the success of Daimler under the forceful direction of Wilhelm Maybach and the excellent sales growth of this company that many attributed to their racing triumphs, eventually led to a change in the board policy at the Benz company. Karl Benz decided to retire in 1903 at this time and the new generation of Benz cars carried much larger engines and competed, with only modest success, in the hectic motor racing of the period. Their 60 horsepower 8-litre car won the Prince Henry Trial in 1907, but little else during the early years. They became more and more committed to the sport and their racing models grew to alarming proportions. The formidable Blitzen Benz of 1909 had a capacity of 21.5 litres from 4 OHV cylinders and developed 200 b.h.p. It achieved world fame as a record breaker when Barney Oldfield recorded a flying start mile of 131.72 m.p.h. in 1910.

Maybach's success with his own design of Daimler owed a little to the shrewd commercial presentation of the new 'Mercedes' model to the public, but much more to the excellence of the car itself. Emil Jellinek, a Hungarian entrepreneur ordered a relatively large number of these new cars on the understanding that he would receive the sole selling rights in America, Austria, Belgium, France and Hungary. Moreover he demanded a change of name to that of his daughter, Mercedes, It was not entirely sentiment that motivated this request. He knew that a German-sounding name would be a handicap to sales in some European countries. In Germany the new car was still called a Daimler, but after two years they decided to register the new name as a trade mark and to abandon the brand name Daimler.

In the spirit of the times Maybach designed the 1901 Mercedes as a production car that could be raced. He broke away from the concept of bigger and bigger engines epitomised by the Blitzen Benz since big inefficient engines only increase the weight and size of the transmission, axles, springs and chassis until the exercise becomes self-defeating. He also knew that the tyres of the period were not good enough to cope for long with such enormous weights. Barney Oldfield must have been a very brave man!

In a modest way Maybach adopted the design philosophy that we now see demonstrated in the modern Grand Prix car. He began to discard all unnecessary weight. For his four-in-line engine he adopted mechanically-operated inlet valves, at a time when suction-operated inlet valves were the norm. This made his engine more efficient and able to operate at higher r.p.m. Cylinders were cast in pairs in iron, but a light aluminium alloy crankcase was used. The customary heavy and clumsy serpentine tube radiator was replaced by a honeycomb radiator. Not only was the radiator much lighter but the cooling system content was reduced drastically giving a saving of about 30 lbs in water alone. There was a four-speed gearbox and a final drive by chains. With a power output of 35 b.h.p. from a capacity of 5.9 litres the new car was not quite as heavy as the 4 horsepower Daimler made four years earlier.

The 35 was followed by a 40/45, a 60 and a 90. The important Gordon-Bennett race in Ireland in 1903 was won by stripped and tuned 60 b.h.p. touring cars borrowed from customers since the 90 b.h.p. team cars had been destroyed in a works fire a few weeks before the race.

When Maybach left in 1907 to start his own company, Gottlieb Daimler's eldest son Paul became the technical director. One of his early innovations was to replace the chain drive to the rear wheels with a shaft drive to the rear axle. Similar drives had been tried before by Renault and others and there were still problems to be solved before a reliable shaft drive emerged.

During the 1914-18 war the Daimler Company worked on the application of supercharging to aero-engines. Roots-type blowers were used in an attempt to maintain ground level engine power at higher altitudes. Paul Daimler saw a future for supercharging in post-war racing and sports cars and he encouraged his development department to continue this work in the twenties. He was, of course, not aware of the Chadwick supercharged racing car from Pottstown, Pennsylvania, that had been so successful in American hill-climbs in 1907 and 1908. This work in the early twenties eventually resulted in the fabulous SSK and SSKL Mercedes sports cars that were such a thorn in the side of W.O. Bentley.

The Daimler engineers developed a system of supercharging that is usually described as 'blowing through the carburettor.' The more popular method is to place the carburettor on the inlet side of the blower. To function correctly the Mercedes system requires a sealed carburettor float chamber with the top of the chamber pressurised by the blower. The Daimler engineers had experienced in their road testing a frustrating boost-lag after the throttle was closed at the approach to a bend. With the large volume induction manifolds used at that time this is not surprising. By blowing through the carburettor a pressure build-up occurred upstream of the throttle plate during overrun and this gave a much improved throttle response when the driver floored the accelerator after a bend.

A two-litre blown Mercedes won the Targa Florio and the Coppa Florio in 1924. The more famous of the supercharged Mercedes sports cars, the SSK and the SSKL were made after the amalgamation of the Daimler Company with Benz, but the team of Daimler engineers provided the expertise that made these cars so memorable.

Paul Daimler's early attempts to produce supercharged production touring cars resulted at first in a reputation for unreliability. One of the troubles, plug-fouling at low throttle openings, only demonstrated that plug technology had not yet found an answer to widening the operating temperature range of their plugs. The way of the innovator is fraught with pitfalls like this. There were other troubles with the early supercharged cars and the Board of directors made an approach to a young Austrian engineer called Ferdinand Porsche who had already made a reputation as the designer of fine cars for Austro-Daimler.

At the end of 1922 Paul Daimler resigned from the company his father had established in 1885 and in April 1923 Dr Porsche left Austro-Daimler to take up his new appointment as Chief Engineer at Stuttgart-Unterturkheim. What a bargain that was! When one thinks of the tens of thousands of man-hours devoted on design committees today before a single new model rolls off the assembly line one finds it difficult to comprehend how Ferdinand Porsche was able to direct design teams while they produced 65 entirely different vehicles, touring cars, sports cars, racing cars trucks and tractors — and this accomplished in less than six years! No wonder that he thought it advisable to take a short vacation before moving to a new appointment with the Steyr Company in his native Austria.

Porsche had not been too happy working for the much enlarged amalgamated Daimler-Benz Company which showed the usual disorientation that occurs at such times. He need not have worried about the future products. Fine engineers such as Hans Nibel carried on where he left off. They introduced independent front suspension, swing-axle rear suspension and a new design of straight-eight engine. To the typical German the Mercedes is the finest car in the world and it was in the late twenties that the image of Mercedes began to be firmly established, as makers of luxury cars and as makers of the finest in sports cars. There has always been this dichotomy. Our interest in this book, however, is only in their sports cars.

The famous S Series sports cars were designed by Ferdinand Porsche. The blower design was based on the earlier work by Paul Daimler. All the S Series had a supercharged SOHC six-cylinder engine. A unique feature for the period was the casting of cylinder block and crankcase as a single unit in aluminium alloy. Aluminium cylinder heads with durable valve inserts were still in the future and Ferdinand Porsche, confined to the technology of the period, used a cast-iron cylinder head. The use of these two materials with different coefficients of expansion, particularly on such a long engine, gave them much trouble at first with leaking head gaskets. This and other problems were solved in the painstaking manner characteristic of the man and the engine soon achieved a reputation for reliability in service. The Roots blower was mounted vertically in front of the cylinder block and was driven through a pair of bevel gears and a multi-disc clutch from the front of the crankshaft. The fan was also driven through a clutch from the front of the camshaft. This was designed to be disengaged at high speed when not required, thus conserving power. It is intriguing to those accustomed to carrying out their own maintenance that the S Series engine only required one special tool for maintenance. The cylinder head, though, was so heavy that lifting gear was required to remove it.

The S model was introduced in 1926, the year when the amalgamation took place. It had a wheelbase of 3.4 metres (11 ft 2 in) and an engine capacity of 6.8 litres (415 cu in). A low centre of gravity (low for the period) resulted from the use of underslung rear springs. The power with natural aspiration was 120 b.h.p., increasing to 180 b.h.p. with the blower engaged. The top speed, using the blower, was about 100 m.p.h., a very impressive performance in 1926. In 1927 the S Model won the Nurburgring Grand Prix of Germany, a race for sports cars, with two more S Models finishing in second and third place.

Competition, chiefly from Bentley Motors, speeded the development of a 'super' model, the SS and in 1928, the SSK (K for *kurz*, short) with a wheelbase shortened to 2.9 metres (9 ft 6 in) and the supercharged power increased to 250 b.h.p. from a bored out version of the original engine. The new capacity of 7.07 litres (430 cu in) was retained for the ultimate development the SSKL (L for *leight*, light). Hans Nibel was now the design head at Daimler-Benz and his lightened chassis frame had so many holes down the sides that it looked like a slice of gruyère cheese. In a final attempt to crush the opposition this potent vehicle was fitted with the 'Elephant' blower, an oversize blower giving a boost pressure 0.83 bar (12 lb/in^2). This blower raised the maximum power to 300 b.h.p., but this could only be used for short periods when required to pass a competitor. This car won the Mille Miglia on its first outing and would have had many more victories in later years if the effects of the thirties depression had not begun to bite so savagely. In 1931 Bentley Motors went into liquidation and Bugatti seemed to have lost his sense of direction. Only Alfa Romeo seemed to be able to finance an active racing department and this was not a rewarding exercise when the opposition had disappeared.

The ear-splitting scream of the SSKL with the blower in action is now only a memory, but the Daimler-Benz Company were more soundly based financially than many smaller companies. They weathered the difficult times of the early thirties and concentrated on the manufacture of luxury cars. Even in hard times there are still a few buyers left for cars in the top class.

THE TYPE 300

Before Hans Nibel's untimely death in 1934, he designed the advanced Type 170, a 1.7 litre Mercedes touring car with an all-independent suspension system and was responsible for the design of the new racing car that was to start a new era in Grand Prix racing. Fritz Nallinger became the new Engineering Director. His chief assistant was Rudolf Uhlenhaut, who was gaining valuable experience to be applied later when he directed the design team working on the highly successful 300 SL in later years.

From the end of World War 2 it took Daimler-Benz only twelve months to get their bombed-out factory turning out a dressed-up version of the pre-war Type 170. Five years later they were so soundly based that their minds turned once more to the concept of a sporting model. In 1951 they introduced the Type 300 luxury car to be followed by the 300S in 1952 and the 300SL sports car in 1954. Daimler-Benz were once more making a real sports car.

THE 300SL

The new sports car had a great appeal to engineers. The author knew several who could not resist the attraction of its engineering excellence. One Texas engineer actually bought two, a black one and a white one. The appeal to the public in general was the performance and the good looks. The coupé body with its gull-wing (up and over) doors was enhanced by a shape that was both aesthetic and efficiently streamlined. The final touch of showmanship was the large Mercedes three-pointed star in the centre of the radiator grill. The tubular frame had enormous strength. The body sills so wide the driver and passenger had to learn how to slide their posteriors across them when entering the vehicle. Few people found this objectionable. In fact when the body shape was changed in 1956 to provide more normal side-hinged doors and narrow sills there were many voices raised in protest.

The engine of the 300SL was developed from the six-cylinder 3-litre engine already used in the Type 300. This was a SOHC design with a robust seven bearing crankshaft. In the 300SL the engine was tilted at 50 degrees to the vertical as shown in the cross-section of Figure 14.21. This helped to lower the

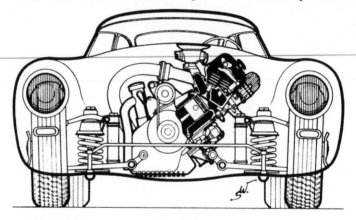

Fig. 14.21   The 300SL sports car, showing a cross-section of the slant-six SOHC engine.

bonnet-line. The joint-face of the block and head was also angled in the opposite direction at 18 degrees to the engine centre-line. An off-set yet compact combustion chamber was formed between the raised piston crown and a side pocket formed between the angled head and the cylinder block. A new head was made for the sports car engine in aluminium alloy. The ports were enlarged and an additional boss was provided to take the direct fuel injection nozzle.

As a design study it is of interest to consider why the decision was taken to abandon the well-tried system of carburation for direct fuel injection, a system remarkably close to that used in Diesel engines. The answer lies in the experience gained by Dr Nallinger in his pre-war work on the Mercedes Diesel. Experience

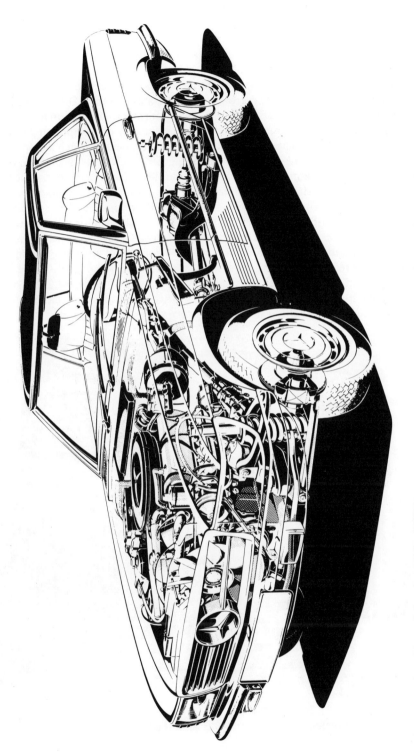

Fig. 14.22 Ghosted drawing of the 350SL.

often guides us in our decisions, sometimes unconsciously. Mercedes had a long working partnership with the Robert Bosch Company who had designed jerk-type pumps for Diesel engines for thirty years and were able to develop a suitable pump and injectors for petrol (much more abrasive than Diesel fuel) in a relatively short time. Part of the pump development programme involved a control system that compensated for changes in ambient air temperature and density. The combustion chamber is a hot dirty environment for such a delicate device as a fuel injector, but the weight of long experience won through. It is of interest though that Daimler-Benz turned to the less hostile location of port injection on later models. With fuel injection the power output of the 300SL was 220 b.h.p. (DIN). The suspension system was based on the firm's racing experience. Front suspension was by coil springs with two wishbones per wheel. Rear suspension was the controversial system using coil springs and swing-axles. Experience showed that the combination of a low roll-centre at the front and a high one at the rear resulted in too much roll-steer effect. Later models changed to a more complex arrangement as shown in Chapter seven (Figure 7.22). This design gave a lower pivot point below the rear drive casing. Roll resistance was also increased by the addition of a horizontal 'compensating spring'.

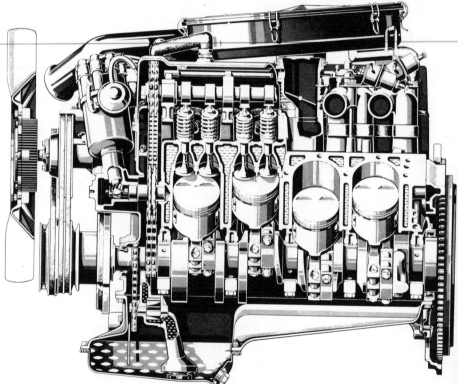

Fig. 14.23   The fuel-injected SOHC V-8 engine of the 350SL.

The transmission had four forward speeds giving maxima, quoting from 'The Autocar' road test of 1955, of 70 m.p.h. in second, 98 in third and 135 in top. The time to accelerate to 100 m.p.h. was 21.0 seconds, an exceptionally good figure for a sports car of that period.

The 300 SLR appeared in 1955. This was an eight-cylinder racing-sports car using an engine that was very close to the contemporary Mercedes Grand Prix car engine. With regret we must omit it from this review since it was not a car sold to the public.

THE CURRENT SERIES

With the introduction of the 230SL Daimler-Benz began to draw together the two major interests of the company. Their interest in racing in the sixties was reduced to a few works-supported entries in Rallies and their new sports car, the 230SL, was soon seen to be the forerunner of the new generation of Mercedes sports cars — the luxury sports car. Perhaps this trend is inevitable. The supply of Spartans who like to feel the wind in their hair seems to be running out. The 230SL, introduced in 1964 was still available as a convertible, but was more popular with coupé bodywork. It had a six-cylinder in-line engine of 2300 cc capacity fitted with Bosch fuel injection. The maximum speed was 106 m.p.h., but the car was obviously not designed with competition in mind. The series has been popular and has been developed over the last thirteen years with progressive increases in engine size and the addition of greater luxuries. The 230 SL was followed by the 250SL, the 280SL and the 350SL. The current model is available with a choice of two engines, a 3.5 litre or a 4.5 litre. The new engines are both V-8s and are fitted with the latest Bosch electronically controlled fuel injection as described in Chapter Five.

Many years had been spent in developing a good well-tamed swing-axle rear suspension for the Mercedes but, as happened to so many chassis designers, a completely new approach was demanded with the introduction of low profile tyres. Swing-axle suspension gives camber changes that are too large for the new tyres. There was very little change in the front suspension; double wishbones being used here, hardly differing in principle from the front suspension on the 1934 Type 170. The rear suspension is the semi-trailing link design which has become so popular in Europe today. With a touch of stubbornness Mercedes-Benz literature insists on calling it 'diagonal swing-axle'. What ever name we use it is still a 'rose'. The author speaks with experience since his BMW is fitted with a similar rear suspension.

The SOHC cylinder head design used on the V-8 engine is the well-tried Mercedes method of valve operation using a rocker to transfer the cam action to the valve rather than a bucket tappet (see Figure 3.9). A longitudinal cross-section of the engine is given in Figure 14.23.

Engine

Number of cylinders	8
Valve arrangement	single, overhead camshafts
Displacement in cu ins	213.6
in litres	3.5
Engine output (DIN)	200 net bhp/5800 rpm
Maximum rpm	6500
Bore/Stroke in	3.62/2.59
mm	91.7/65.6
Compression ratio	9.5:1
Fuel	Premium commercial fuel or benzine — benzol mixture
Maximum torque (DIN ft lbs/rpm	211/4000
mkg/rpm	29.2/4000
Fuel injection system	Bosch, electronically controlled fuel injection with automatic starting and warming up, responding to absolute suction pipe pressure, engine speed, cooling water temperature and air temperature.
Injection nozzles	Bosch
Ignition sequence	1-5-4-8-6-3-7-2
Ignition timing	Automatically, acc. by centrifugal force and vacuum
Crankshaft bearings	5 multi-layer bearings with steel-backed shells
Connecting-rod bearing	Multi-layer bearings with steel-backed shells
Oil filter	Lubricating-oil filter with paper cartridge, full-flow
Oil cooling	Oil cooler in air-stream
Capacity of crankcase	Imp/U.S. pts 13.2/15.9 9.7/11.6

Engine *continued*

Cooling	Water circulation through pump drive, by-pass thermostat, visco fan
Electric system	12 Volts, three-phase current generator 770 Watts max
Battery capacity	66Ah

Power transmission

Clutch	Single-plate dry clutch
Transmission	MB-4-speed-transmission, fully synchronized in all gears, floor-type gear shift
Transmission ratios (4-speed-transmission)	Optional *MB-Automatic transmission, floor-type gear shift*

I	3.96	3.98
II	2.34	2.39
III	1.43	1.46
IV	1	1
R	3.72	5.48

Climbing ability		
I	43 %	43 %
II	41 %	42 %
III	22 %	22 %
IV	13.5%	13.5%

Top speed in the individual gears	*Approx. m.p.h.*	
I	34 m.p.h.	27 m.p.h.
II	56 m.p.h.	56 m.p.h.
III	93 m.p.h.	93 m.p.h.
IV	130 m.p.h.	127 m.p.h.

Rear axle ratio	3.46	3.46
Engine speed at 60 m.p.h.	2945 r.p.m.	3085 r.p.m.

Chassis

Frame	Frame-floor unit, closed central member, box-shaped side and cross linked by welded sheet iron floor plates, self-supporting body, Engine-transmission block resting on two rubber bearings, on front axle carrier; in the rear with one rubber bearing on the chassis.

Chassis *continued*

Front wheel suspension	Independent suspension through twin wish-bones with anti-dive control device, coil springs with progressively acting rubber helper springs, dual-effect hydraulic telescopic absorbers, anti-roll bar, front axle carrier suspended front side members through rubber bearings
Rear axle	MB-diagonal-swing axle, coil springs with progressively acting rubber helper springs, dual-effect hydraulic telescopic shock absorbers, anti-roll bar limited slip differential optional
Brake system	Hydraulic dual-circuit brakes with vacuum booster; disc brakes front and rear.
Steering	MB-Power steering with automatic bleeding.
Tyre size	205/70 VR 14 with tubes

Dimensions	inches	metres
Wheelbase	96.9	2.46
Track front	57.2	1.45
Track rear	56.7	1.44
Overall length	172.1	4.37

Dimensions *continued*

width	70.5	1.79
height (unloaded)	51.2	1.30
Turning circle diameter	ft (approx) 33.9	metres (approx) 10.0
Tank capacity incl. reserve	Imp/U.S. gal 19.8/23.8	
	Imp/U.S. gal 2.9/3.4	

Weights	lb	kg
Kerb weight (DIN 70020)	3405	1543
Permissible total weight	4355	1977

Performance

Top speed with MB	Manual transm. 130 mph app. Autom.transm. 127 mph app.
Power/weight ratio	lb/HP (DIN) 14.8
Acceleration (0-62 m.p.h.) when shifting through gears	8.8 seconds approx.
Fuel consumption according to DIN 70030+)	m.p. Imp/U.S. gals 22/18 (measured at 68 m.p.h.)
Overall consumption at cruising speed	m.p. Imp/U.S. gals 25/21

+At ¾ of top speed (max. 68 m.p.h.) with 10% added.

THE PROTOTYPE C111

In 1969, Daimler-Benz revealed an experimental sports car, the C111 shown in Figure 14.24 fitted at this time with a 3-rotor Wankel engine mounted behind the driver and later to be fitted with a 4-rotor version of 350 b.h.p. (DIN). There was much speculation at the time that a Mercedes might be seen again in sports car racing, but the vehicle has, so far, been nothing more than a design exercise. It is interesting to note that the wedge profile body is fitted with gull-wing doors as in the original 300SL.

The development of the Wankel engine has been overshadowed in recent years by two problems, high fuel consumption and poor emission control. Not all workers in this field have been discouraged but Daimler-Benz have decided to

Fig. 14.24 The C111 experimental sports car, first used with 4-rotor Wankel power and now used as a mobile test bed for a 3-litre turbocharged Diesel.

discontinue development work on the Wankel engine and to put renewed effort into a Diesel engine programme. The company still denies that the C111 has any future as a production car and they are currently using it as a mobile test bed for a turbocharged 3-litre 5-cylinder Diesel engine. The car has already broken the long-distance Diesel-engined car world record by completing 10,000 miles at an average speed of 156 m.p.h.

Mr Van Winsen, who was responsible for the development of the new turbocharged diesel, believes that a Mercedes sports car powered by this unit will be produced by 1979 and that this new sports car will have no difficulty in meeting the tighter emission and fuel consumption regulations that will be in force in the United States at that time.

'Diesel engines we can make without headaches,' says Mr Van Winsen: 'Petrol engines are more of a problem.'

THE PORSCHE

This story must start at the turn of the century when Ferdinand Porsche, in his late twenties, began to compete in early motor races with cars of his own design. In 1905, after taking his doctorate in engineering, Dr Porsche became the chief engineer for the Austro-Daimler company. An Austro-Daimler won its class in the 1922 Targa Florio and Hans Stuck drove one to success in the European Hill Climb Championship. Between 1922 and 1928 Dr Porsche was in charge of the design office at the Daimler Motoren Gesellschaft and as already related in the Mercedes Design Study he supervised the design of 65 widely different classes of vehicle. It was a very tired man who eventually returned to his native Austria to work for the much smaller Steyr company. Before leaving the amalgamated Daimler-Benz company he was responsible for the design of the SSK Mercedes sports car.

In 1930 Dr Porsche formed his own company in Stuttgart. His intention was to act in a consultative capacity and to build up a design and development service for the benefit of the expanding motor industry. In 1933 he was asked to design a new Grand Prix car for a newly formed group of car manufacturers to be called Auto-Union. This was the famour P-Wagen with the controversial combination of a heavy rear engine and swing-axle rear suspension. Despite the handling problems associated with this fascinating vehicle that started life with a 295 b.h.p. engine and finished in 1937 with 520 b.h.p., Dr Porsche was still convinced the combination could be made to work. Since he had already designed about 80 vehicles by this time, very few of us would have had the temerity to contradict him. Consequently, his next major design assignment, one of the most famous in the whole history of the motor car, is now known affectionately as 'the Beetle'. Inevitably he designed it with a rear engine and swing-axle rear suspension.

After the war with the German automobile industry in ruins Dr Ferdinand Porsche, Jnr., usually called 'Dr Ferry' to distinguish him from his father,

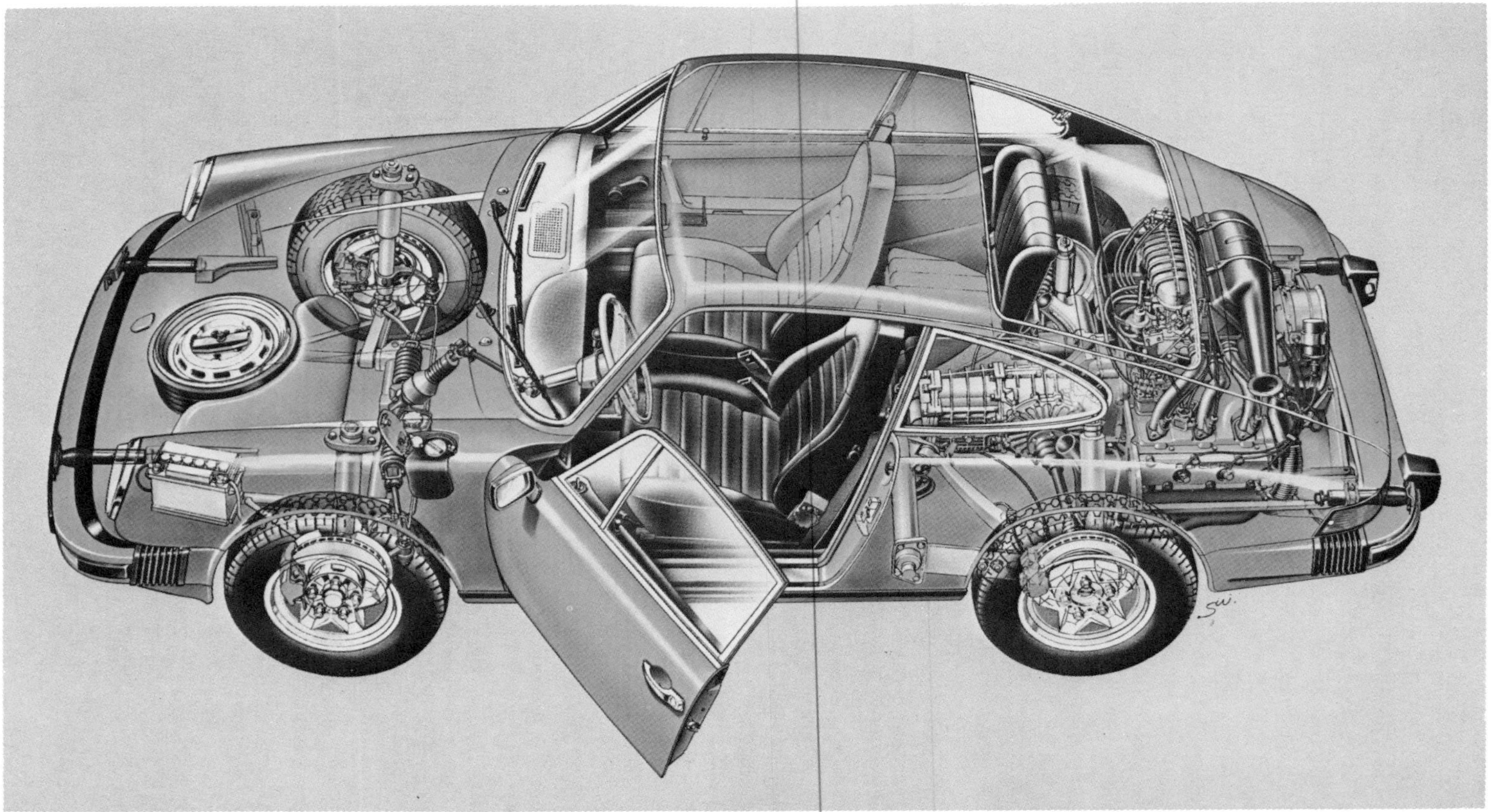

Fig. 14.25 Ghosted drawing of the Type 911

decided the only hope of re-creating the pre-war Porsche Technical Office was to design a sporting vehicle based on the Volkswagen. His father, Professor Porsche was no more optimistic but they hoped that sufficient second-hand VW would be available to make a start. They must have been surprised at the rapid recovery made by the VW factory and the first post-war Porsche, designed by Dr Ferry, went into production in 1949.

The Porsche Technical Office existed before the war purely as a design and development establishment. The Porsche baulk-ring synchromesh had been designed and covered by world patents at this time. In 1948 an agreement was signed with the newly established Volkswagen company in which VW had full use of all Porsche patents free of charge. In exchange Porsche were to receive a royalty on every VW built. It is this dichotomy within the Porsche company, its manufacturing interests on the one hand and its design and development function on the other, that explains the employment of more than 1,000 technicians and engineers in the research complex at Weissach. This research and development complex is well outside the industrial area of Stuttgart-Zuffenhausen where the Porsche cars are made.

The manufacturing side of Dr.Ing. h.c. F.Porsche Aktiengesellschaft turns out about 15,000 cars per annum. Porsches have never been inexpensive, but they would certainly be more expensive if the lavish facilities at Weissach were supported entirely by the sale of Porsche cars. The research centre has 13,400 sq metres (144,000 sq ft) of workshops, foundries, test-rooms and laboratories. There is a 'Can-Am' high-speed circuit and a Mountain circuit and all the rolling dynamometers, exhaust emission test equipment, arctic weather chambers, etc that one would expect to find at the research establishment of a large manufacturer. It is here that the motor racing development and testing work is carried out, the story of which has been so admirably told by Paul Frère in 'The Racing Porsches'.

The history of Porsche as a manufacturer from the post-war start in 1949 to the present day is one of a gradual shedding of the 'hotted-up VW' image and the establishment of a true identity. The Porsche 911, which has now been in production for eleven years, does not employ a single component in its entire body and chassis from the VW Beetle. It is therefore ironic that an entirely new Porsche is now being marketed in Europe that is constructed from many components used in the current Audi and VW cars. The original 924 project, using a water-cooled front engine driving the rear wheels, was undertaken on behalf of VW, who later decided not to proceed to production. Porsche, however, saw possibilities in this new car and have proceeded to establish a new production line to make the 924 as a medium-priced sports car using many mass-produced Audi and VW components. They have also developed a water-cooled V-8 version, the Type 928. The author is not yet familiar with these new cars and does not propose to discuss them in this study.

THE TYPE 911

There is something logical in the Porsche philosophy of avoiding the idea of annual model changes. Every attempt is made to identify weaknesses that are thrown up by customer liaison, to work on these problems and introduce changes and modified components as soon as they have been approved by the development department. Every attempt is meanwhile made by the staff at Weissach to improve the reliability, road-holding, handling, braking, etc based on new information emanating from racing experience. Henry Ford also saw the logic of continuity when he refused to replace the Model T. He did very little, though, to improve the car. Porsche avoid this mistake. The original Type 911 in 1966 had a 2-litre engine. Since then the engine size has increased to 2.2, then 2.4 and is now available in 2.7 or 3.9 litre form. A ghosted view of this most popular of Porsches is given in Figure 14.25

The engine

Porsche have used horizontally opposed air-cooled engines since the early post-war days. The first VW-based Porsche was a flat-4. Since then there have

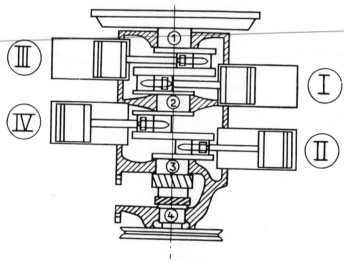

Cylinder I:	flywheel side	right	Main Bearing 1: with shoulder, solid
Cylinder II:	pulley side	right	Main Bearing 2: split
Cylinder III:	flywheel side	left	Main Bearing 3: solid
Cylinder IV:	pulley side	left	Main Bearing 4: solid (pulley side)

Fig. 14.26   Simplified layout of a flat-4 engine. The same layout, with main bearing between pairs of opposed connecting rods is used on 6, 8 and 12 cylinder Porsche engines.

been 6s, 8s and 12s. The racing engines, including the flat-12 in the fabulous Type 917, have all been described in Paul Frère's book. What is difficult to describe in a few words are the benefits that accrue when a company is able to test their products in the harsh fire of competition. Some large companies claim that modern laboratory techniques make racing and rallying completely outdated as test methods. They could be right, but it is difficult to infuse a competitive spirit into a computer-controlled series of laboratory tests. Motor racing soon reveals if your product is much inferior to the opposition. Laboratory testing only tells you how good your own product is.

Porsche use both methods, but their racing programme involves a considerable expenditure. The publicity gained by these racing successes is difficult to evaluate in financial terms, but it is very reassuring to the owner of a Type 911 to know that similar engines to the one in his car have been tested in long distance races and with the engine tuned to produce much more power than in the production model.

Figure 14.28 gives a longitudinal and a transverse cross-section of the Turbo engine which is similar in basic layout to the Type 911. For those overwhelmed by the mass of detail Figure 14.26 shows how banks of cylinders on one side are staggered relative to those on the opposite side. This is the earlier flat-4 engine. American readers familiar with the V-8 should visualise the flat-6 as a V-6 with the included angle between banks increased to 180 degrees. Perhaps this description appeals more to our Irish readers! A flat-6 fits into a rear-engined sports car as admirably as a flat-12 into a Formula 1 racing car. Dr Porsche always had a firm commitment to air-cooling. The advantages of air-cooling are:

1. Low weight (even alloy radiators are heavy),
2. Greater reliability, since that constant source of trouble, the burst or leaking hose, is absent.

The disadvantages are:

1. Slightly higher internal operating temperatures than those in a water-cooled engine of the same specific power output,
2. A higher level of mechanical and combustion noise, since there are no water jackets to help damp out some of the noise.

Air-cooling on the Type 911 is provided by a large ducted fan mounted above the engine and belt driven from a pulley on the front of the crankshaft. A SOHC head is used, rockers being used to transfer the cam lift to the valves which are at an included angle of 55 degrees. The two camshafts are chain-driven from the crankshaft. The cylinder barrels are in aluminium alloy with chrome-plated bores. The crankcase, which is made in two halves, was originally an aluminium alloy casting but, as a result of racing experience, it is now a much lighter magnesium alloy casting in the 2.7 litre engine. The Bosch K Jetronic fuel injection has already been described in Chapter Five. To comply with future legislation in several countries to reduce the lead content of fuels the Porsche 911 is now designed to run on 2 star petrol.

Transmission

The transaxle used on the type 911 (Figure 14.27) is cast in silicon aluminium alloy. The gearbox is overhung behind the final drive section. The gear selector rod can be seen at the bottom of the box. The Porsche design of automatic transmission is available as an optional extra.

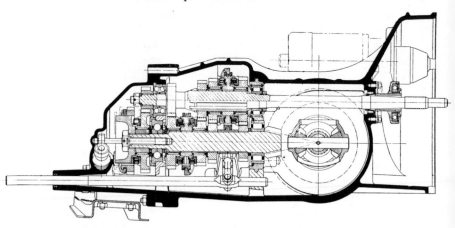

Fig. 14.27   Gearbox and final drive unit as used on the Type 911.

The body

The Porsche is a small car compared with the Jaguar, the Lotus and the Mercedes. Porsche sports cars have always been small high performance sports cars with two comfortable front seats and two tiny seats in the rear for children. The Porsche 911 is 14 ft 1 in long and 5 ft 3½ in wide. The Jaguar XJ-S is 16 ft long and 5 ft 10½ in wide. The Jaguar has 75 per cent more power than the Porsche, but it weighs 45 per cent more in road trim with two people aboard. These figures are not given to denigrate the Jaguar, only to show that Porsche have always believed that 'small is beautiful'. Drag coefficients as low as 0.31 have been achieved by several racing Porsches, but the addition of aerofoils and other spoiler devices to aid stability at speed increased this figure. In the same way, but less seriously, the addition of those bulky '5 m.p.h. collision' bumpers has increased the total drag of the latest 911 slightly. The coefficient in the region of 0.32 is still very low for a production sports car.

The body is well equipped and carries the usual Porsche high standard of finish. The galvanised under-body is guaranteed for six years. Besides the normal coupe body, those with a taste for fresh air can choose the Targa model which carries a detachable roof section that can be stored in the boot. The fixed roof section acts as a roll-over bar.

The suspension

The suspension has been described in Chapter eight. In recent years Porsche have concentrated, not only on high cornering power, but on safe predictable handling. Under moderate cornering forces the car understeers to a small extent. Acceleration through a corner gives a slight roll-steer effect. With a Porsche it is always safest to brake before a bend, then to accelerate through it. If a need to lift-off then occurs the behaviour remains stable and predictable.

At speeds above 120 m.p.h. the standard Porsche body, with no aerofoil, can be a little twitchy, especially in a cross-wind. The Turbo with a maximum speed exceeding 150 m.p.h. has a substantial aerofoil blended attractively into the body to create the necessary downthrust for high speed stability.

General specification

Engine

Cylinders	6, horiz opposed
Capacity	2687 cc (163.97 cu in)
Bore/stroke	90x70.4 mm
	(3.54x2.77 in)
Cooling	Air
Block	Light Alloy
Head	Light Alloy
Valves	Sohc per bank
Valve timing	(at 1 mm valve clearance)
inlet opens	6° atdc
inlet closes	50° abdc
ex opens	24° bbdc
ex closes	2° btdc
Compression	8.5:1
Induction	Bosch K Jetronic fuel injection
Bearings	8 main
Fuel pump	Bosch electric
Max power	165 bhp (DIN) at 5800 rpm
Max torque	173.5lb ft (DIN) at 4000 rpm

Transmission

Type	5 speed manual
Clutch	Sdp diaphragm spring

Internal ratios and mph/1000 rpm

Top	0.821:1/23.1
4th	1.000:1/19.0
3rd	1.261:1/15.0
2nd	1.833:1/10.3
1st	3.181:1/6.0
Rev	3.325:1
Final drive	3.875:1

Body/chassis

Construction	All steel integral
Protection	Floorpan, sills and wheel-arches galvanised; PVC underseal; all cavities Tectyl treated. 6 year warranty

Suspension

Front	Independent by MacPherson Struts, longitudinal torsion bars, anti-roll bar.
Rear/Cap	Independent by semi-trailing arms, transverse torsion bars, and anti-roll bar

Steering

Type	Rack and pinion
Assistance	No
Toe in	Nil
Camber	0° $0'$
Castor	6° $5' \pm 0^\circ$ $15'$
Rear toe in	0° $20'$

Brakes

Type	Discs, front and rear
Servo	No
Circuit	Dual, split front/rear
Rear Valve	No

Wheels

Type	Light Alloy, 6 in rim
Tyres	185/70 VR 15
Pressures	29 psi front; 34 psi rear

Electrical

Battery	66 Ah, 12V
Polarity	Negative
Generator	Alternator
Fuses	25
Headlights	60/55 W Halogen

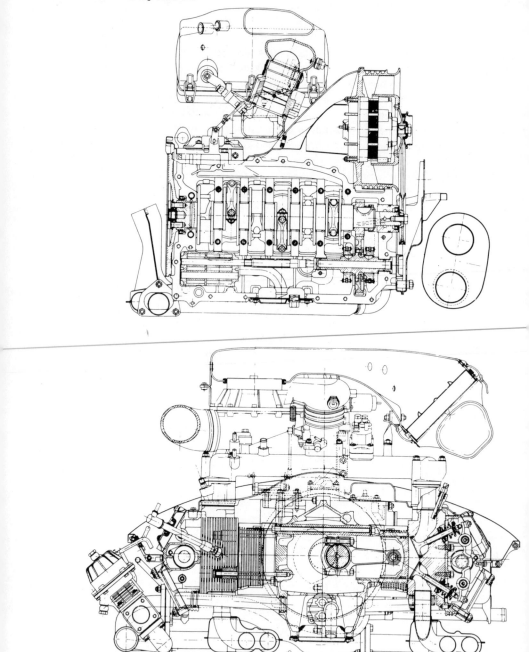

Fig. 14.28 Longitudinal and transverse cross-sections of the Turbo engine.

THE CARRERA

The name Carrera once indicated a highly competitive racing sports car that yielded very little of its performance and handling to creature comforts. The latest Carrera has a top speed in excess of 140 m.p.h. and can accelerate from zero to 60 m.p.h. in 6 seconds, yet the same lavish equipment available on the Type 911 is standard equipment on the Carrera. With thermostatic heater control, even an electrically-heated outside door mirror the new Carrera combines the luxurious interior comfort of the Type 911 with the handling of a racing car.

The Carrera is equipped with wider wheels and tyres at the rear. The front wheels on the Carrera are 185/70 VR 15 on 6 inch wide wheels, identical in fact to those at both ends of the Type 911. At the rear 215/60 VR 15 tyres are fitted

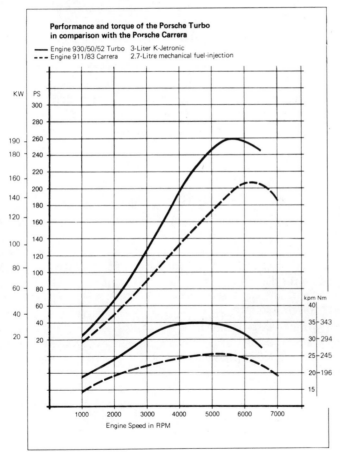

Fig. 14.29   Comparative power and torque curves for the 2.7 litre Carrera and the 3 litre Turbo.

to 7 inch wheels. Forged aluminium alloy wheels are used on the Carrera to resist the higher stresses liable to be applied with the higher performance. With the increased output of 200 b.h.p. from the 3-litre engine and an increased area of rubber at the rear the traction and cornering power of the Carrera is even more impressive than that of the 911. The rear wheel arches are widened to take the wider tyres.

THE TURBO

The engine

The principle of turbocharging has been discussed in Chapter Thirteen. Full use of the experience gained in turbocharging the Type 917 racing sports cars has been made in applying the technique to the new Turbo model. Longitudinal and transverse cross-sections of the Turbo engine are given in Figure 14.28. The turbocharged Type 917 produced anything from 175 to 200 b.h.p. per litre, depending upon the boost control setting. the Production model is controlled to a boost pressure of 0.8 bar (11.8 lb per sq in). This modest amount of supercharge increases the maximum power of the 3-litre engine from 205 to 260 b.h.p., as shown in Figure 14.29. An interesting aspect of the boost control system is the useful lift given to the power curve in the middle speed range. At 4,000 r.p.m. the power is increased by 50 per cent. At 6,200 r.p.m. where the Carrera engine peaks the power increase is less than 25 per cent. Tuned in this way the mid-range acceleration is much improved yet the maximum power output is kept within safe limits.

The transmission

Apart from the use of a high strength silicon aluminium alloy in the transaxle casings the transmission layout is largely similar to that of the 911. The final drive ratio varies depending upon the choice of tyre section since the rear wheels can be fitted with either 50 Series or 60 Series tyres. Wider gearwheels are used in the Turbo gearbox to withstand the increased torque. A five-speed gearbox is not required on the Turbo since the low speed torque is so good.

Suspension, wheels and tyres

Suspension layout is largely similar to the Type 911. The rear radius arms are made as aluminium castings of generous section to give increased strength. The rear hubs are also more robust, being the pattern used on the Type 917. Bilstein gas-filled dampers are used and the suspension geometry is designed to suit the ultra-low profile tyres. As in the Carrera forged aluminium alloy wheels are used, the front being 7J section, the rear 8J. 205/50 VR 15 tyres are fitted at the front and a choice between 225/50 VR 15 or 215/60 VR 15 at the rear.

Body

The body changes introduced with the Turbo are pronounced flares at the wheel arches, a small spoiler added to the front apron and a very elegant aerofoil at the rear. The widened wheel arches are neatly blended into the body contours. The rear 'spoiler' (the name used by Porsche for what is technically an aerofoil) is not only aesthetically pleasing but with characteristic ingenuity the Porsche engineers have incorporated in the upper surface additional cooling vents to improve engine cooling when idling, to cool the air conditioning condenser and, by means of a separate passage, to admit air to the engine cooling blower.

All windows on the Turbo are tinted. The rear window has its own wiper. There is two stage heating of the rear window and single stage heating of the front screen. Interior heating is thermostatically controlled and the external mirror is not only heated but can be adjusted manually by the driver from an internal lever. Headlamp washers are also a part of comprehensive equipment. In keeping with the image of this new leader in the Porsche range the Turbo has a Blaupunkt stereo-casette player and radio with 4 speakers and an electric aerial. With all this lavish equipment the kerb weight of 1195 kg (2635 lb) is remarkably low.

Performance
The maker's figures for the Turbo maximum speed is in excess of 250 k.p.h. (155 m.p.h.). The acceleration time for 0-100 k.p.h. (0-62 m.p.h.) is given as 5.5 seconds, which appears to put it ahead of all the European competition.

Index